Microsoft Teams
User Guide 2024

The Complete Guide for Beginners & Experts to Master Microsoft Teams

Copyright © 2024 **Morgan Skye**

All Rights Reserved

This book or parts thereof may not be reproduced in any form, stored in any retrieval system, or transmitted in any form by any means—electronic, mechanical, photocopy, recording, or otherwise—without prior written permission of the publisher, except as provided by United States of America copyright law and fair use.

Disclaimer and Terms of Use

The author and publisher of this book and the accompanying materials have used their best efforts in preparing this book. The author and publisher make no representation or warranties with respect to the accuracy, applicability, fitness, or completeness of the contents of this book. The information contained in this book is strictly for informational purposes. Therefore, if you wish to apply the ideas contained in this book, you are taking full responsibility for your actions.

Printed in the United States of America

TABLE OF CONTENTS

TABLE OF CONTENTS III

A QUICK LOOK 1

CHAPTER 1 2

EXPLORING MICROSOFT TEAMS 2

    SYNOPSIS 2
    INSTALLING AND DOWNLOADING MICROSOFT TEAMS 2
    KEY CHARACTERISTICS OF MICROSOFT TEAMS 4
    A BRIEF OVERVIEW AND EXPLORATION OF TEAMS 5
    REGARDING TEAMS CALENDAR 10
    ACTIVITIES 12

CHAPTER 2 13

EXAMINING INNOVATIVE FEATURES IN GROUPS 13

    SYNOPSIS 13
    A COMPONENT OF MY COLLABORATIVE LOOP SYSTEM 13
    TO-DO LIST LINKS THAT ARE EASY TO RECOGNIZE 15
    LOCATING CHAT ROOMS OR CHANNELS IS MADE EASY 16
    ABOUT MARK TEAM NOTIFICATIONS 16
    CUSTOMIZE A PRE-ESTABLISHED LIST OF RESPONSES 17
    THE LATEST VERSION OF THE ONEDRIVE SOFTWARE 17
    THE MEET APP 18
    THE MOBILE APP STREAM 19
    THE BROWSER INTEGRATION 20
    IMPROVEMENTS TO THE LIVE CAPTIONING 21
    ACTIVITIES 22

CHAPTER THREE 23

CREATION OF TEAMS AND CHANNELS 23

    SYNOPSIS 23
    ESTABLISHING A GROUP 24
    OUT OF A COLLECTION 26
    RIGHT FROM THE START 27
    MAKING USE OF THE TEMPLATE 29
    TAKING PART IN A GROUP 31
    MANAGEMENT OF TEAMS AND CHANNEL 32
    THE MANAGEMENT OF THE TEAMS 33

Setting up Tags	36
Concerning Channels	36
Breaking up with a team	39
Hide a team from view	39
Taking a group out	39
Activities	40

CHAPTER FOUR 41

ABOUT CHATS AND CONVERSATIONS WITHIN THE TEAMS 41

Synopsis	41
Conversations that take place within Teams	41
Message sending and receiving	43
Starting a new conversation	44
Increasing the enjoyment of your conversations	45
Organizing the conversations	46
Getting files and sharing them via chat	47
Addressing a specific person	49
Editing, removing, and bookmarking posts	49
Private messages exchanged	52
Activities	55

CHAPTER FIVE 56

COMPREHENDING MEETING AND CALL CONFIGURATION 56

Synopsis	56
Opening of the meeting	59
Start an on-demand call	60
A meeting schedule	68
Attending a scheduled meeting	70
Sharing a screen	72
Participating in meetings by delivering live presentations	75
Generating ideas in a meeting	77
Complicated meeting circumstances	82
Activities	87

CHAPTER SIX 88

MICROSOFT TEAMS: MANAGING PROJECTS 88

Synopsis	88
The Setting Up	88
Regarding the Conversation	89
File sharing	89

- Including instruments from external sources 90
- Activities 91

CHAPTER SEVEN 92

TEAM MICROSOFT PLANNER USERS 92

- Synopsis 92
- Regarding My Day 92
- Concerning My Tasks 94
- Concerning My Plans 95
- Accessing My Teams 98
- Important setups 99
- Comparing new planners to older ones 100
- Activities 101

CHAPTER EIGHT 102

MICROSOFT EDUCATION: EXPLORATION OF ADVANCED FEATURES 102

- Synopsis 102
- Adding notes to a PDF 102
- About reminder 105
- Extend the feature until the deadline date 105
- Responses in bulk 106
- Coloring book that promotes awareness and introspection 107
- About Personnel reflect 109
- Lowering noise levels to make reading easier 110
- Notification of missing attachment 111
- A revised feature for student editing 112
- Using tables 113
- Updated Turn in festivities 113
- The school connection app 114
- Activities 118

CHAPTER NINE 119

UNDERSTANDING HINTS AND TECHNIQUES 119

- Synopsis 119
- The essentials 119
- Mute unrelated conversation threads 120
  - *Turn a post into a task* *120*
  - *The hub of activity* *121*
- How to set up the windows that pop up 123
- The out-of-office message's scheduling 124

ADDING FRESH TABS	125
USING THE SEARCH BAR	127
ACTIVITIES	130

CHAPTER TEN 131

CONCERNING THE TROUBLESHOOTING OF TEAMS 131

SYNOPSIS	131
ARE TEAMS NOT OPERATING AS THEY SHOULD?	131
DOES SPELL CHECK NOT WORK CORRECTLY?	132
ACTIVITIES	135

CHAPTER ELEVEN 136

ADD-ONS FOR TEAMS APP INTEGRATIONS 136

SYNOPSIS	136
APP INTEGRATIONS	136
Utilizing the Meet application	*137*
OneDrive applications	*137*
The Viva's insights	*138*
The Microsoft SharePoint	*140*
ACTIVITIES	141
GENERAL SUMMARY	141

INDEX 142

A QUICK LOOK

If you're new to Microsoft Teams and need a little extra assistance using it, this is the guide for you. For instance, you might not know what's going on or even how to utilize it if your business just started utilizing it. Imagine your team being more productive, more in communication, and better at managing projects. Microsoft Teams 2024 can assist you with achieving all of those goals. Staying up to date with the newest tools can make a big difference in your success. The ins and outs of utilizing Microsoft Teams in 2024, including all the new features and collaborative workgroup techniques, will be covered in detail in this book. With Teams, you can increase productivity, communication, and teamwork. This book will provide you with the necessary tools and information to ensure that you are making the most out of Microsoft Teams. Therefore, regardless of why this book is necessary, there is something here for you to improve your teamwork. Knowing how to utilize Microsoft Teams can help you achieve more and work in teams more effectively. If you want to get the most out of this book, take your time going through each chapter, working through the exercises, and applying the teachings to your everyday work. Before you know it, you'll be an expert at using Microsoft Teams to improve the productivity and effectiveness of your team. This book covers the most recent improvements and changes to Microsoft Teams, a popular platform for teamwork. It is meant to act as a thorough guide that shows you how to effortlessly use every Teams function.

Are you feeling ready to use Microsoft Teams? Let's move forward now.

CHAPTER 1
EXPLORING MICROSOFT TEAMS

Synopsis

This first chapter will walk you through setting up Microsoft Teams and using its main functionalities, like the Teams Calendar that lets you collaborate with colleagues and manage your calendar. Microsoft Teams is a collaboration tool developed by Microsoft. It provides a single area where people may interact, have audio and video chats, share files, and collaborate on various tasks and projects. Whether it's a tiny company, a huge corporation, or an educational institution, the purpose of teams is to facilitate communication and teamwork among members of an organization.

Installing and downloading Microsoft Teams

Look for a Microsoft Teams download using your browser. Next, choose "Download app for desktop" and "Download Microsoft Teams Desktop."

Successively, select "Download Teams for home" or select Teams for work or school. Hold off while Microsoft Teams downloads.

Click the Open button to begin installing Microsoft Teams after the download is complete. The installation process should take one minute.

After installation, sign in using your Microsoft account. It will activate the Microsoft Teams app. You can now join meetings and start conversations with teams.

Key characteristics of Microsoft Teams

So what are some of the key benefits of Microsoft Teams?

1. **Conversation:** Users can share files, communicate with coworkers one-on-one or in groups, and express themselves using gifs, stickers, and emojis.
2. **Meetings:** Teams enable users to arrange and participate in meetings with coworkers or outside parties by providing audio and video conferencing features. Screen sharing, virtual backdrops, and recording features are supported.
3. **Channels:** Teams group discussions and documents into channels that are devoted to particular tasks, divisions, or subjects. Channels offer a disciplined method of working together and maintaining the order of conversations.
4. **Integration with Microsoft 365 Teams:** allows users to create, edit, and share files within the platform by integrating with other Microsoft Office programs including Word, Excel, and PowerPoint.
5. **Partnerships:** On documents, several team members can work together at once. Outlook, OneDrive, SharePoint, and other Microsoft 365 services are all easily integrated with Teams. The Teams interface now makes it simple to access files, calendars, and other resources thanks to this integration.
6. **Ecosystem for apps**: Users of Microsoft Teams can improve their experience and connect with other tools they use in their workflows by utilizing the many third-party integrations and apps that the platform offers.
7. **Accessibility:** Both Windows and Mac users can download the desktop version of Microsoft Teams. Additionally, there is a web version that can be accessed via browsers and mobile apps on iOS and Android devices. Particularly since the pandemic, when remote work and virtual cooperation have proliferated, it has significantly increased in favor.

A Brief Overview and Exploration of Teams

Now, we'll open Microsoft Teams through the portal, walk through a few basics, and examine the user interface. We're going to look at our app launcher, which is located under Microsoft Teams right here. It's crucial to remember that our access method at the moment is a web browser. You can also download the desktop application to gain access to Teams. The UI is the same. The first thing you'll notice when you open Teams is that this left-hand menu, which runs vertically along the left-hand side, contains the principal activity. These are all the elements that comprise a team.

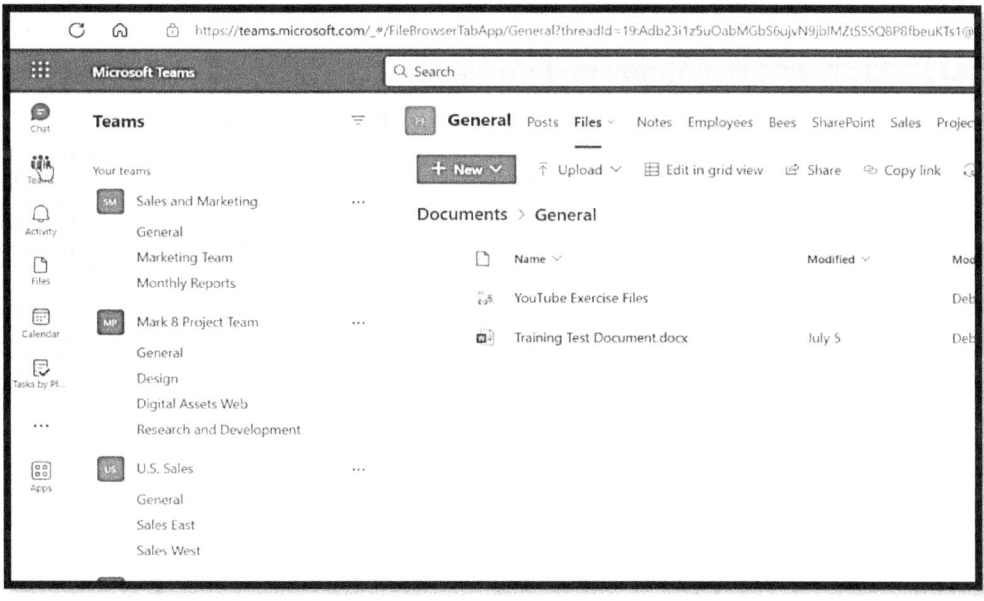

The purple-highlighted one is the one you are now clicking on. When we click on Teams, a long list of all the teams that we can access emerges. By default, it will choose Teams. For example, sales and marketing collaborate. These little folders you see underneath them are meant to serve as a roadmap for certain conversations. A team channel is the name given to them. As a result, the marketing team has its own channel within the sales and marketing team. This is where any marketing-related information, correspondence, and posts would be shared. We have a separate channel where all conversations on monthly reports take place. You can find as many channels as you'd like below, enabling team members to concentrate heavily in particular fields. Right now, one thing you'll notice is that all newly created teams have a general channel by default. This is where all general talks will take place, and you can see that a debate is currently in progress by clicking on one of the teams below. This brings us to our next point: you can see that there are numerous tabs at the top of the general channel (this is true for all of our channels). This looks more like what you see when you first launch a new channel. Posts and Files will be the only two tabs available at the top. All talks now take place at the bottom of the post area, as indicated by the new conversation button. This is where you would talk to your teammates if you wanted to. The Files tab makes it simple for us to browse any shared files within this team channel, which gives us quick access to the projects we're working on at the moment. We can add other tabs by clicking the plus button that appears next to it, and we may access a variety of apps from here. The most important thing to remember from this is that there are several tabs that go across the top of each channel. We also have teams and channels. Later on, we shall discuss this topic in further detail.

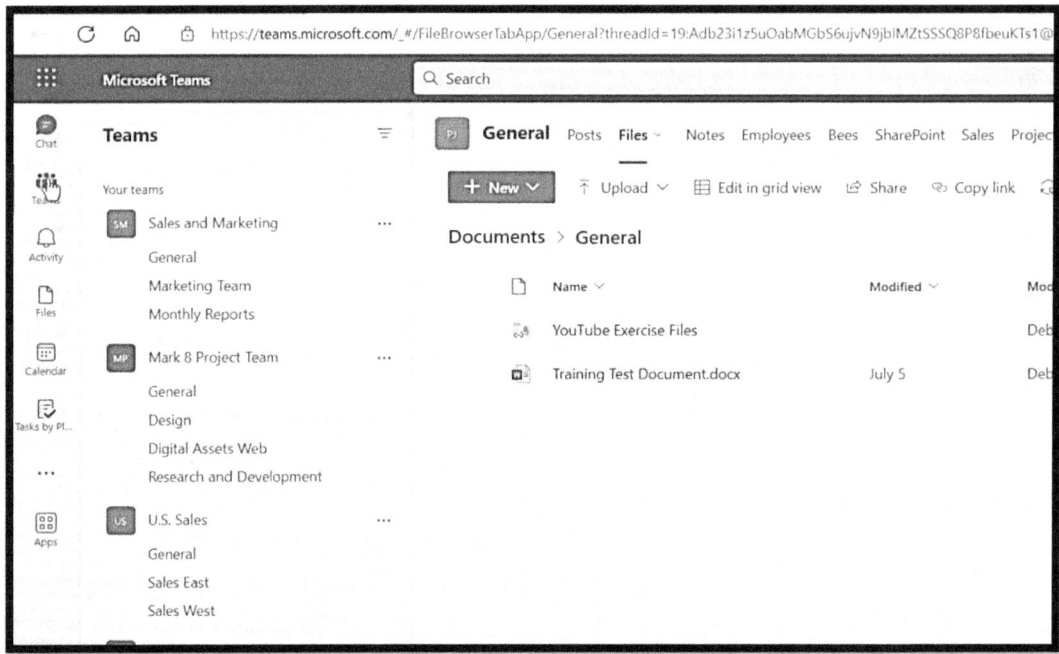

Additionally, you'll notice that when you hover your mouse over each team and each channel, three dots appear on the side of the screen. Clicking on these dots will bring up a small contextual menu that offers you additional options for managing your teams and channels as well as for carrying out actions. Keep in mind that we'll be coming and going from this as we work through this section.

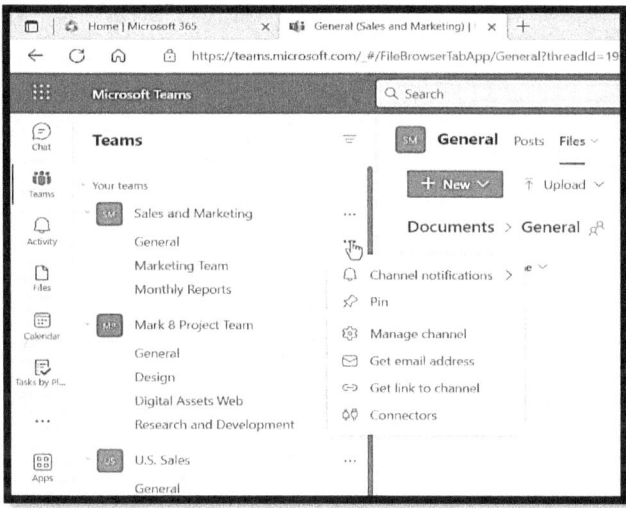

Chat is the icon directly above. We meet here for our intimate conversations with individuals. You can use this feature to have private chats if you would want to speak privately with only one person of a team rather than messaging everyone in the channel.

You can see all of the updates happening on all of your teams by selecting the Activity option here, which is a feed. You may come here and instantly check who has mentioned you, whose team and channel you need to reply to, which is very helpful if you have people @ mentioning you.

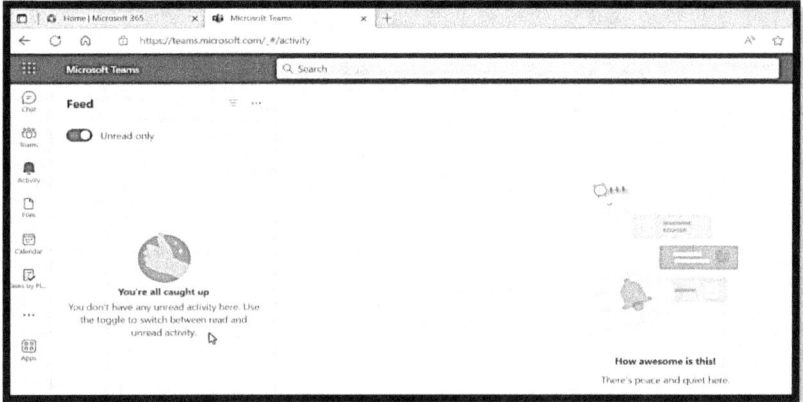

There's an area called Files underneath that. This will merely direct us to the team's file library, where we can view all of the shared files that our teams have access to. We can also use this to filter the files according to various file kinds. We can add papers directly from our PC into this file library or choose to simply view all the Word files. Clicking the "New" drop-down allows us to create new workbooks, presentations, and documents. Once more, we will go over all of this in much greater detail in a moment.

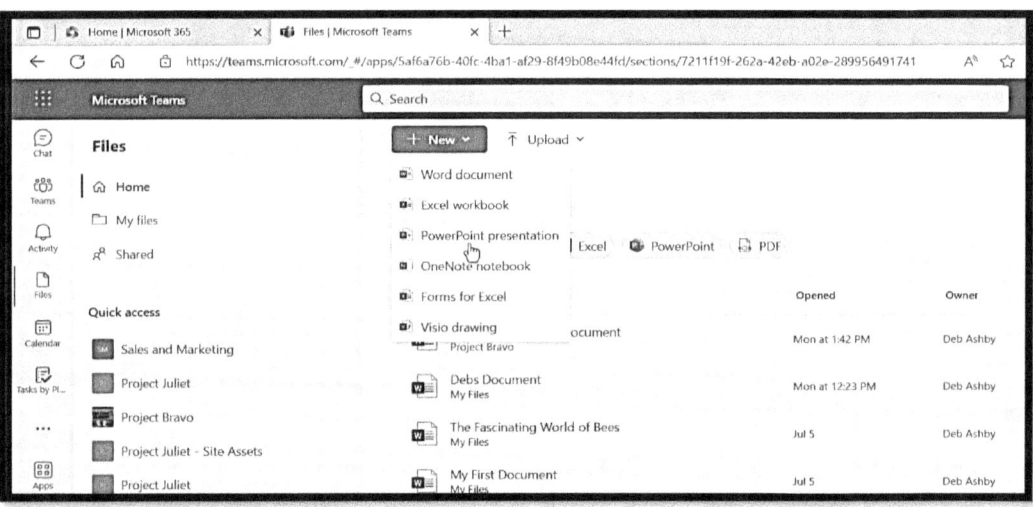

The calendar of a team is also available to us. If you'd like to share a calendar with your team, this is fantastic.

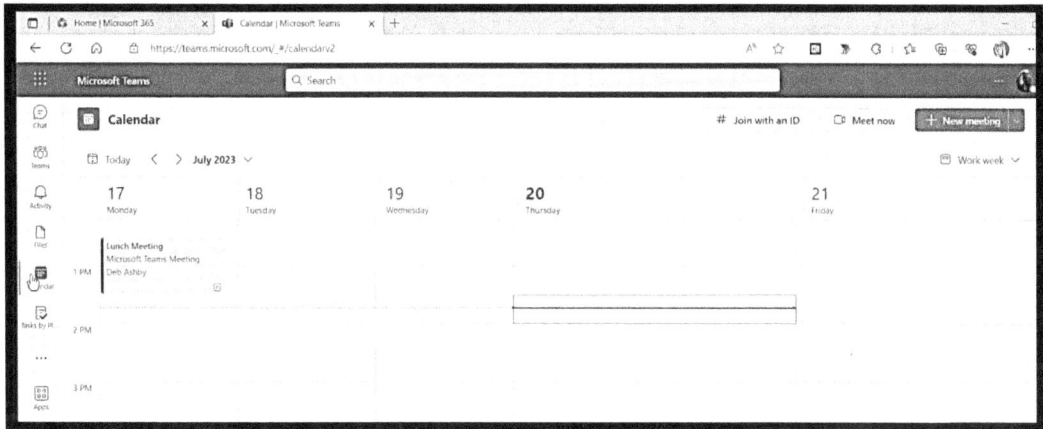

Then, there's something titled Tasks by Planner underneath that. Using the Apps option at the bottom, you can add an additional application that we added to keep track of all the work that our team completes. Clicking Apps provides us with access to every third-party app that we can add to teams to enhance our functionality and expand our experience.

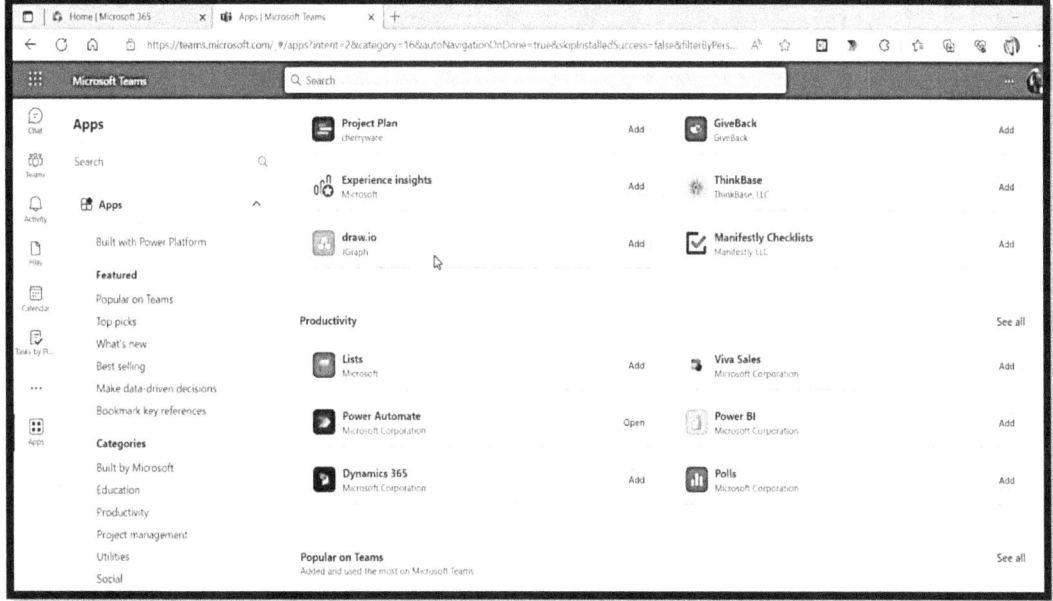

The final thing to talk about is the search bar, which is situated right at the top. Here are several keyboard shortcuts and little hints that will help to make things lot easier to find. You can search for a variety of items across all of your teams with this universal search. We will discuss this in more detail later on.

Regarding Teams Calendar

We also have an easy-to-use calendar. You have the following three options: Meet now, create new meetings, and sign up with your ID.

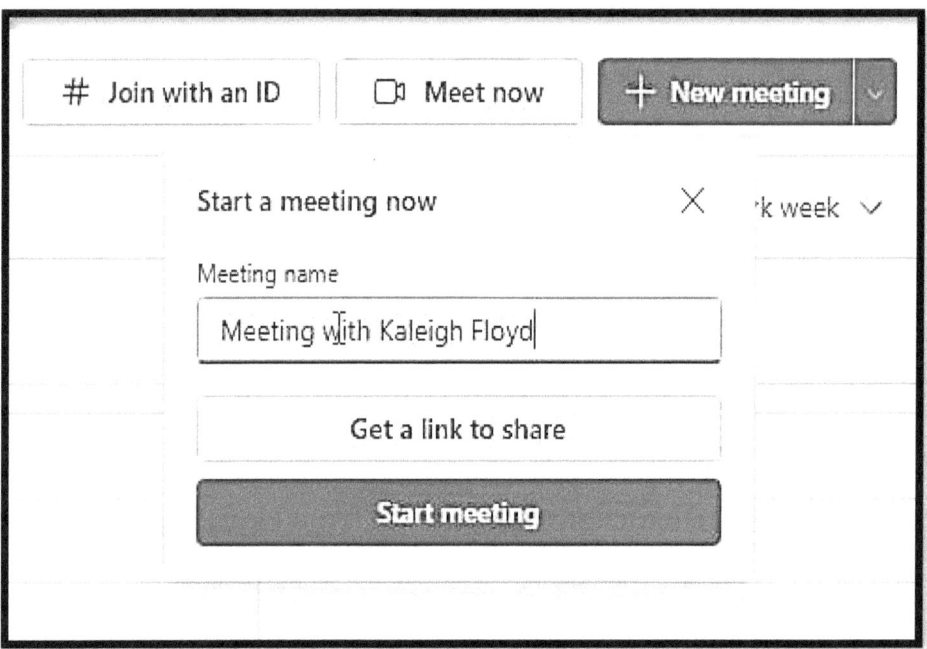

If someone has given you a specific ID, you can select to join their meeting when you join with that ID. You can obtain the link to the meeting right here and forward it to someone. If you choose to Meet Now, it will initiate a brief meeting at that same moment. That is, if you desired a hasty and spontaneous meeting at that very moment. Next, there's the New Meeting Schedule. If you click on it, a box will open with options for adding a title, needed attendees, and whether or not you want attendees to select whether or not to attend the meeting.

Following that, you will specify the day and hour of the meeting. Additionally, you may select if the meeting will repeat itself, whether it will take place on a daily, weekly, or monthly basis, and whether you would like to link it to a channel. In the event that you link it to a channel, each member of that team will receive a customized invitation. You can also decide on the meeting's location and whether or not it will be conducted online. You can choose to have a lobby where attendees can wait for the meeting to start while holding an online meeting. You can now opt to allow only organizers and co-organizers to bypass the lobby by selecting this last button. By doing this, you provide the meeting's organizers and co-organizers an opportunity to speak with attendees before allowing others to join.

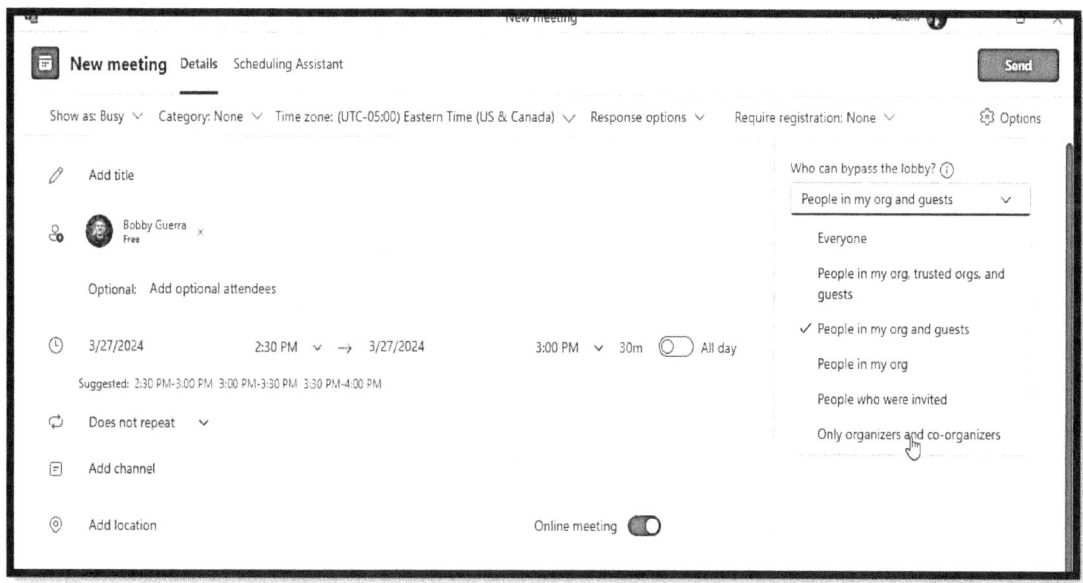

After that, you have the meeting's specifics and the choice to create an agenda. When you're finished collecting all of this data, you can opt to send them a meeting invitation, which will be sent to them right away and appear on your calendar.

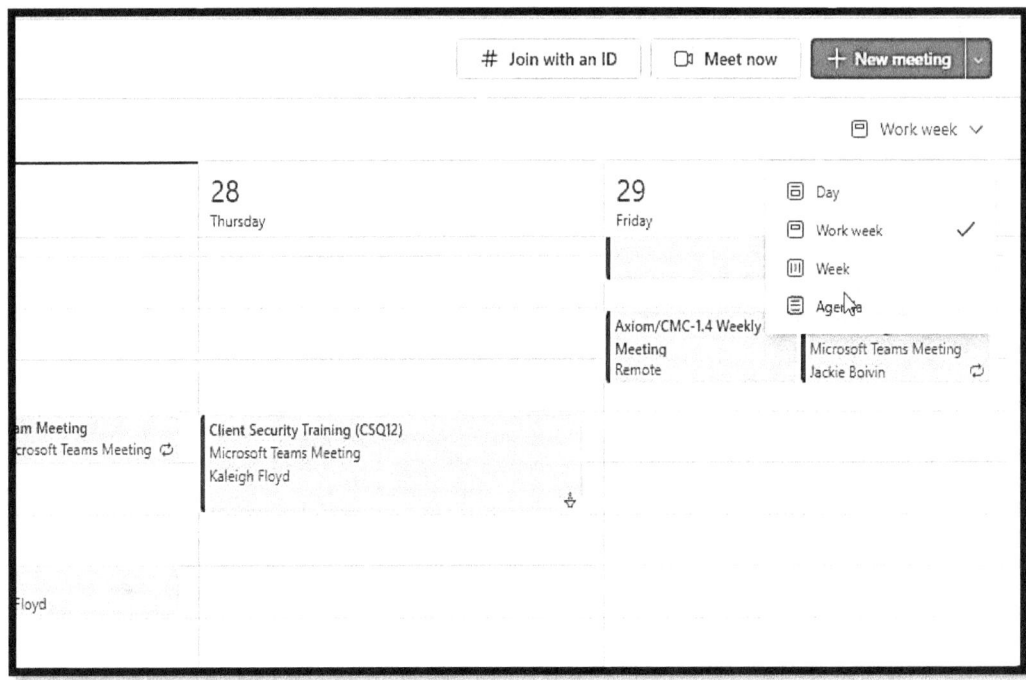

There are other ways to see your calendar: you may view it based on the Work week or use the new Agenda view, which just shows the locations of your meetings. Should you select the last option, those days will not be displayed as there are no booked meetings. You'll want this view, especially if you're trying to find appointments quickly.

Activities

1. On your PC, download and install the Microsoft Teams desktop application.
2. Modify the Teams application's design to your taste.
3. Delve into the many calendar views and options available in the Microsoft Teams app by opening the "Calendar" section of the app.

CHAPTER 2
EXAMINING INNOVATIVE FEATURES IN GROUPS

Synopsis

Chapter 2 covers the latest features added to Microsoft Teams, such as the Collaborative Loop, direct task list linkage, improved search capabilities, browser integration, and live captioning. These new features have the potential to further improve processes and teamwork. In this chapter, we'll be showcasing Microsoft Teams' most recent features. This includes extra apps including Meet, Stream, and OneDrive; you may customize your own reaction tray; Loop components are added to channels; and much more.

A component of my collaborative Loop system

Channels and chat both now support components. Clicking "Start a post" at the bottom will allow you to choose a topic. The "Collaborate with Loop" feature can be added by clicking this plus button. This is how the user interface of the new Teams was harmonized.

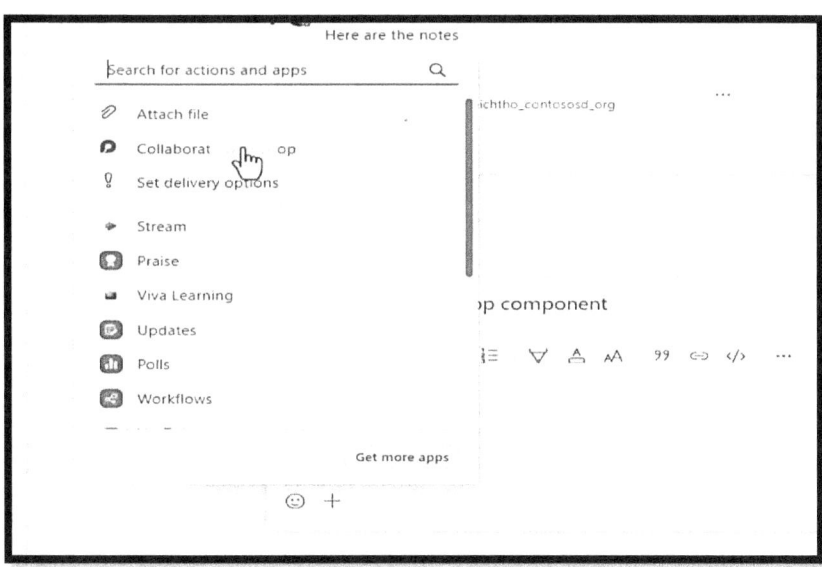

These options—list checklist, Q&A, tables, and task list—all function collaboratively, just like Loop does in all the other programs, including Word, Outlook, and Whiteboard. For example, you can make your first component from a task list. After giving it a title, begin adding tasks to this. You can view your task planning here if you add a new assignment and quickly submit this message. Now that the loop component is in the main channel, anyone may go there and add to it as well, making collaborative loop component creation simple.

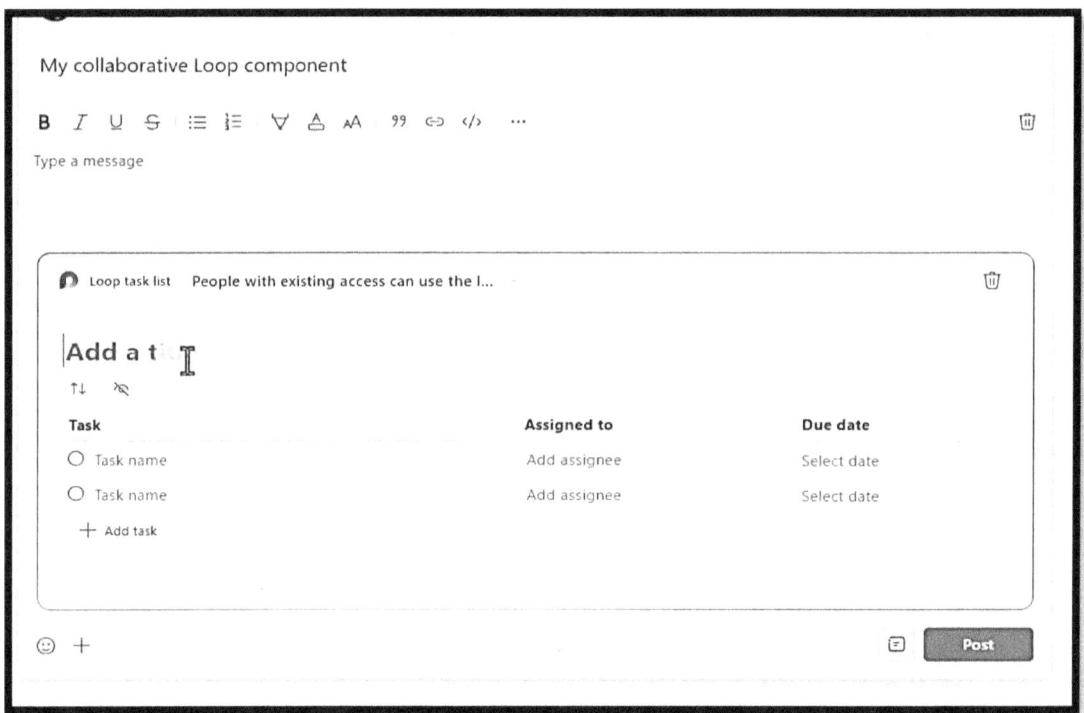

There are a lot more loop components that you can perform; this is just an example of what you can accomplish. You may view who has shared access and shared locations, as well as copy components with a single click by selecting "Copy Component" and pasting it into an email. Loop offers a plethora of enjoyable activities; however, it should be noted that it is currently supported in Teams channels.

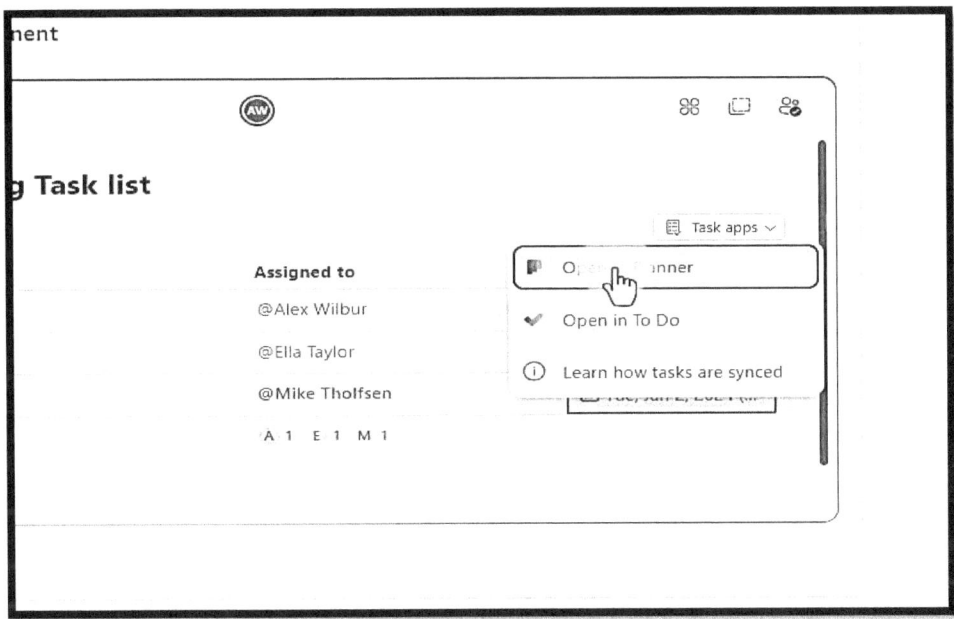

To-do list links that are easy to recognize

The direct connection between the elements of your task list and the planner or to-do list should now be visible to you. This subsequent addition is also a product of Loop.

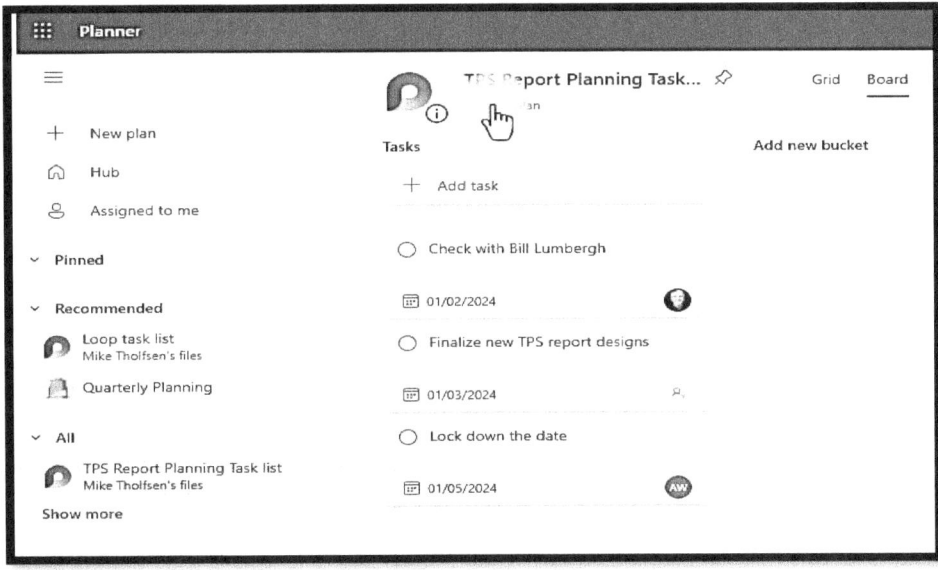

This is where the Tasks app is located. By selecting "open in Planner" with a click here, you can see that the Loop component immediately creates a Planner board. This also has the benefit of automatically adding the job to the to-do list. When you open the to-do list (a free service that comes with Microsoft 365), you may see the date that it was added automatically. This makes it easier to find stuff within a discussion or channel.

Locating chat rooms or channels is made easy

The use of this is really easy. Pressing CTRL+F will, assuming you are in a channel, open a window on the right that lets you search inside of it. Several examples show up when you type something in. You can click to navigate directly to that message and find what you're looking for if you press Enter. You'll notice that it appears quickly. This works in a chat similarly. When this chat window opens, put "report" into it with CTRL+F, and then hit Enter. There are a ton of postings in this conversation about the report. You can now navigate around after finding the exact instance you're looking for.

About Mark Team Notifications

The fourth new feature allows you to mark all team notifications for a certain team as read with a single click. Let's say that the Product team has three different notifications up top. The three notifications will be marked as read and become invisible immediately upon choosing "Mark all as read" from the three-dot menu.

Customize a pre-established list of responses

Hovering your cursor over a debate will reveal a limited number of responses. Clicking the plus sign on the happy face will set this response. Over here, there's another little smiley face that says, "Customize default reactions." Four default options will appear when you click on it. Next, you can click Save after adding your own and disabling some of these. The default responses that show up when you hover over a message are now these.

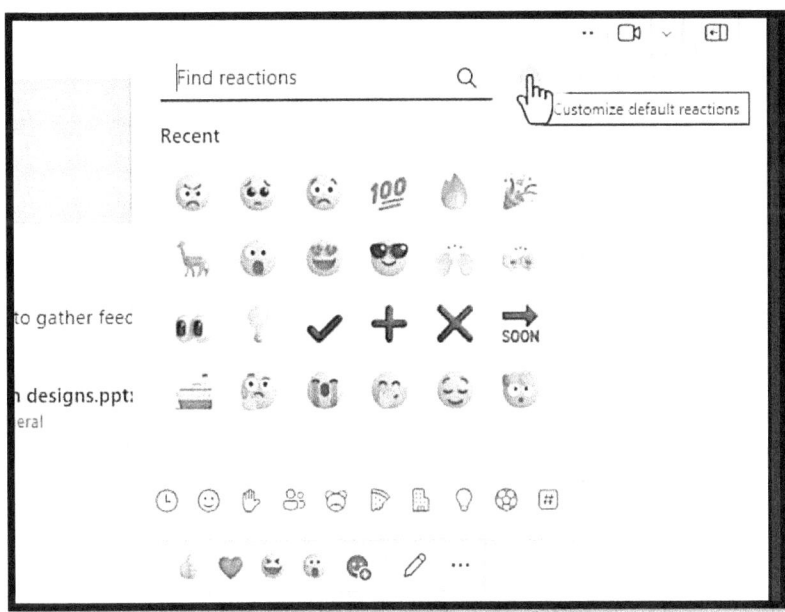

The latest version of the OneDrive software

The Files app on the left-hand rail is the OneDrive app, which now pulls in the entire new OneDrive. Your OneDrive, which is the same OneDrive that appears on the web version of OneDrive, will load when you click on it. The Upload button allows you to add and upload new files. This is where you can access all of the filtering, including Word, Excel, PowerPoint, and more. You can browse by meetings or people and instantly access all of your other teams from here. You can now swiftly access other files thanks to this, and Teams comes equipped with all the functionality of the newly launched OneDrive.

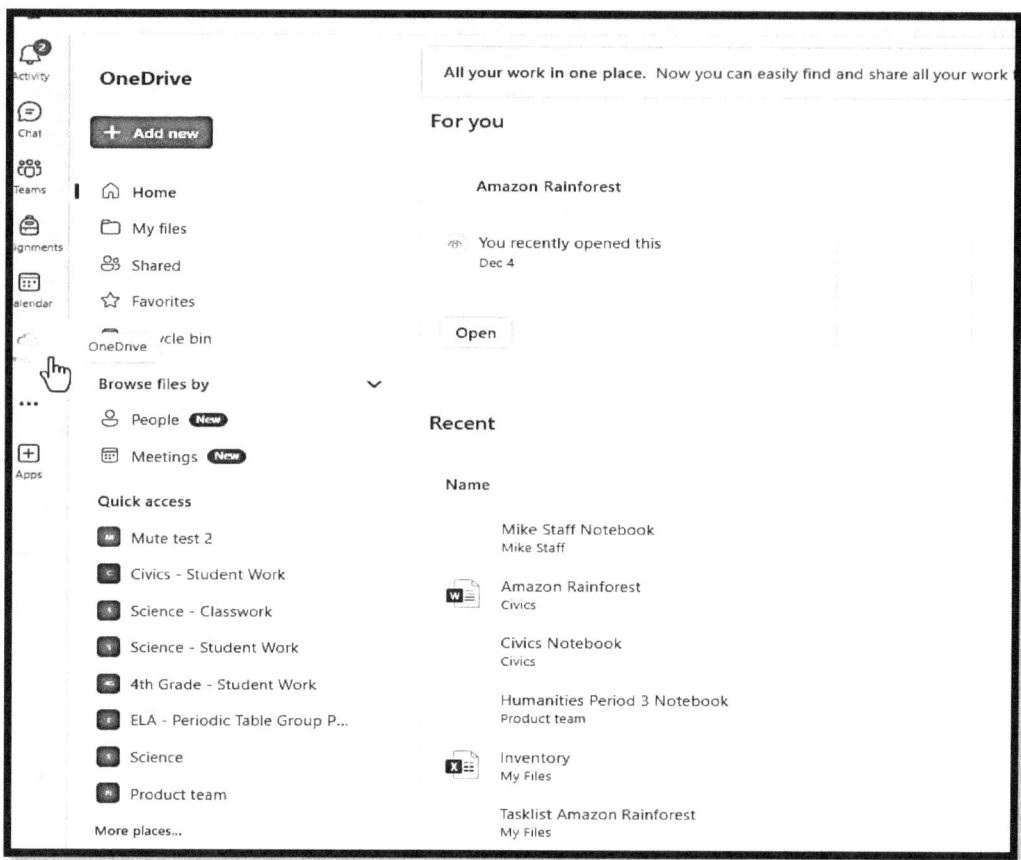

It should be remembered that if you collaborate with others, the classic files will still appear first. If you're a teacher working with class teams and you have queries regarding the course materials, you can still access the files in the general channel. A unified OneDrive that gathers all of your files in one place can be seen on the left.

The Meet app

This is now included in the updated Teams. By selecting Meet, you can download this app, which is the meetings app. To ensure that it remains in place, you can right-click on this and pin it. This area holds everything pertaining to your meetings, both past and present. This is also where you may get recordings of recent meetings. Just click on that option if you want to view the summary.

Rescheduling and sending reminders are only two of the Meet app's many fantastic features. If some people haven't responded, you can remind them about the meeting by selecting the "Send Reminder" option, which will open a chat box. This is a practical way to remind individuals to respond. There's also the option to reschedule right there; selecting it will bring up the meeting and give you the option to reschedule. The Meet app is now available for anybody to add, and as we showed before, you can right-click on it to instantly pin it.

The Mobile App Stream

Microsoft Stream, our video solution for use in corporate and educational settings, has a redesigned homepage in the main web area. To add something to Teams, you'll need to right-click on it and pin it.

You may share videos, record your screen, and create playlists, among other things. This is where all of the videos that you have submitted and those that have been suggested to you are compiled. You can choose to see it in grid or list view. To access everything on Stream in one location, you may examine items that you have made, look for recorded meetings, view playlists if you have any, and view shared files or favorites. The homepage of Microsoft 365 appears to be very identical to that of previous software versions, with the exception that Teams now shares the same feature set and user interfaces. Additionally, you may pin this with a right-click, exactly like you have in the past. If you would rather not pin it, you may just say "unpin" to make it vanish.

The Browser integration

This new functionality allows the Edge Browser and Teams discussion to be instantly connected. When you click on a link, for instance, everything from the Wikipedia page opens up right here and the context of the chat appears to the right.

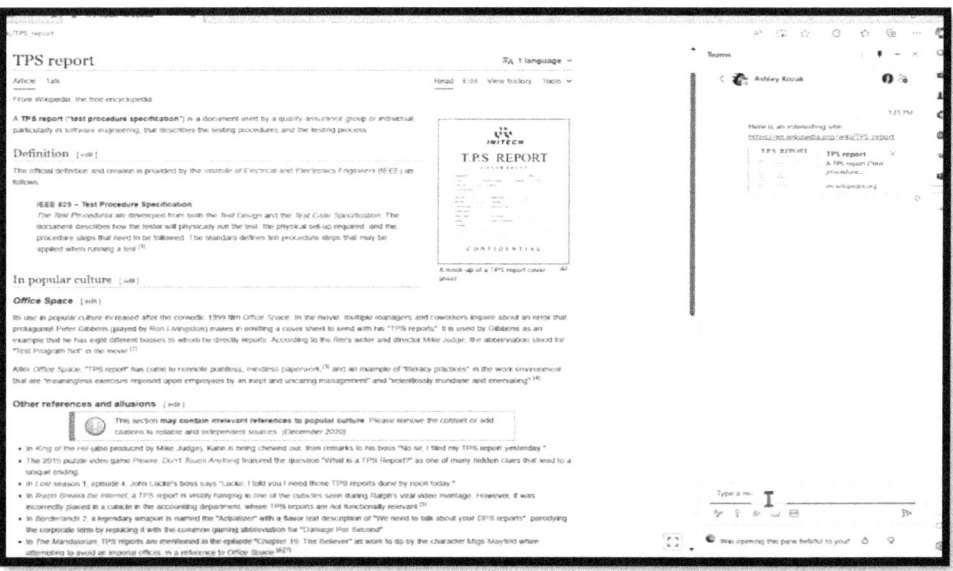

You may see an exchange you had with someone about a certain topic; you can also talk to them when that website is open. The webpage is interesting. It's a handy method of merging your conversations, and if you're in a channel, it will start doing the same thing where the website appears right next to the conversation and the context.

Improvements to the live captioning

This relates to improvements to the layout and positioning of live captions. Let's say you turn on live captioning during a meeting. Choose Language and Speech from the three-dot menu to activate Live Captions. You'll see that the live captions are playing at the bottom when you select your preferred language.

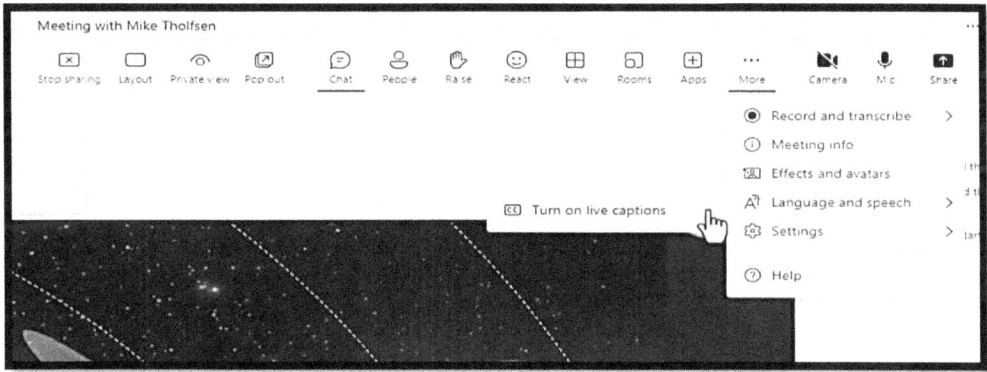

There are numerous new caption settings on the right. Once you click Settings, you can adjust the font size, color, height, position, and language. You can also see a preview of the final product while you make adjustments.

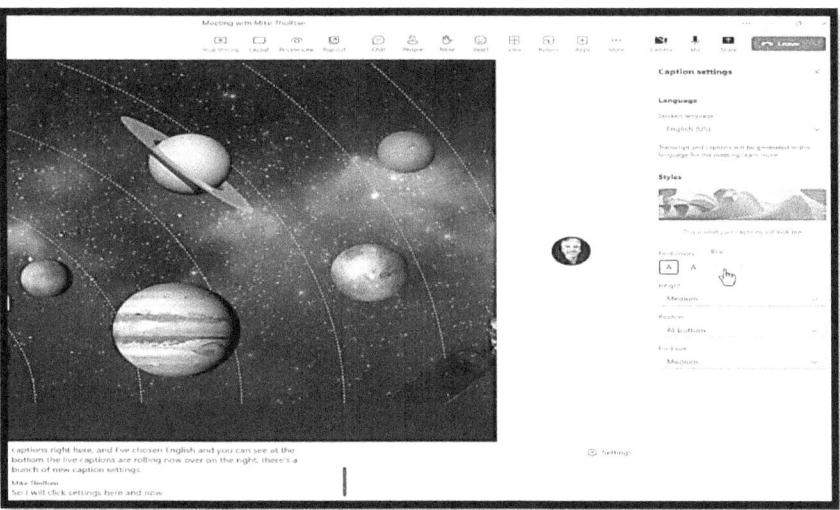

Everything's height is adjustable. If you want your captions to be up at the top, you can make it a little bit longer, smaller, or medium. The captions will now go right across the top. You can put it at the bottom or top. Finally, altering the text size is another option. For your live captioning, you have a plethora of alternatives at your disposal.

Activities

1. Start a fresh Collaborative Loop and extend an invitation to your group to participate.
2. Play around with the various Collaborative Loop features, such commenting and work assignment.
3. Examine the ways in which Collaborative Loop and other Microsoft 365 apps interact.

CHAPTER THREE
CREATION OF TEAMS AND CHANNELS

Synopsis

Creating and managing Teams and Channels—described in depth in chapter 3—allows for more efficient communication and organization. You will get knowledge on how to create Teams from various sources, oversee team members, create tags, and modify channel configurations. Teams are quite intriguing because there are multiple channels within each team. When you go to a team in Microsoft Teams, you'll see that a general channel is required. You can make as many subchannels beneath the main channel as you'd like, depending on how your team works and how you want to arrange content. It's crucial that you understand that you may manage your teams, examine your pending invites, and view your teams' stats by clicking the three dots at the top of this page.

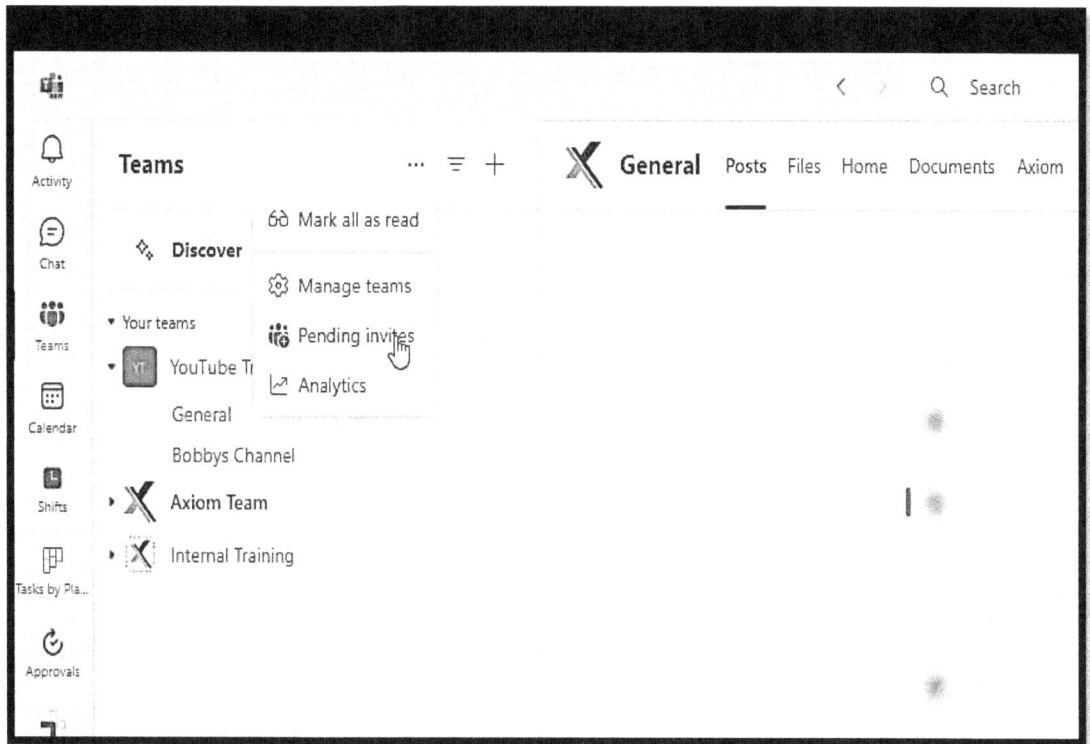

Public and private teams are the two types of teams you may create with Microsoft Teams. The difference between the two is that a private team requires an invitation from you, the team owner, in order for someone to join. Moreover, private teams are concealed from view, whereas public teams are accessible to every employee in the organization without permission to join. Let's now examine an example of each. A "Join or create a team" button can be found at the bottom of the Teams screen, which shows all of our teams on the left.

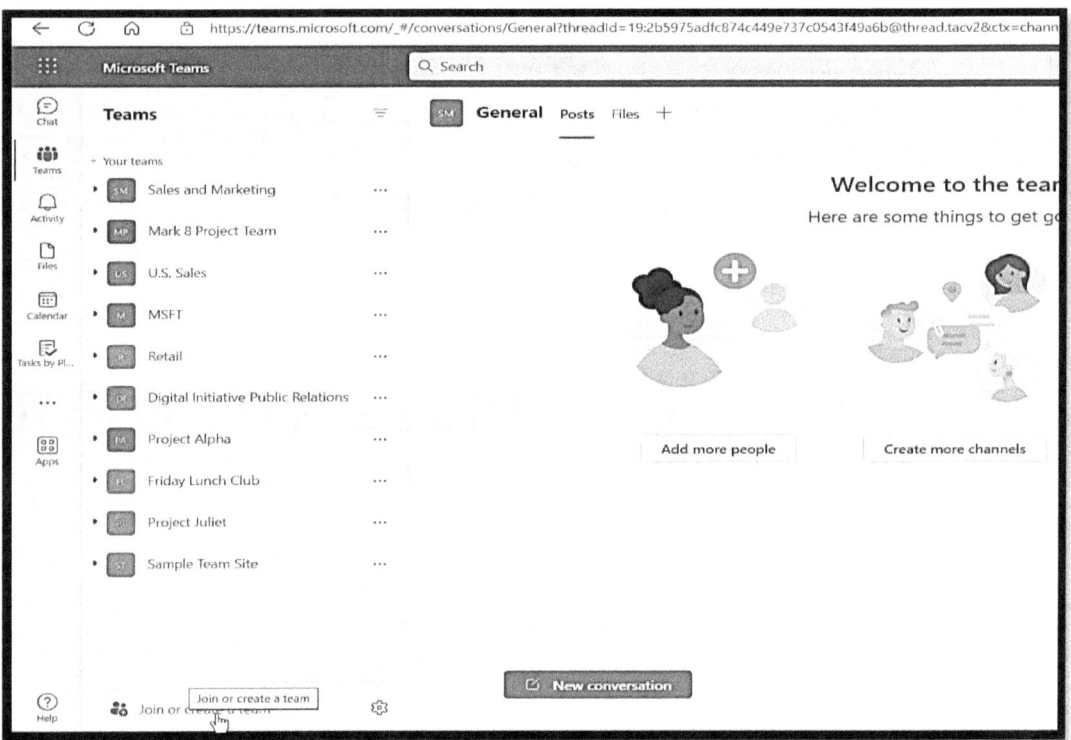

Establishing a group

The page that displays when we click on this has two options. The option on the right is to join a team with a code. Later on, we will discuss this in more detail, but for now, let's focus on the formation of a team. To accomplish this, click the "Create a team" button. A few alternatives will then be displayed to us on how to proceed.

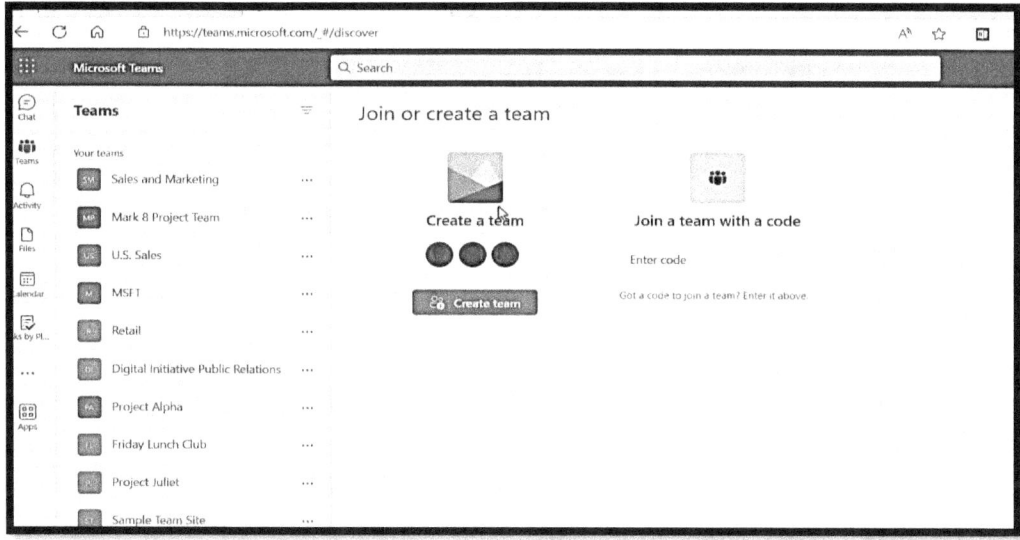

We can start from zero and build a simple team that only provides the framework; but, starting from scratch necessitates adding each member of the team by hand.

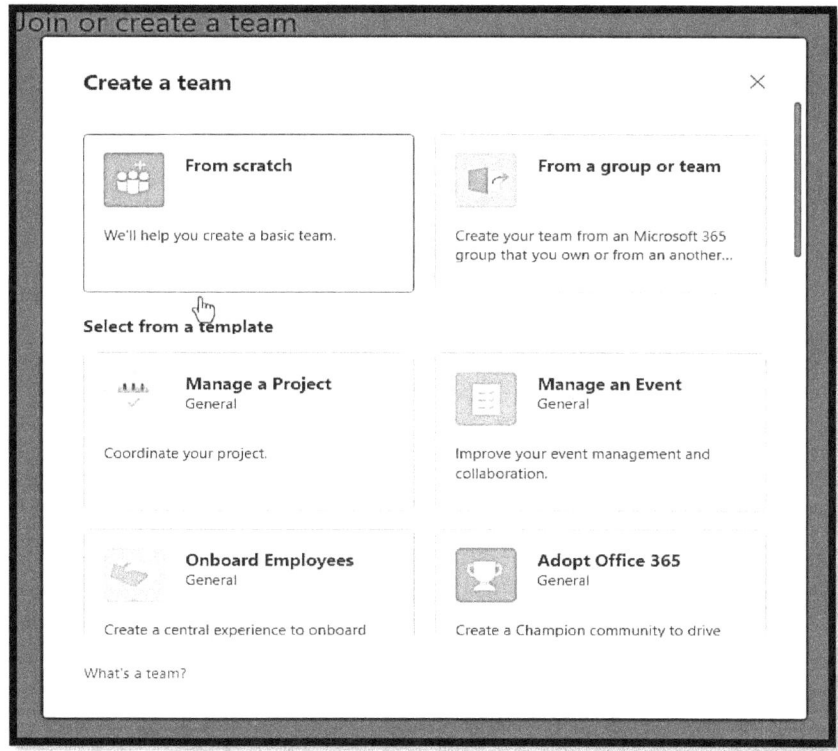

The alternative option available to you is to build a team based on an already-existing Microsoft Teams team or Microsoft 365 group. For example, if you already have an Outlook group with, say, ten members, you could save some time by building a team based on that group, which will include every member.

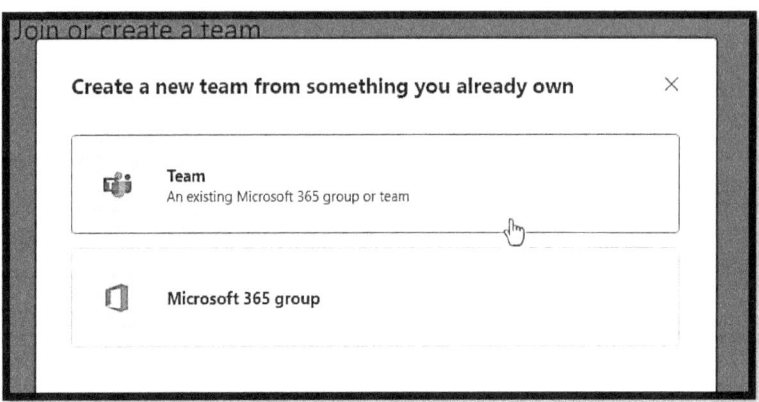

Our third option is to create a team using one of our many templates, as you can see by scrolling through. You will have to choose which of these themes works best for you, but first let's have a look at a few examples. The channels that you will receive are outlined in these templates, which are pertinent to the team's subject matter.

Out of a collection

Click from a group or team and choose Microsoft 365 group to create a team based on a Microsoft 365 group for this example. We can view the groups we've made in Outlook from there. Choosing one of these groups, clicking "Create," and that's it is as simple as pie. We have our normal General channel open so we can start conversing with team members. The new team is at the bottom of the teams list. If we click the three dots next to the team and choose Manage team, we can view every member, guest, and owner of the Microsoft 365 group. We have the ability to view each member as the owners. Obviously, if we want someone to be a co-owner, we can shift them to the top half of the screen by just giving them more access to "Own". This method of forming a team will save you time if you already have a Microsoft 365 group set up and you just want to copy over the members and settings.

Right from the start

Let's look at one more strategy for team building. The "Join or create" button will be selected once more, and a new team will be formed from scratch. We can now decide whether to create a team that is private, public, or organizational in nature.

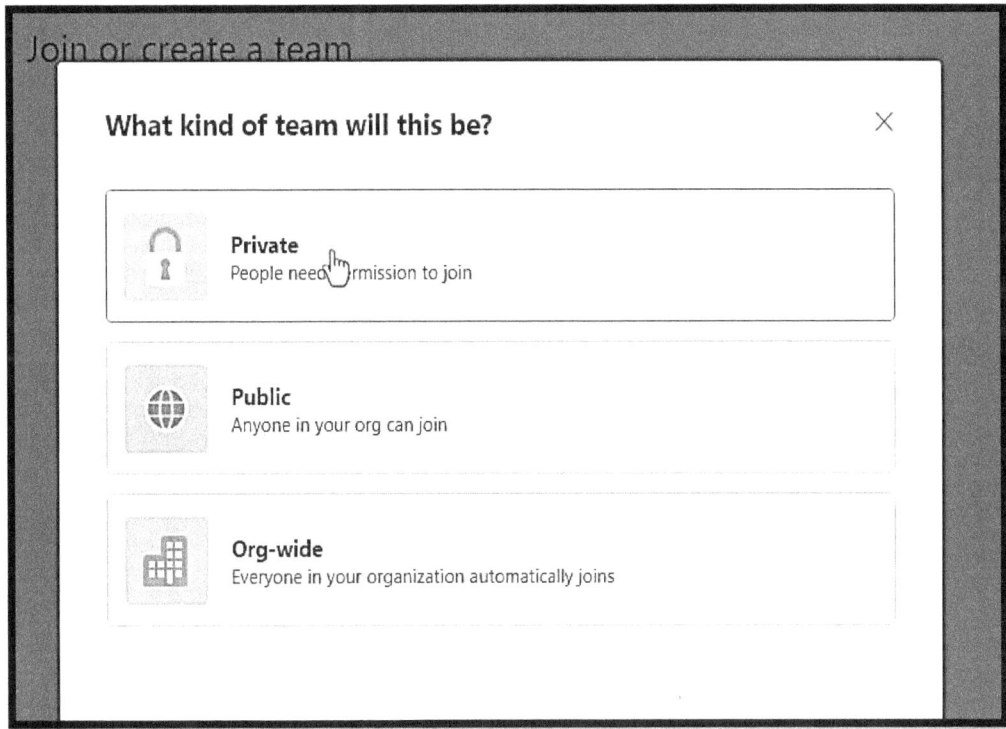

As we earlier stated, these differ in that:

1. Individuals must be granted permission to join a private group.
2. Any member of your organization can join a public group by clicking the join button.
3. When you create a group that is open to the entire organization, everyone on the list will see it as soon as it is created. This is because everyone is automatically a member of that team.
4. To join a public team, one must physically press the join button; to join a private team, one must receive an invitation.

We're going to start from scratch with a public team for this example. Our team has to have a name. Once more, you can click "Create" after adding a description.

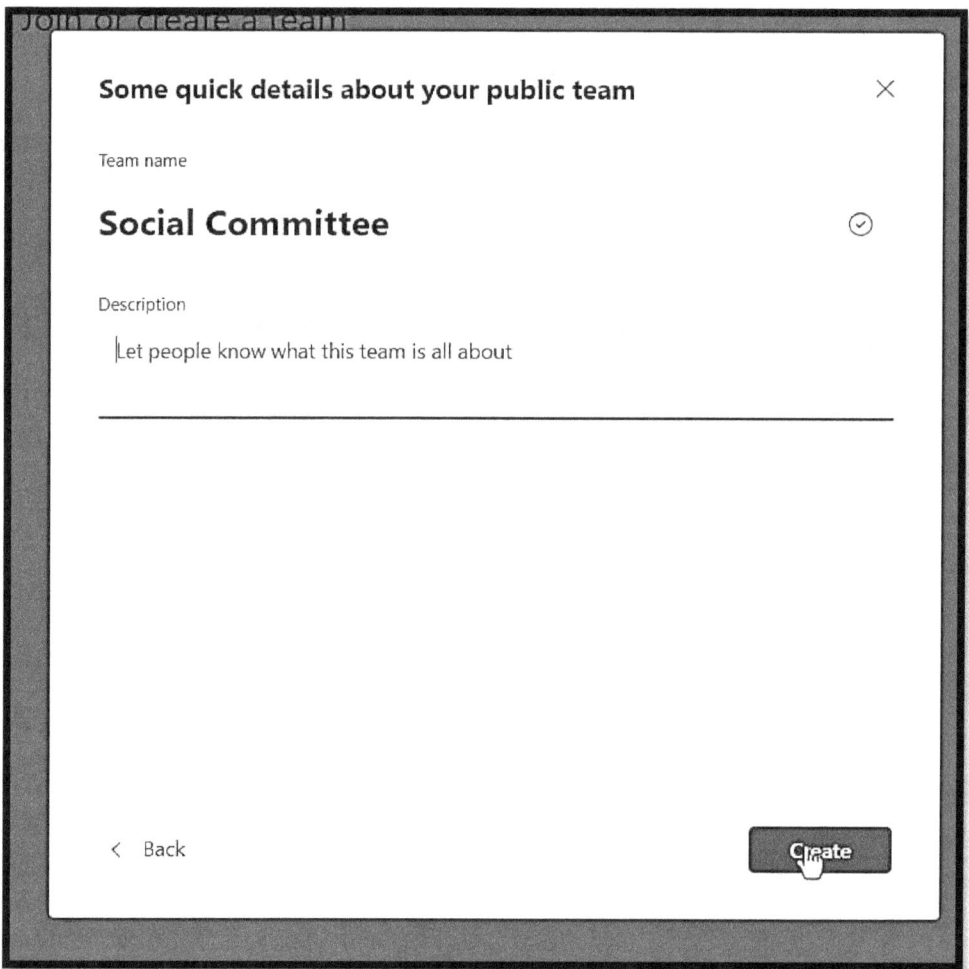

After it has created the team, it will ask us to select members to join it. Once more, you can begin entering the name of a member of your organization and then click the "Add" button to include them. At this point, you can either leave them all as members or turn any of these individuals into owners and grant them little more access. We'll select "Close."

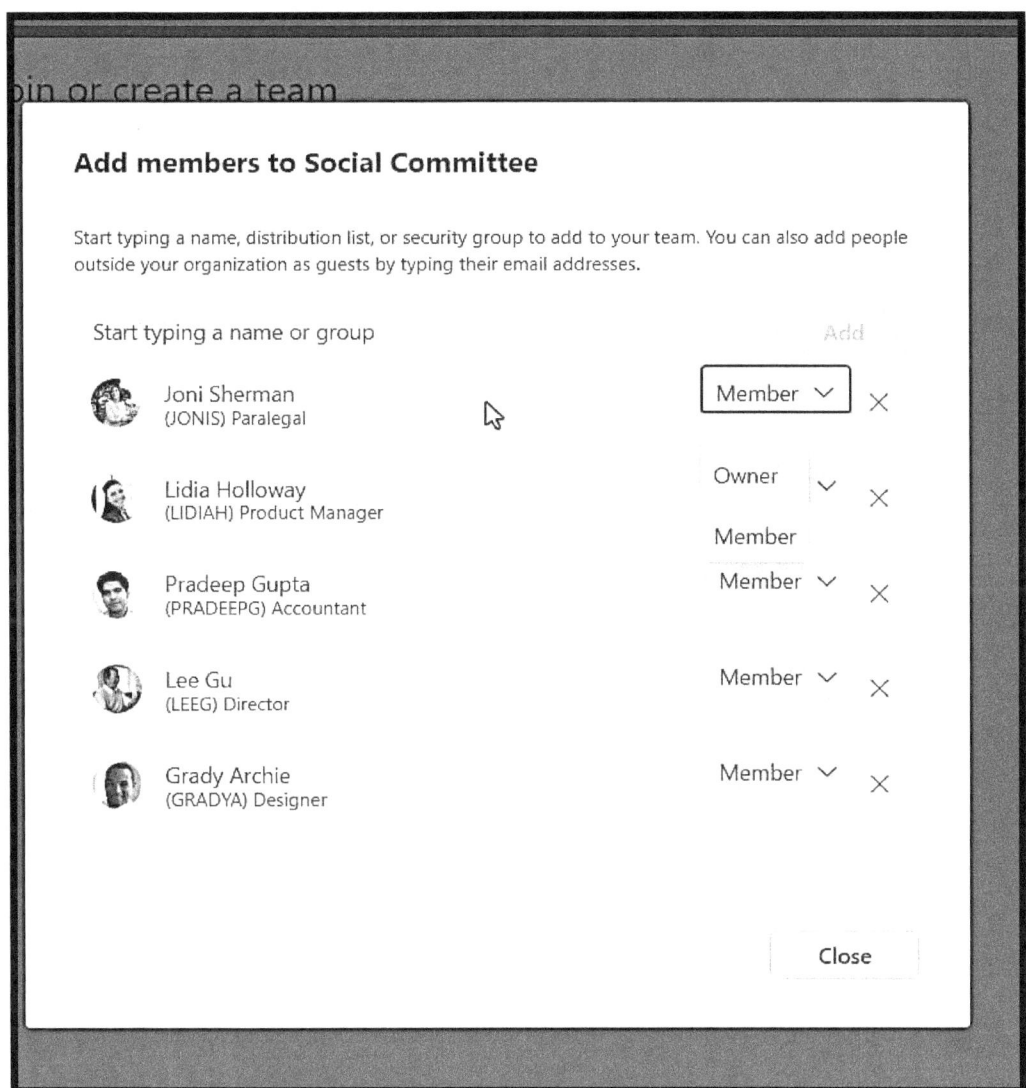

Our new team is now visible at the bottom, and we have a general channel again so that we may initiate communication.

Making use of the template

The final strategy for team formation is to use a template. This example shows us the channels that we will be able to access: General, Announcements, Employee Chat, Trainer, and Training. We will also click the "Onboard Employees" template. It will add nine applications for us as well.

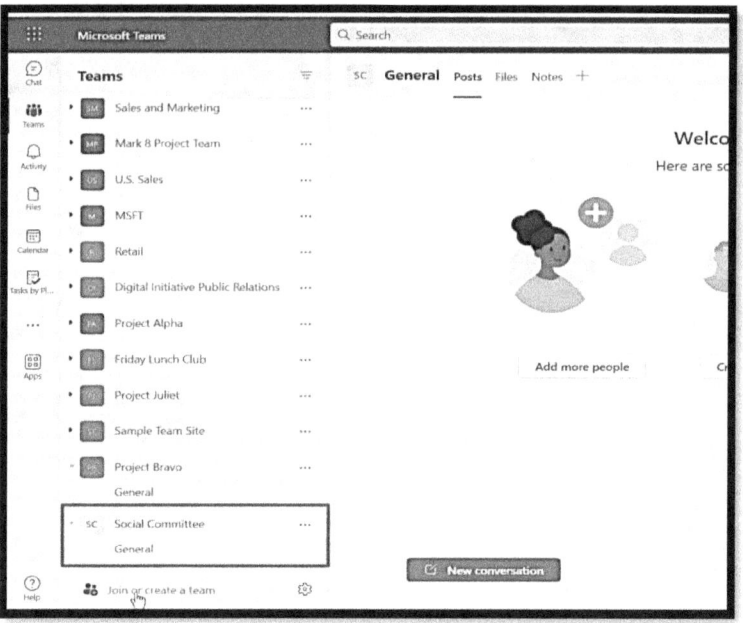

We'll select the next option, and in this example, we'll also make our team public. At this point, we can give our team a name. You can rename these channels if you extend customized channels, so you're not limited to the default names. Following that, we'll click "Create," and the team will be formed. Recall that we are forming a public team once more.

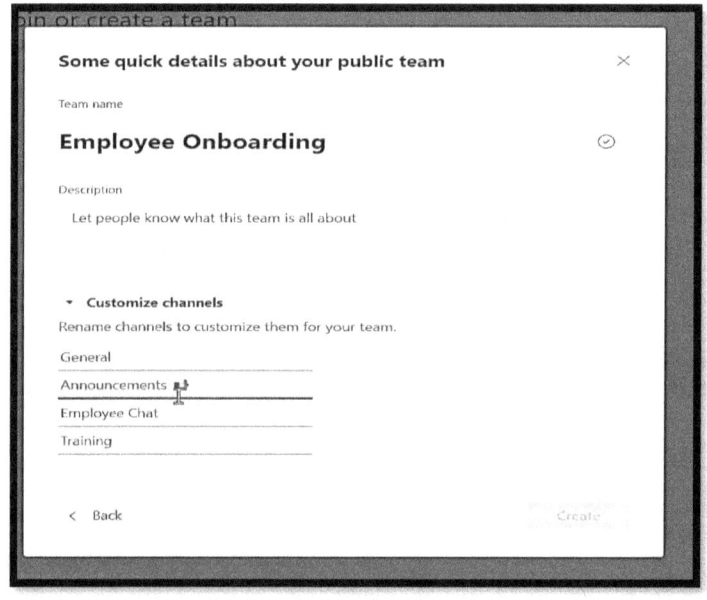

When you use a template like this, it adds a lot of features, including connectors to other programs, and creates all the channels so you can dismiss this window and carry on working, but it will take a little longer to construct the team. But when the team is formed, you will be informed. The bottom of this page indicates that an Employee Onboarding system has been created.

Taking part in a group

Going back to the "Join or create a team" area, things have changed. Let's say that our squad is now called "Music and Movie Recommendations." This is a publicly accessible team that another one of our employees built. A public team will appear in this window exactly where it is formed. All you have to do to join this team is move your mouse over and choose "Join team."

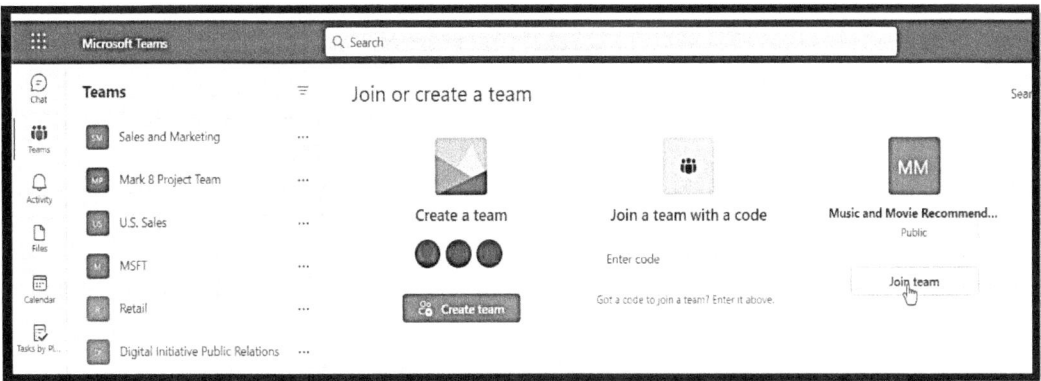

We can see the team for music and movie recommendations at the bottom of our team's list now that we've joined that team. That's how you become a member of a public team; however, joining a private team works a little differently. The team owner must extend an invitation to you in order for you to join; this will appear as a pop-up. In addition to the pop-up in the corner, you'll now notice that there's a notification or alert in the activity area. If you click on it, you'll be notified that you've been added to the team, and you can now access that team by going to your Teams and scrolling to the bottom. Alternatively, you can use a code to join a team. The team owner has the ability to provide you with a code. Let me give you an illustration of this. We can create a unique Team Code under this section under the Settings tab by going to one of our teams, clicking the three dots, and selecting Manage Team. From there, we may invite anyone to join the team by sharing their

Team Code with them. To join the team, those individuals would just need to go to the "Join or Create team" option, copy this code, and paste it into an email or channel.

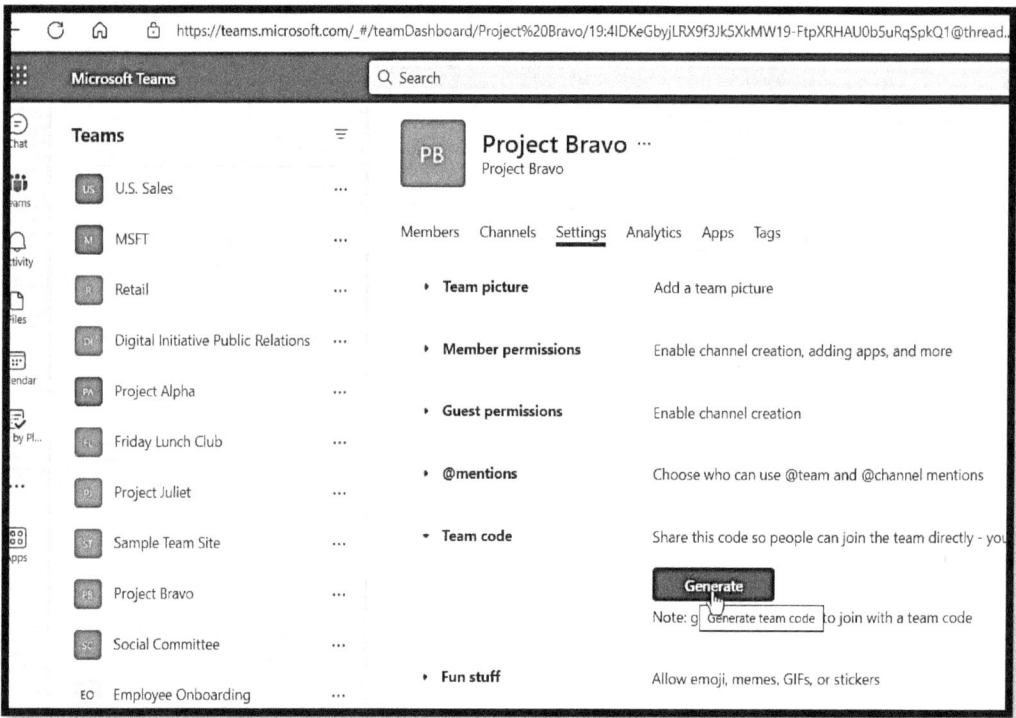

As you can see, there are various methods for joining and forming teams in the public and private domains.

Management of Teams and Channel

Understanding some of your Microsoft Teams team and channel management options is essential. For example, if you're currently on the general channel in a team and you should be familiar with the fact that three dots signify the existence of a menu that will provide us with further options. By selecting the three dots here, you can view the range of tools available to you to help you manage this team.

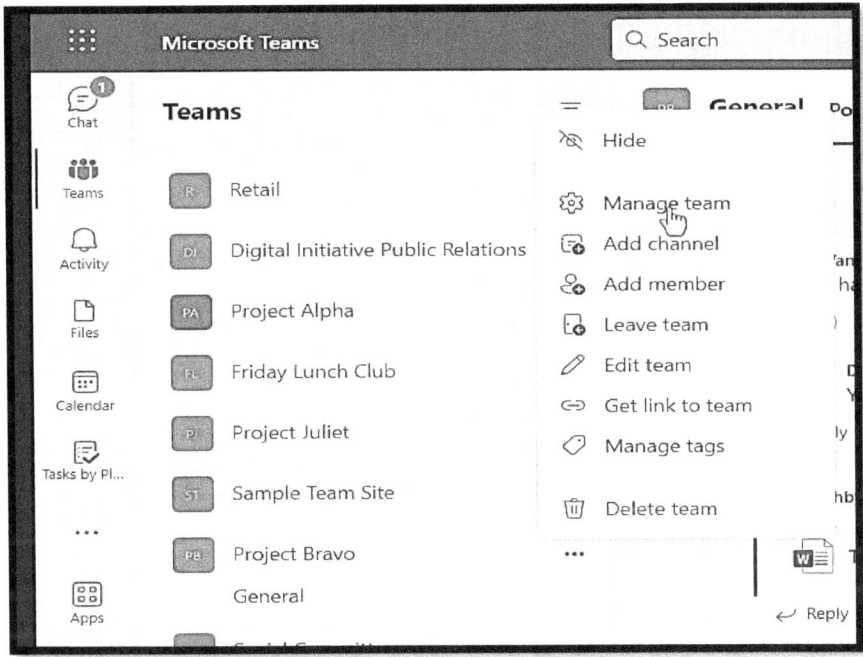

The management of the teams

First, let's look at it by choosing "Manage team." This time, the top is covered in many tabs. If you're ever in need of knowing precisely who is a part of this particular team, the first tab we have is called Members, and it divides it down into owners, members, and visitors for your convenience. From this location, you may view the owners and members. Since you have already seen how to promote or demote these people, as an owner, you can simply use the column to demote your co-owner back to member status.

A search box is also located at the top. When you drag your mouse over any member of your huge team, a small pop-up window appears with a preview of the many activities you can make. You can also use this feature to search for specific members. From this screen, you can message a member, start a video conference, and send them a quick note. Additionally, all of their contact details are visible to you. Sometimes, this is helpful. You can add new members with ease by selecting the "add members" link located in the upper right corner.

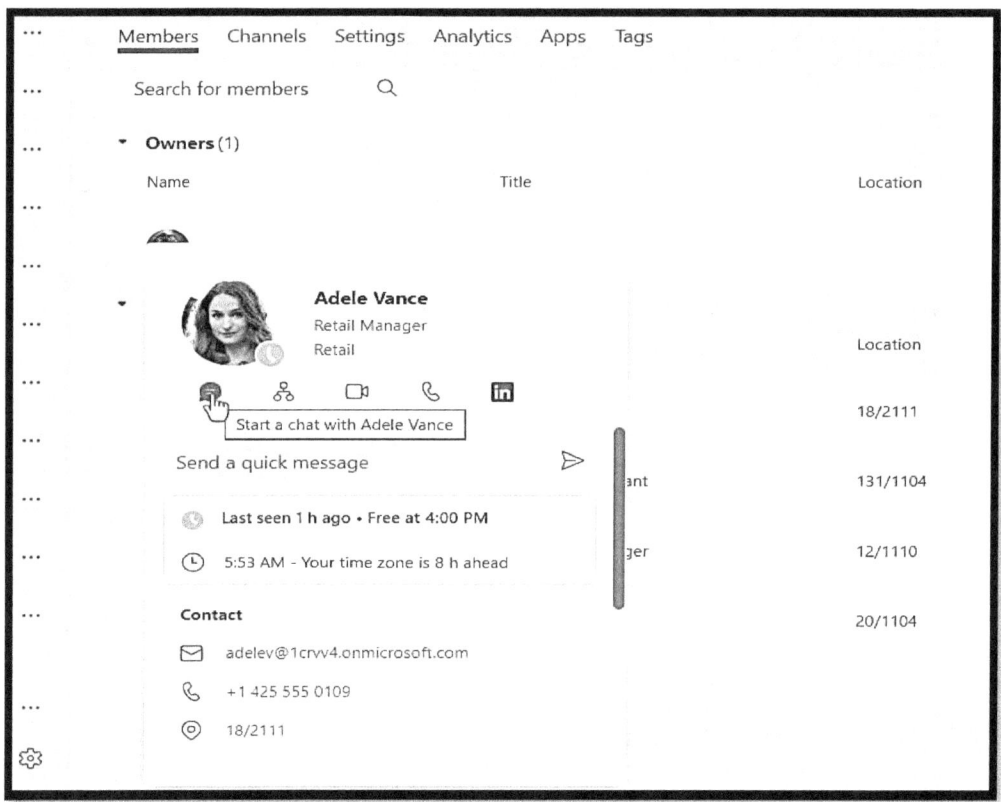

Let us return to the Manage team and navigate to the Settings section. This is where you may adjust every setting for your group. You can alter this avatar, for instance, to a different image instead of the plain, default one. Select "Change picture," add a photo, and then select "Save." Permissions for members can also be specified. This is a set of checkboxes that you can enable or disable for this team based on what you want.

We have all of them toggled on, for instance, so that members can add and edit channels, make private channels, remove and re-add channels, and so on. Take a quick look at these; it's possible that you want to prevent users from being able to do things like delete and restore channels. If so, you can deselect that option, so make sure to verify and make any necessary modifications. You also have a guest permission section, where you can specify exactly what you want visitors to be able to perform.

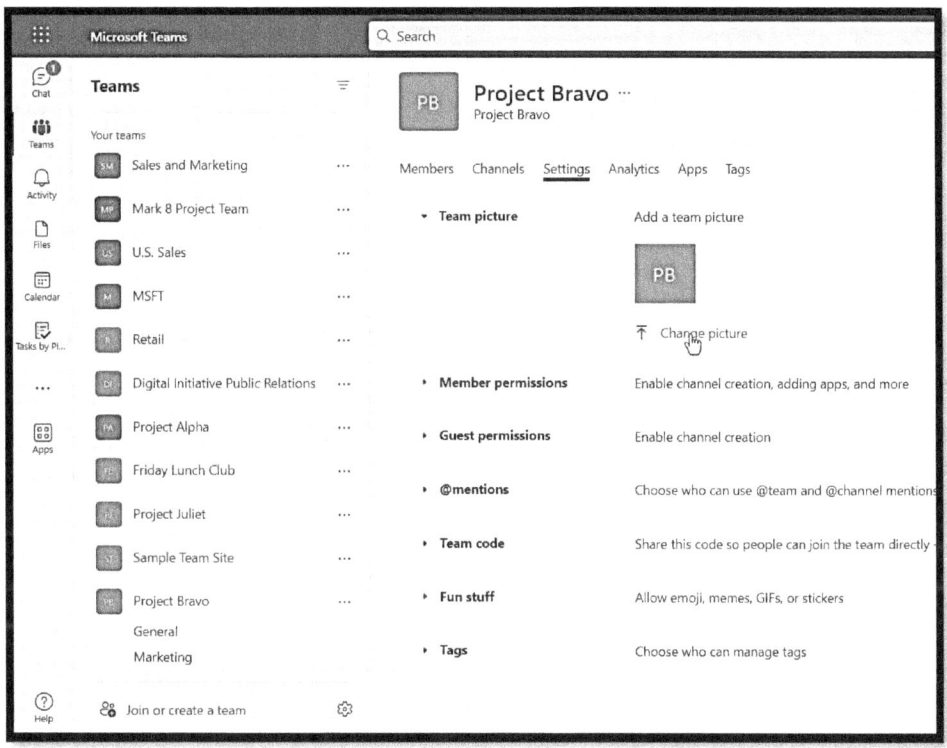

In the @mention area, you can define who can use @team and @channel mentions. As you may remember, you have the ability to @mention both specific people and the entire team in order to message every member of the team. The same can be applied to a particular channel. This is where you have a unique code linked to the team that you may share with others to extend an invitation to join (we looked at this section previously). This has a "Copy" button that makes copying and pasting into an email really easy.

Have a quick look at the stickers, gifs, memes, and emoji categories under the "Fun Stuff" category. By default, every item in this list is selected. In the final section at the bottom, devoted to tags, you can designate who will be in charge of overseeing all of the tags connected to this team. As you can see, tag management is currently under the purview of the team owners. To access the Analytics page, which is helpful for reviewing data or a team overview, keep going through these tabs. The Apps page shows you all of the installed apps currently on your device.

Setting up Tags

You can add a new tag by going to the Tags section. You can quickly communicate with a large number of individuals at once by using tags. If you were to establish a tag for "sales assistant," for example, it would effectively group all of the people who have the same job title—let's use "sales assistant" as an example—with several employees.

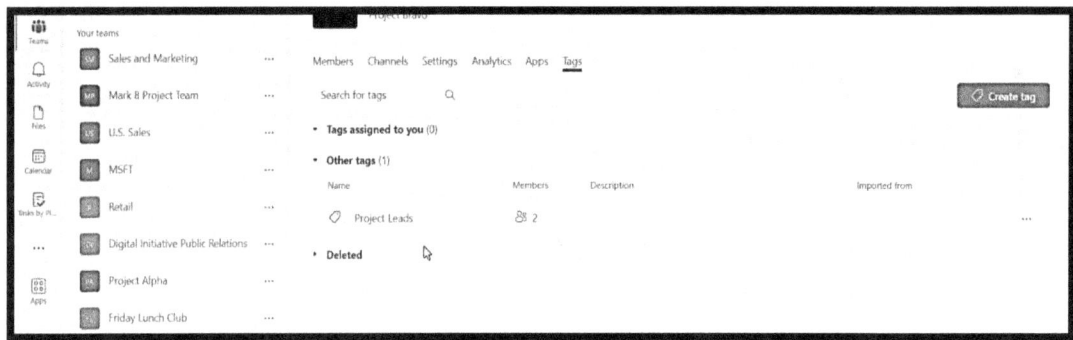

Let's create a tag named Project Leads, add people to it, and then describe it. Once they're made, we can use them in posts similar to @mention. Go to the Tags page to manage your tags and create new ones. Remember that in addition to those team settings, we also have channel settings.

Concerning Channels

You have a little page within a channel that has postings. They work much like a miniature bulletin board that you can personalize with different messages that are important for the team to know. Click this button to start a post. You can then add more content and enter the message in the subject line. You can choose whether to post this in multiple channels, only in this channel, and whether you want the moderators and yourself to be the only ones allowed to respond. Though they are simply between you and the other person, these are more akin to direct discussions, so bear that in mind as you consider your other options. If you have been invited to a team but haven't seen it yet, you can click on the three dots above and choose Pending invites. This is mostly for communications and announcements inside the team. When someone invites your team to a shared channel, the invite will show up there, and by clicking those three dots, you can access the Analytics section. You can see how many people are actively contributing to your team, how many posts and replies there have been, and if the channel is secret or public. You have a lot of options within Teams to adjust the parameters for the team. You can modify member permissions, add or remove channel material (such stickers and memes), allow users to add or remove apps, and upload custom applications by clicking the "Manage team" button. Members have the option to allow or prohibit the creation of private channels.

You have the option to create private channels inside a team. This suggests that just as there are public and private teams, there may also be public and private channels that are below those teams; therefore, you will need an invitation to get in contact with them. It's vital to keep in mind that Microsoft Teams and SharePoint integrate seamlessly, so when you build a team using Microsoft Teams, a SharePoint site is built instantly. We recommend that you connect them since it will be very beneficial for your team. Additionally, you ought to store your data in places where only the people you want and no one else should be able to access it.

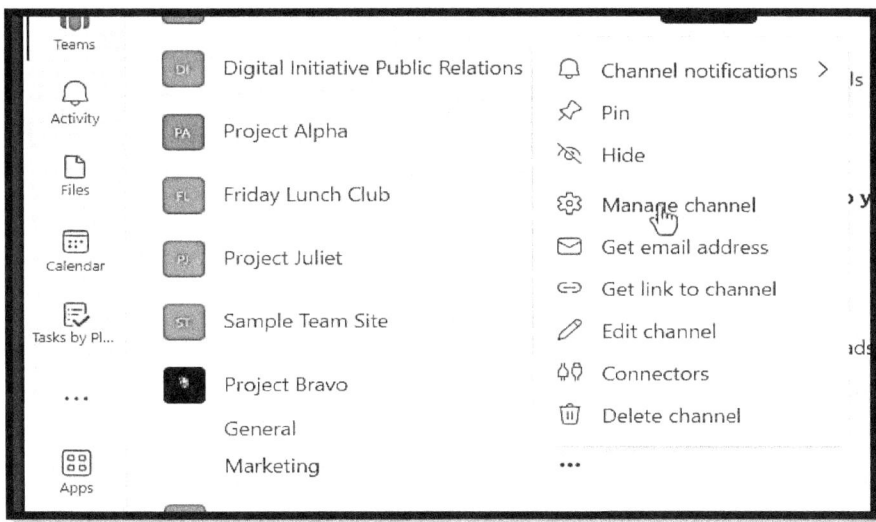

You may view all of the channels that are a part of this team by selecting the Channels option at the top of the page. The main channel will be visible to you, and from here you may also add more channels.

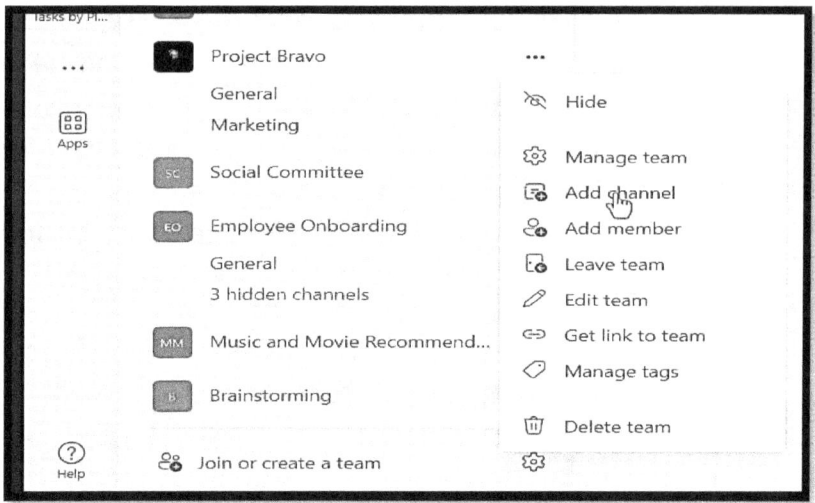

You can make a brand-new channel specifically for this team by clicking the "Add Channel" button. If you needed a marketing channel, you could create one; give it a description, and set the access level to standard so that all team members could use it. You may select from a few options by clicking the drop-down menu, and once you've finished, you'll notice that this channel has been added. You can access more options by clicking the three dots that appear next to a channel. For instance, you have access to some channel metrics and may manage your channels, set permissions, and even impose moderation on channels if desired. The last thing to note is that you may establish things like new channels without necessarily entering the "Manage team" page; you can just click the three dots, where there is also an "Add Channel" option.

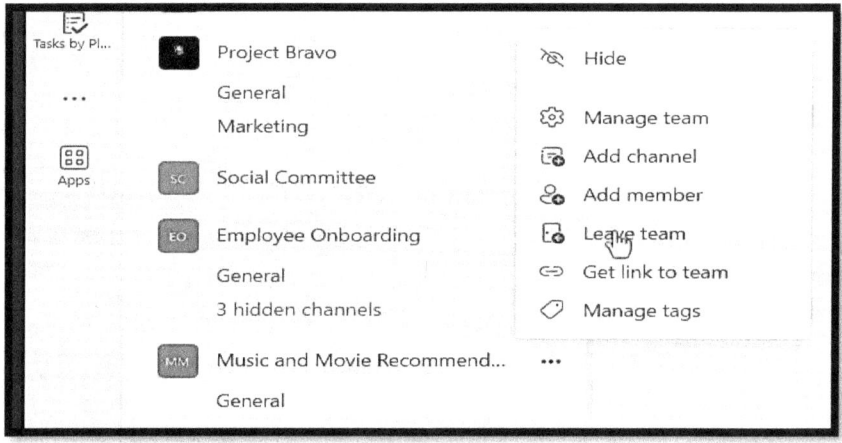

Within Teams, you have three options: you can delete, conceal, or leave a team. Teams are often created because they are related to certain projects that we will eventually finish and no longer have to be a part of. It should be emphasized that only the team owner has the final say over whether or not a team member may eliminate their own teams.

Breaking up with a team

Let's talk about leaving a team now. We'll look over a team you didn't put together for this. Assume for the moment that you would like to leave the team and that you would not like to add this team to your list. To complete the process, simply click the three dots, choose "Leave team," and indicate that you want to depart. The team will thereafter be removed from your list of teams when you do that. That is the extent of its contents. Returning to a team from which you previously left since this is a public team, if you choose to go back to the "Join or Create a team" option and decide you want to rejoin, you might notice it there. To return it to your team's roster, just select "Join team."

Hide a team from view

The next thing to do is to hide a team. Let's say you would want to hide the team from your list rather than remove it because you have a lot of teams here and just want to show the ones you use regularly. To make a team disappear from the list, pick the team again, click the three dots, and then click the "Hide" option. At the bottom is a small, hidden team space. You can see any teams you have hidden by expanding it. Just click the three dots and choose "Show" to bring the team back up in the main list of teams and reveal them once more.

Taking a group out

Your last option is to delete a team. As we mentioned earlier, you may only remove teams that you have created. In the event that you did not create the team, clicking the three dots at the top will not allow you to delete the team; however, if you did create the team and would like to do so, selecting the three dots at the top will expose a "Delete team" option at the bottom.

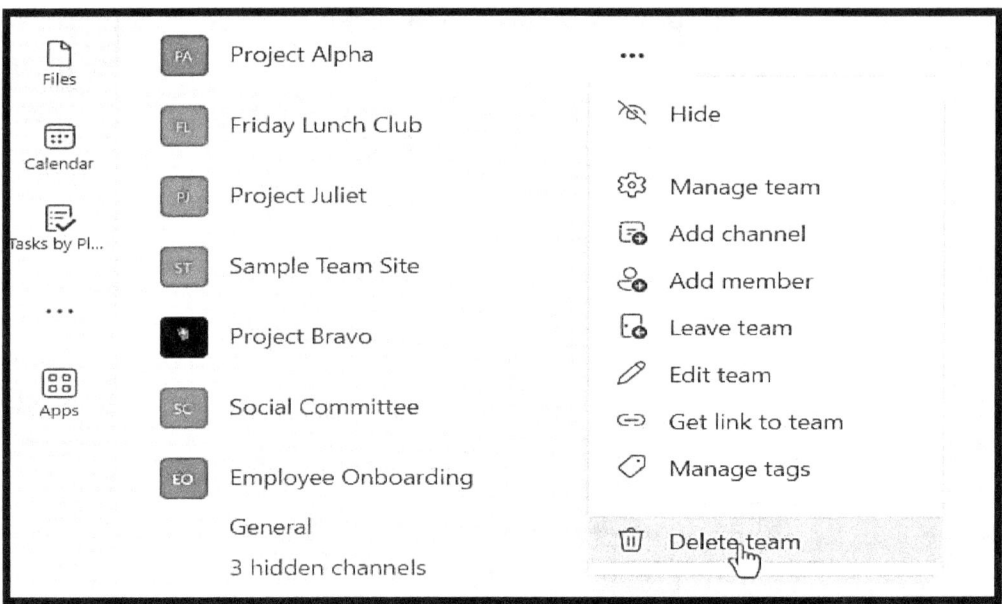

This will be erased along with all of its contents. Select that choice, check the box to indicate that you realize that everything will be deleted, and then click "Delete team." Be careful that when you delete a team, it will be deleted for everyone who has access to it, not just you. If you simply want to remove the team from your list, often hiding the team is preferable to removing it. It's time to move on to adding tabs to the top and searching now that you have a solid understanding of how many various elements function in Teams.

Activities

1. Using a pre-made template, form a new team.
2. Establish a new channel for an already-existing team.
3. Keep an eye on the additions, deletions, and role changes that occur within the team.

CHAPTER FOUR
ABOUT CHATS AND CONVERSATIONS WITHIN THE TEAMS

Synopsis

Good communication is crucial in Microsoft Teams; Teams Chats are discussed in chapter 4. You will learn how to create and format messages, share files, and use more advanced features like bookmarking important topics and tagging people in them. Conversations in chats take place between you and one other person, or between you and two or three others, but we don't recommend getting too involved. Like text messaging, a chat should be an easy and rapid way to connect with someone.

Conversations that take place within Teams

Choose "New chat" from the menu in the top right corner to begin a new conversation.

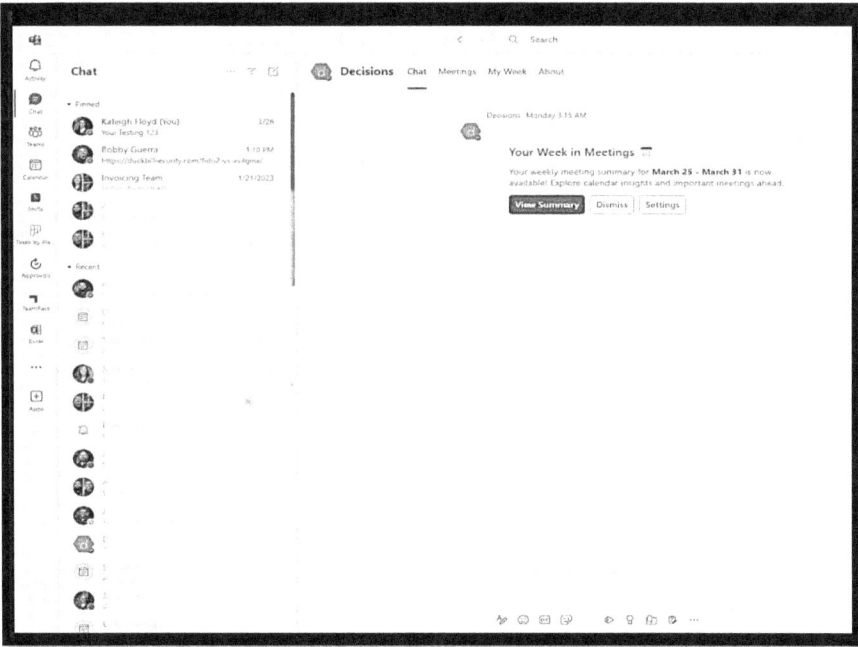

It breaks out into this adorable little window and creates a new window all by itself. You can select the person you wish to chat to from this list and begin typing directly to them. You have additional options if you click on the three dots that are close to the place where you just started a new chat. If you wish to delete all of your notifications, you have the option to mark them all as read. Additionally, you'll see that some of your discussions are at the top while some are at the bottom. Your pinned chats are the ones at the top, and you can pin any chat by right-clicking on it and selecting "Pin." You'll also notice some more options when you right-click. You can select to open the chat in a new window at the very top, which will cause your conversation to appear in a separate window when you click on it. You can also mute, hide, and modify the apps within the chat.

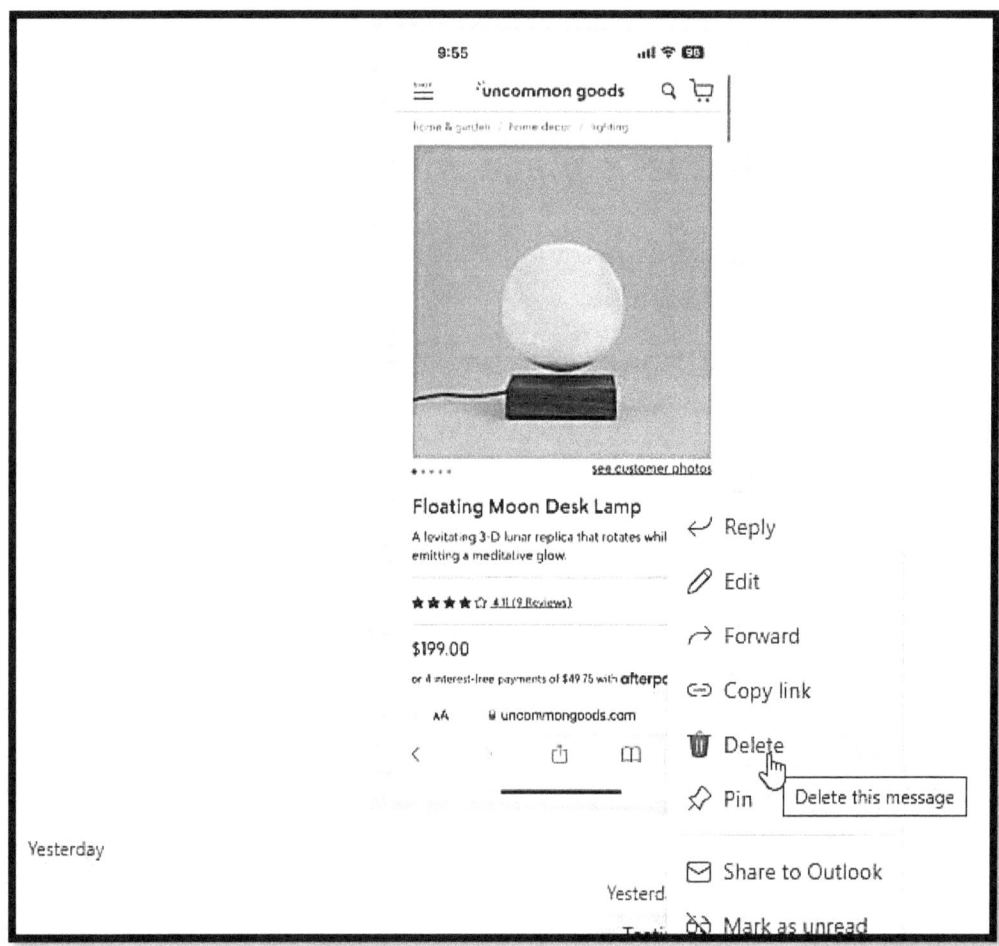

There's one thing about messaging and discussions that you should know. Instead of advancing the cursor to the next line as it would when typing text on a Word document, pressing Enter in Microsoft Teams just transmits the message. The fix for that issue is to use the formatting button. This format button (little A with pencil) allows you to expand the Box and access a wide range of formatting options if you were typing anything and wanted to go on to the next line. When entering something, we highly recommend pressing the enter button to get several lines because it moves the cursor to the next line. Another fantastic feature is the ability to add things like cells and label messages as important. To erase a message, simply click the top delete button, and the message will be removed. Additionally, you should know that by doing a right-click on a message, you can remove it.

When you do this, the message's receiver is notified that it has been removed, but the other recipient cannot see the contents. Furthermore, you have the option to use the right-click menu to pin that specific message. The link to the message can also be copied, and this transfers the complete link to the chat window. The last option is to forward the message, which duplicates it and enables you to send it to a different recipient along with the precise message's sender information. If you simply wanted to copy some information to someone and didn't feel like texting it out properly, you could just click forward, send it to the person you want to send it to, and it will convey the message to them. Note that the message's contents are listed after the writer's name. It also contains the transmit date and time of the message.

Message sending and receiving

Posting and receiving messages in groups is a pretty simple procedure. As before, this pane on the left shows us every team to which we have access, and when we expand a team, we can see every team channel underneath that team. Remember that a general channel is created automatically when you form a new team. One of the ways we can talk to one other is through this. Let's just take a quick look at our message sending and receiving options at this time. We shall examine this option in a later section. We can also create our own channels.

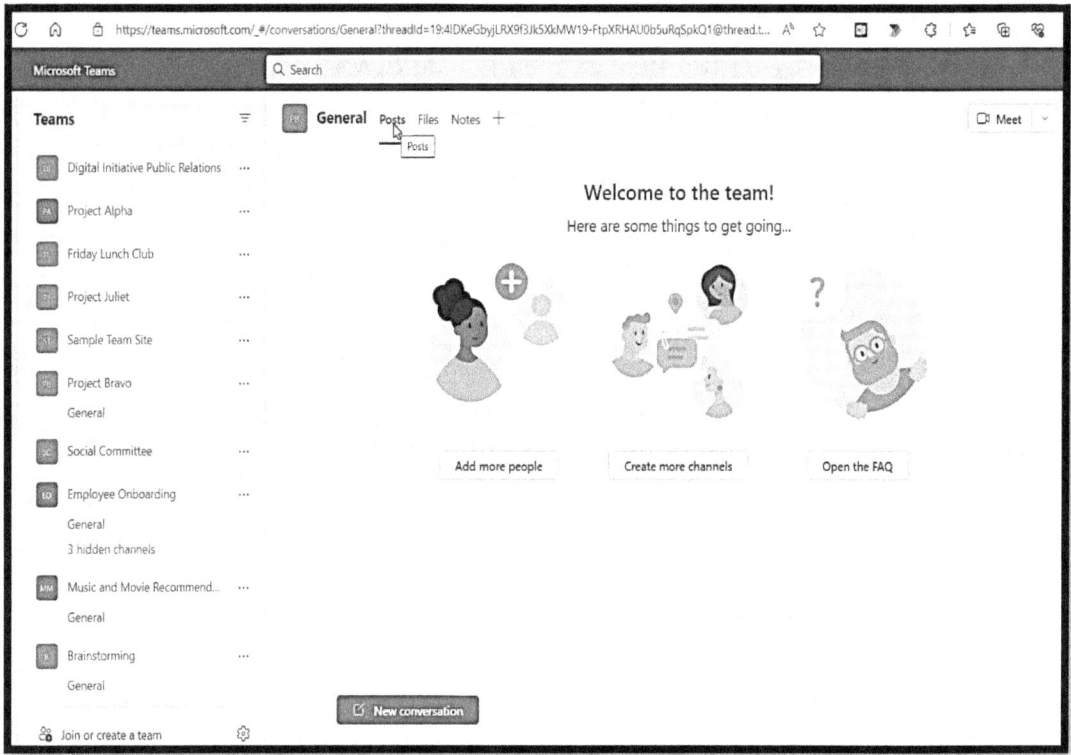

When you go to the General Channel, the first thing you'll notice is that there's a Posts tab at the top in addition to the channel name. Here, you can submit images, gifs, stickers, emojis, and other amusing items in addition to chatting with your coworkers and attaching files.

Starting a new conversation

To start a new chat, navigate to the bottom of the screen and click the "New conversation" button. This could result in the opening of a small conversation box with some icons underneath. Now that you have written a message, you have two choices for sending it: you may publish it to the channel so that your colleagues can reply, or you can select the small paper aircraft icon on the right-hand side. As an alternative, you can use the keyboard's Enter key.

When a message is received, a little pop-up notification will appear in the lower right corner of the screen. Notably, Teams chats include a threaded conversation layout that facilitates easy identification of the individuals who are responding to one other.

Increasing the enjoyment of your conversations

In order to reply to someone, first ensure that you have selected the relevant field and then type your message. If you would want to add some individuality to this message, you have a few alternatives.

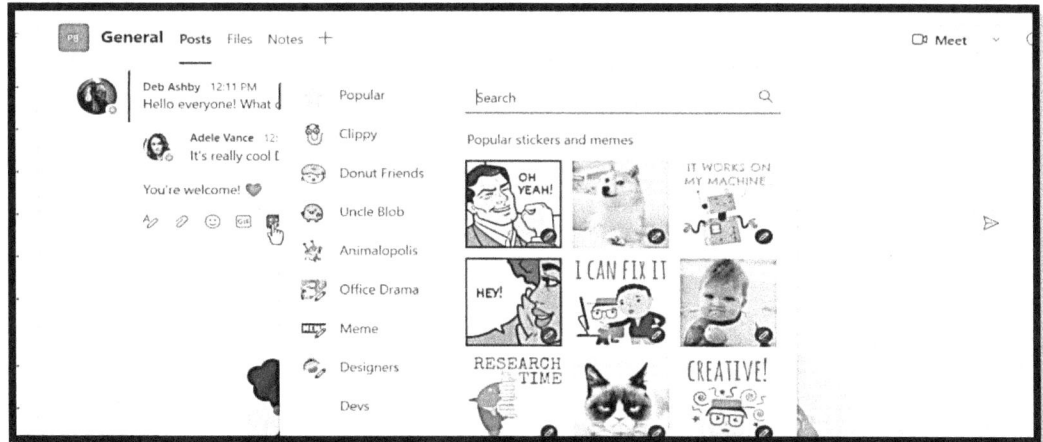

You could, for instance, add an emoji, so that when you click the emoji button, a long list of various smileys and other items are added. Additionally, you have the option to add a GIF, so when you choose to open this, a variety of small GIFs can be added to your talks to lighten the mood a bit. The sticker option, which is your last chance to add some individuality to your messages, is broken down into various categories and consists of amusing tiny notes that you can send. Once you've added the desired one, click the Send button to send it to the other person.

They will receive a pop-up notification in their teams letting them know you've replied to their message. Sometimes you'll see that this person has begun a new post and hasn't replied to the prior thread in the chat, only sending through a fresh message. Additionally, you'll notice that a small toolbar appears when you hover over someone's message, allowing you to reply to their post. If you find something interesting in their post, all you have to do is click the thumbs up button to show your approval.

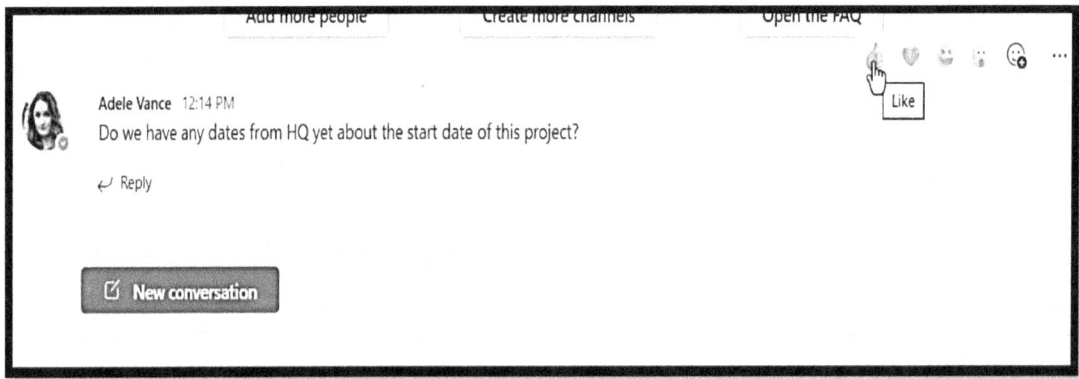

Organizing the conversations

You can reply to their messages again now, but this time you have to click on the format message option underneath. A more spacious reply box will show up, and this window has all of your formatting options.

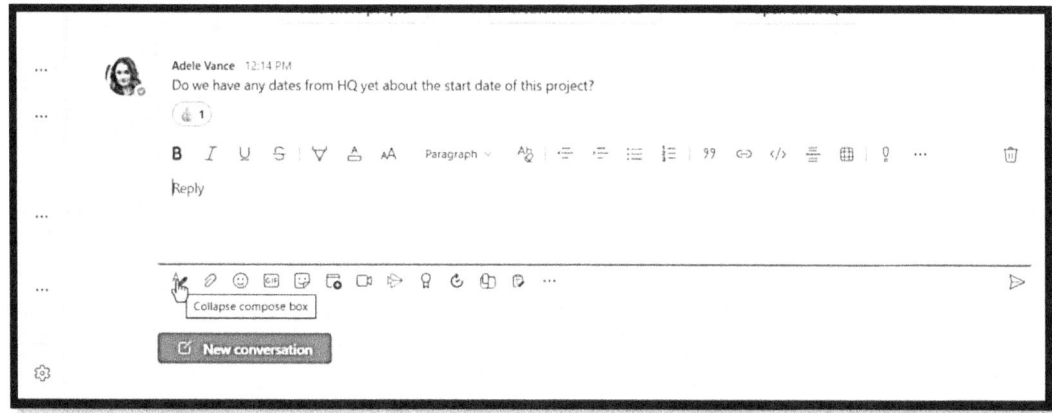

If you want to format your message rather than just use the same font and style throughout, click the format option. You can change the font's color, add bullet points, quotes, tables, and make your work bold, among other things. You can also choose to erase the draft of a message at any point while you're writing it by selecting the trash can symbol located on the right side of the screen.

Getting files and sharing them via chat

Remember that file sharing is supported here as well. This is where you'll notice the paperclip icon when you start a new chat. Upon clicking this, a few options will appear, including the ability to upload files directly from your PC, search through files published by other teams and channels, browse recently posted files, and open OneDrive.

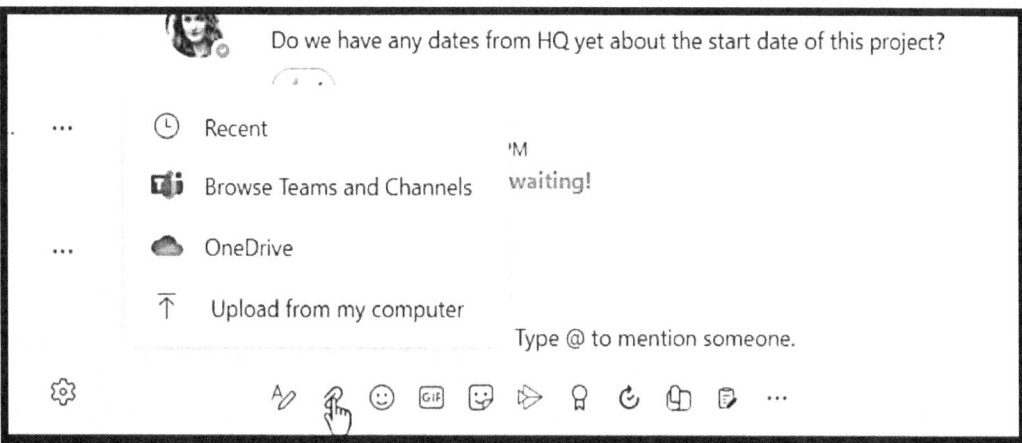

You can send documents from a Files folder on OneDrive by going there. You have two choices when you click on that: you may share a link or upload a copy. If you decide to upload a copy, the document will load into the message and you can send it through as usual, allowing everyone in this channel to view it.

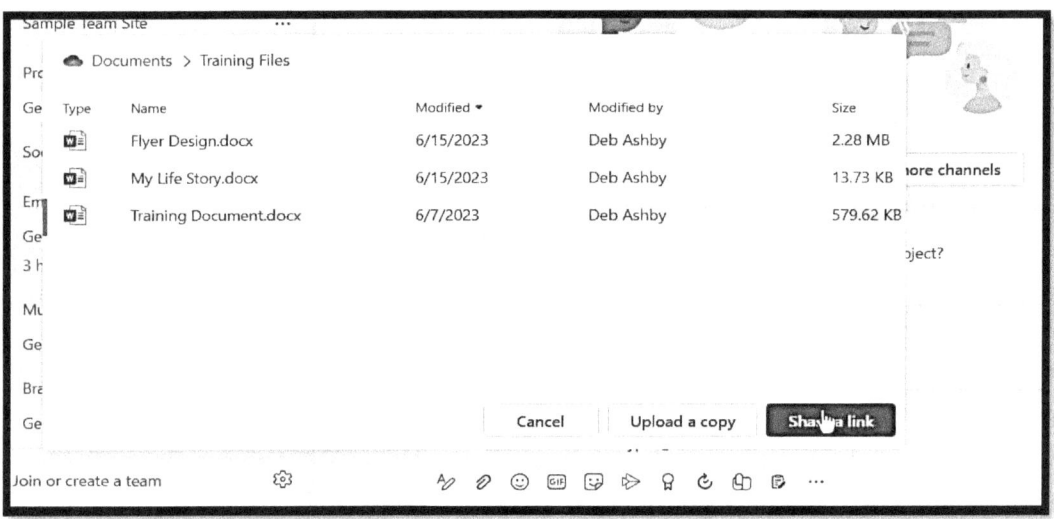

It's also important to note that when you share documents in this post area, they upload and are accessible via the items tab at the top. This means that you can easily view all of the items you've posted in this channel by going to Files and finding them all there. It simply implies that you may find your files without having to navigate up and down in a chat.

Addressing a specific person

You can also use @ mentions in your discussions. Let's say you want to add someone to the conversation and reply to a post again. To choose an individual, start entering their name, or just type @ to bring up a list of alternatives. Sending and receiving messages basically only involves typing in your message and hitting Enter to send it.

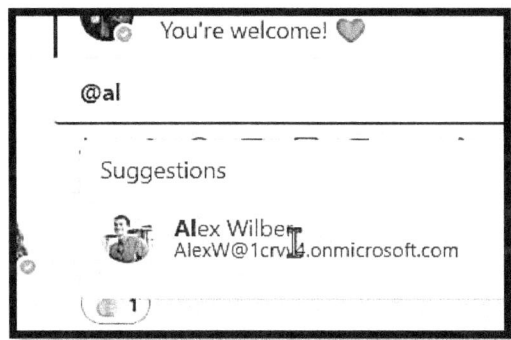

After adding the last name, you can backspace to erase it, so that, for example, it merely reads Alex rather than Alex Morgan. Remember that it's not always necessary to provide your entire name in these @ references; occasionally doing so seems a little more formal. If you've ever used any similar programs, you should have no issue understanding this.

Editing, removing, and bookmarking posts

In this section, we'll examine bookmarking, editing, and deleting entries. By bookmarking messages, you can efficiently mark ones that you might want to go over again later. It is analogous to adding a bookmark to a desired webpage. It's unclear how we designate postings in Teams as favorites at first. Let's look at a channel with a little bit more information. For example, we can move the mouse pointer over a message from someone and see the three dots that show up next to each of our reaction icons, indicating extra options, if we would like to bookmark that message. If you click on more options, the item in this menu labeled "Save this message" describes exactly what you're doing, even if it's not really a bookmark.

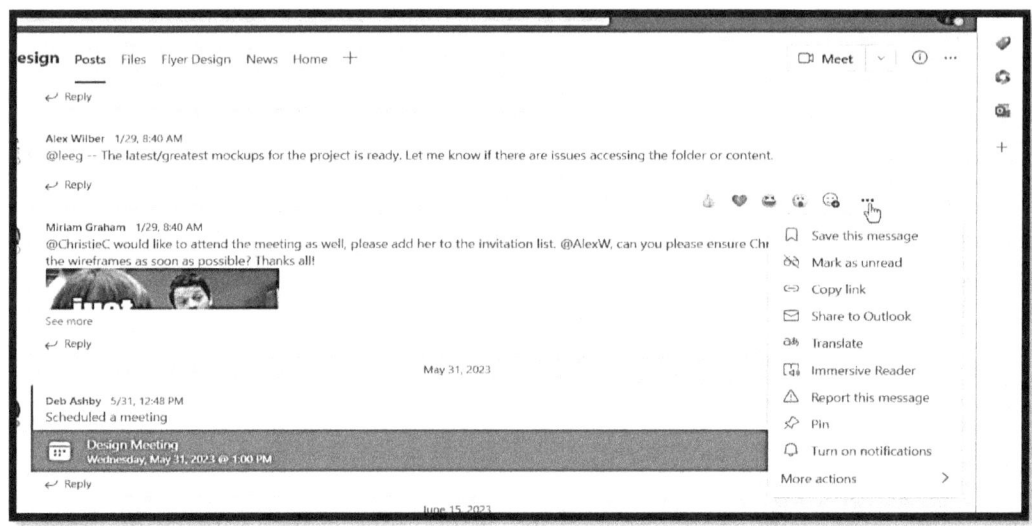

When we select "Save this message," we are notified that it has been stored. To view all of our saved messages, we must locate and click on our profile picture. From there, we can select "Saved."

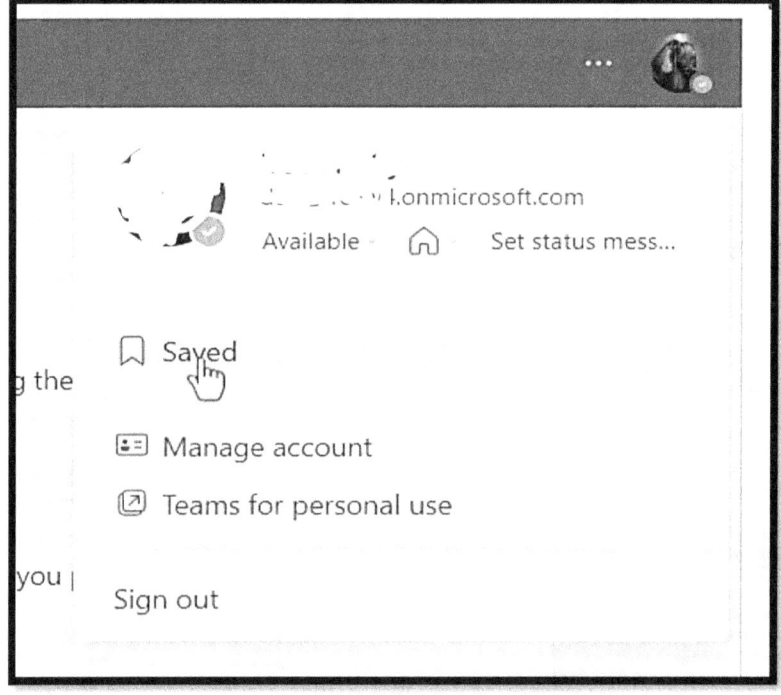

A lengthy list of all the messages we've bookmarked will appear if we select "Saved." Naturally, you can unsave a message by clicking on the small Saved button, which will remove it from your list of saved items.

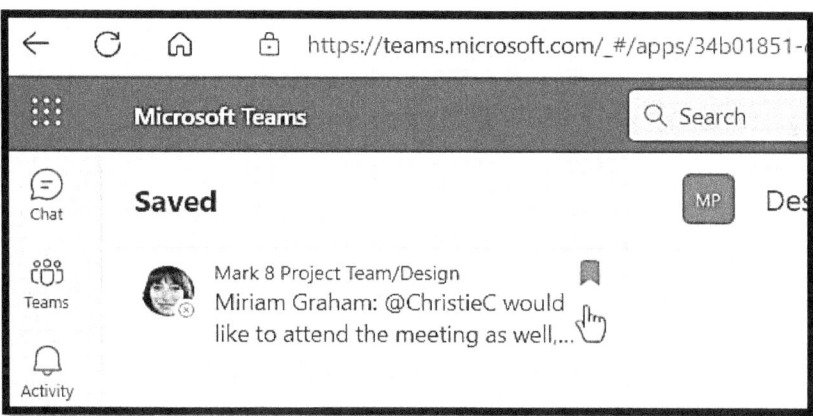

It's time to discuss message editing. Suppose we have a message that we would like to alter. Once more, all you have to do is hover over the message you like to edit. It should be noted that you can only edit messages that you have sent. We'll return to the three dots once more, and this time the menu has a "Edit" option. When we click on it, it takes us to edit mode where we can make edits. After making changes, we click the tick to send the message, and the recipient will naturally receive a notification that it has been modified, allowing them to verify it again.

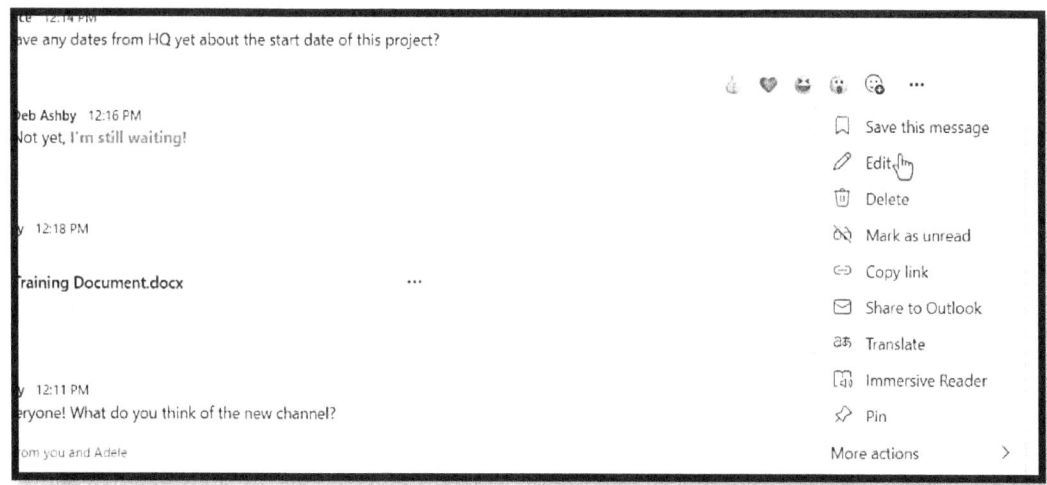

Finally, let's talk about how to delete messages. As one might anticipate, this is also rather typical and straightforward. For the time being, let's assume that we want to delete this message. Again, we'll select Delete from the menu by hovering over the message and selecting the three dots. When we click the Delete button, a quick notification letting us know the message has been removed will show up. Remember that no one else in the channel will know that you deleted this post because only you can see it. If you decide to retract the message, you can do it right there in the chat window using the undo button.

Private messages exchanged

We have been going over the messages we send out to every team member. Every message we share with anyone who is a part of this channel or has access to it can be viewed by them. Since there are times when you would choose to publish a message or chat with a specific team member rather than the entire group, we refer to this as private messaging. While it's not appropriate to speak with every team member, let's imagine that you wished to inquire about the well-being of a coworker who wasn't present in the office yesterday. The team channel is intended for private chats between the two of us; please do not type private messages there. To do this, navigate to the Teams' Chat section. The first item on the left-hand menu is the chat option, which is where you send and receive all of your private messages. You can initiate a new discussion at the top of the window, or you can continue typing in the list of previous conversations you've had with other users.

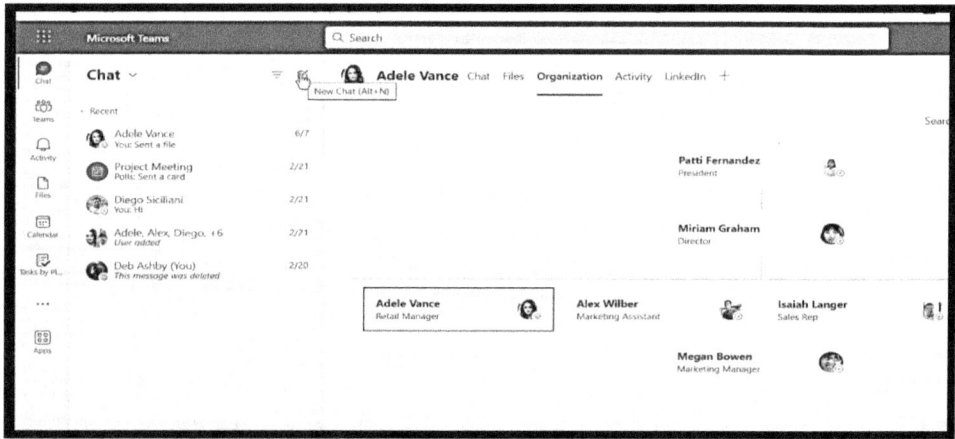

Clicking "New chat" opens a new window where you can enter the recipient of this private message. If they work for your company, you can either type in their name or choose from a list. You are able to have multiple private chats with people at once; Mary, John, or anybody else you like can be added. Suppose you would like to message Mary. In order to avoid cluttering your recent area with new chats with the same person, as soon as it detects that you have already had private messages with Mary, it will take you directly to your most recent exchange. Now, all you have to do is input your message and hit the send icon to send it through. Only Mary will see it and be able to respond. You should also be aware that there are many tabs across the top of the screen when working in private chats. Some of these are customizable, but there are two tabs that are always there: chat and files. This functions a lot like when you are conversing in a team channel. Please be advised that any files provided within this private chat will be displayed. "More" is shown in this private conversation because you have the option to add more tabs across the top. It's also important to note that, should you decide at this point that you would like to speak with this person over video call, there are icons in the upper right corner that let you accomplish just that. You have the option to initiate an audio call or a video call with this individual. That's essentially how private functions chat; we'll look at audio and video calls later.

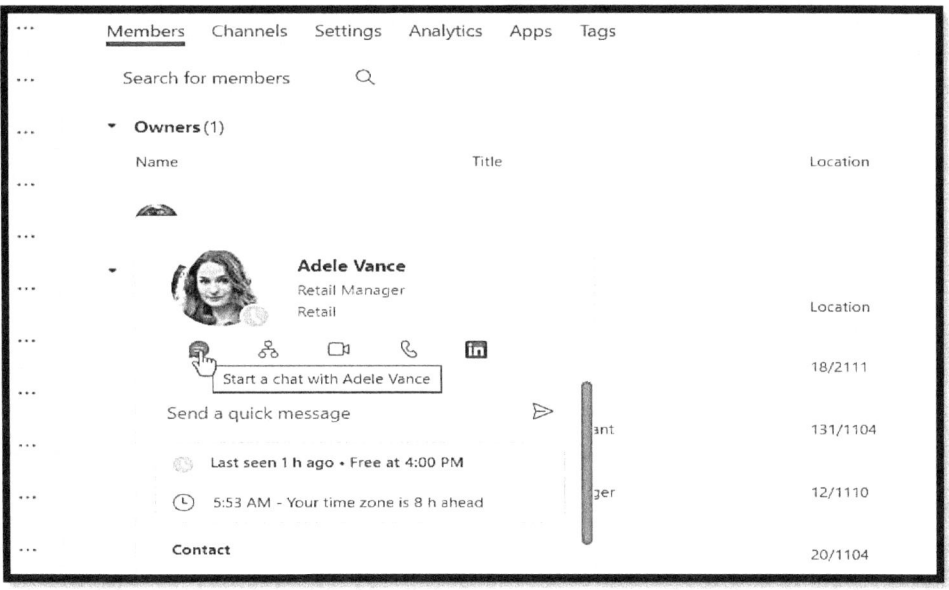

The only other item to note is that there is a small filter at the top that allows you to filter by name by clicking on it. Don't forget about the top option if you're looking for talks you've had with Diego. You may enter in his name and it will display all of the chats he's been a part of. The last thing to note is that you have a few alternatives here if you hover your cursor over any private discussion.

Once more, the three dots will take you to additional options:

1. This exchange might be pinned to the top. To make someone easy to reach in private talks, this is helpful if you speak with them frequently.
2. You are able to flag this discussion as unread. When you do that, the conversation is immediately bolded to appear as though you haven't seen it yet. You can also see that a small notification indicating that you have an unread conversation appears on the chat icon in the menu on the left.
3. Additionally, you have the option to mute the chat entirely. You have the option to silence the discussion if you're attempting to work intently.

Notifying when available is a suitable solution in this case. You have a green tick, as you can see if you look at your profile photo at the top. This indicates that you are available, as indicated by the availability symbol next to your username. However, you have the opportunity to modify this at any moment, so altering your availability status. Occasionally, these will alter automatically based on the events listed in your calendar. For instance, Teams will automatically set you to busy if it detects that you have a meeting scheduled. However, you have the option to manually change your status.

For instance, if you set your status to "Be right back," you'll notice that the icon changes immediately. If you know you'll be away for an extended period of time—let's say an hour—you can even specify how long you want this status to be applied. For instance, if you choose one hour from the list above and click "Done," your status will change to "Be right back for the next hour" and then will immediately go back to available. In the event that someone has completed this task on their own and you need to speak with them about something crucial, you may find the "Notify when available" feature helpful. You will receive a notification and be able to initiate a private conversation with the individual as soon as their status changes back to Available if you have this set on this private conversation.

Activities

1. Launch a fresh chat session in the Teams app with a coworker.
2. Practice utilizing various emoticons and formatting styles in your chat messages.
3. Examine the possibilities in a chat for sharing files and other items.

CHAPTER FIVE
COMPREHENDING MEETING AND CALL CONFIGURATION

Synopsis

You will be guided through the process of setting up virtual meetings and calls in Chapter 5, from initiating an on-demand call to scheduling and attending a meeting. It also teaches you how to use the more advanced features, such screen sharing, live presentations, and brainstorming sessions. Teams, channels, and conversations have all been discussed. Let's get started with that now that launching audio and video calls is among the most popular applications of Microsoft Teams. With everyone going online during the pandemic, Teams has emerged as the standard platform for online collaboration, file sharing, and meetings.

We advise verifying a few settings pertaining to your team meetings once more before proceeding with the process of initiating video and audio sessions. In the upper right corner of the screen, you might notice our profile photo with three dots next to it. You can click here to view your settings.

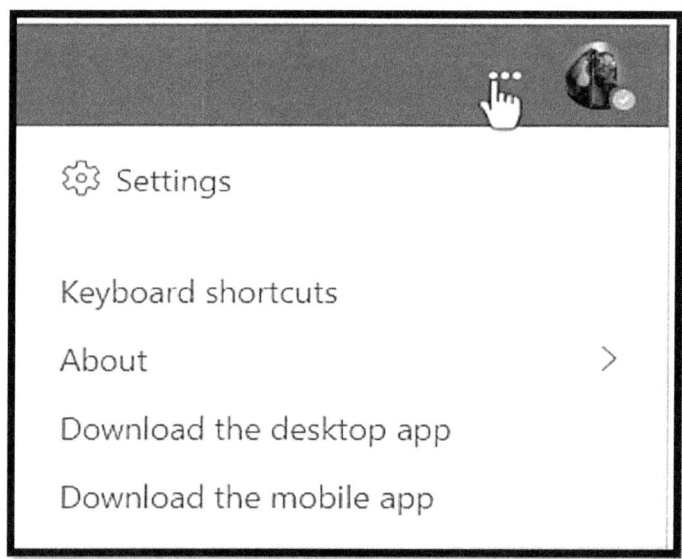

I won't go into detail about every single one of these settings because they are all applicable to Teams. Instead, we'll focus on the ones that have to do with video and audio meetings. However, we strongly suggest that you take a look at all of these settings and adjust them to fit your teams' needs.

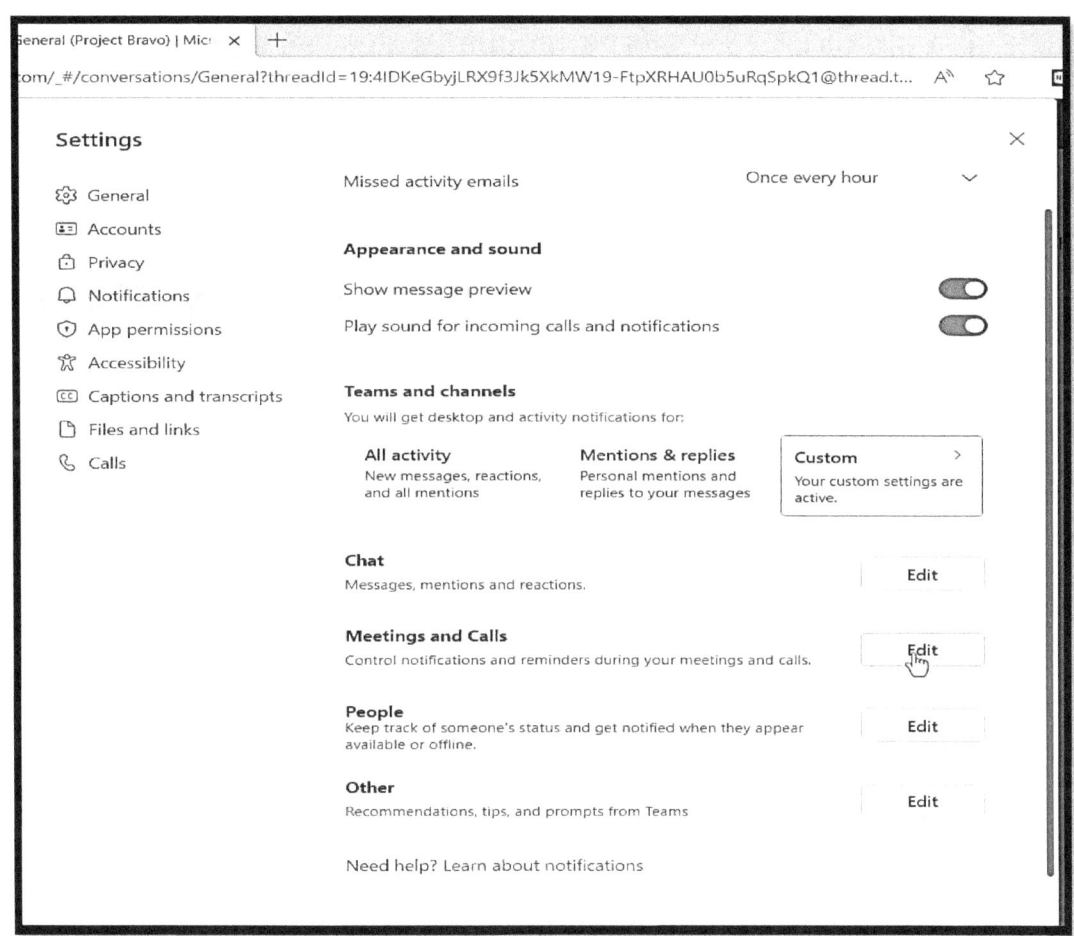

We have a few of items pertaining to Teams' meetings here, so let's head down to Notifications. To manage reminders and notifications before, during, and after meetings and calls, scroll down to the Meetings and Calls section. You can change how you act when you join a meeting by clicking the Edit button. For instance, you may select this option if you'd like everyone to keep their microphones muted. To allow everyone to talk, you may either unmute everyone or put them on silent until you, the meeting organizer, join or deliver a message. Be mindful that this second choice is the default when you're presenting live events or webinars. We have another choice here that is related to Teams' meetings especially, Captions, so let's scroll down under Accessibility. As you can see, this is where you may set your meeting captions to always display. Turning this feature on will cause closed captions to appear on the screen whenever someone speaks in the meeting. This is a terrific aid for those who are hard of hearing or for those whose native language is not English; after all, reading the words rather than trying to decipher a variety of accents and voices can be a real challenge.

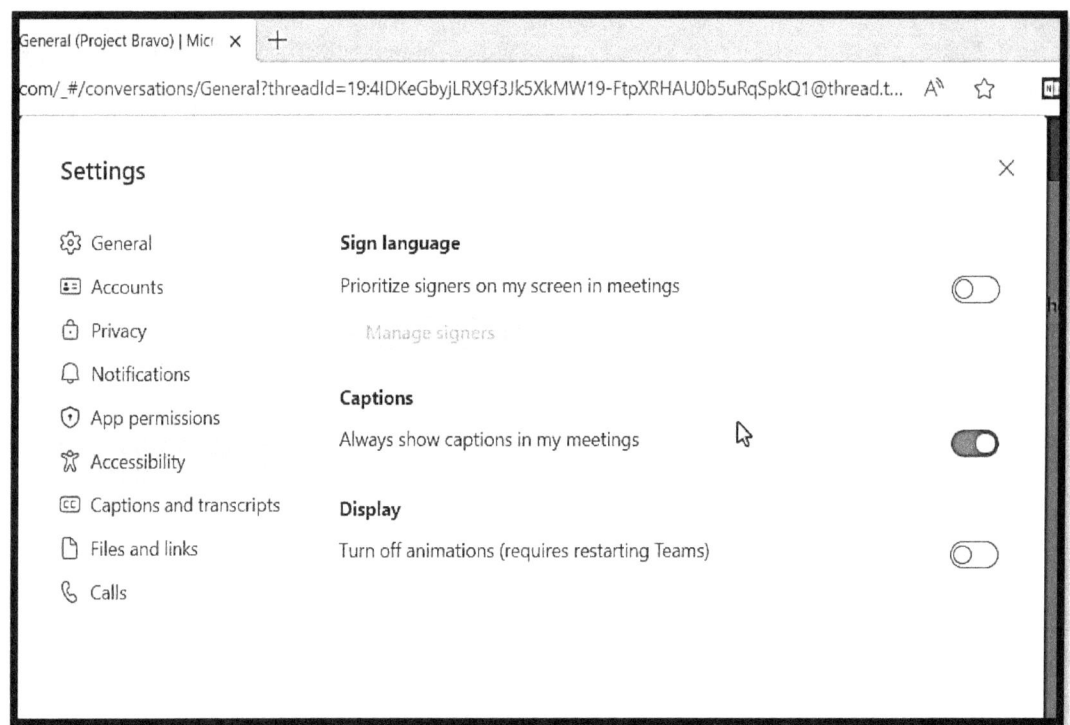

Transcripts and closed captions are also available in this area. You have the option to have Teams recognize your identity in meeting transcripts and captions automatically. Our intention is that your name will appear in the meeting transcript and onscreen captions as a result of it. It is also wise to have the "Filter Profane words" enabled, which we have done. Those are some of the things to consider when arranging a Teams meeting.

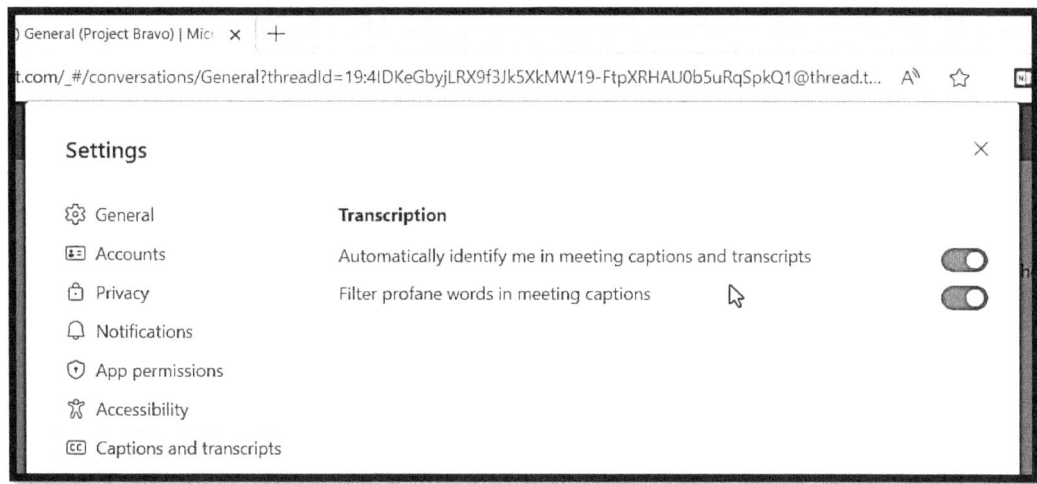

Opening of the meeting

The next thing we should do is find out where each meeting venue is before we start a live meeting. Let's say you are having a group conversation on the general channel when you decide it would be better to have a video meeting. It is possible to start a new meeting in Teams from any channel. The Meet button is shown in the top right corner. You can schedule a meeting for a later time or to meet now by using the drop-down menu. A meeting that is begun with the "meet now" command starts right away, whereas one that is planned will happen at a later time.

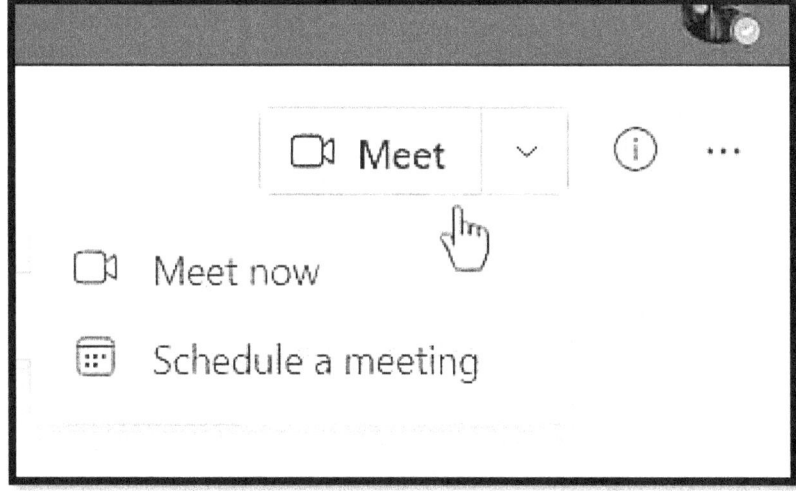

You can also start new meetings from the private chat window if you go over there. You can initiate an audio call or video connection straight away by clicking the small button in the upper right corner.

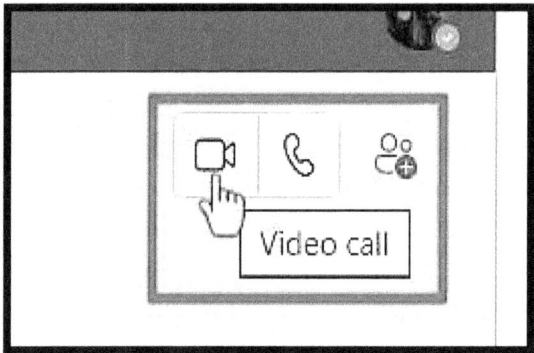

The calendar for your Team is another place you can initiate a meeting. Once you go to the Calendar, you'll see a "Meet now" option in the upper right corner, or you can select to set up a meeting right here. A new team meeting can be initiated or modified using these three sections.

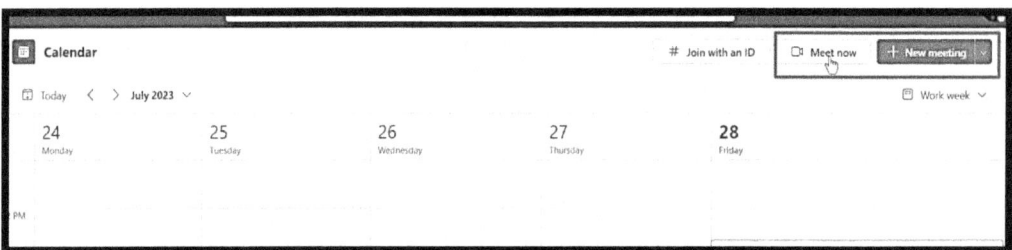

Start an on-demand call

As an example of how to initiate an audio or video conversation on demand, we will now look at how to start an on-demand meeting within a team's channel. Once more, considering the team's background, picture yourself conversing with Mary and Alex on the General Tab when you decide to call a meeting to discuss this in greater detail. In the upper right corner, there is a Meet button with two options: Schedule a meeting and Meet now. To initiate a meeting immediately, select "Meet now." You can then access the video settings from there. Choosing a background filter, naming the event, turning on or off the camera, and configuring the audio are all examples of meeting settings.

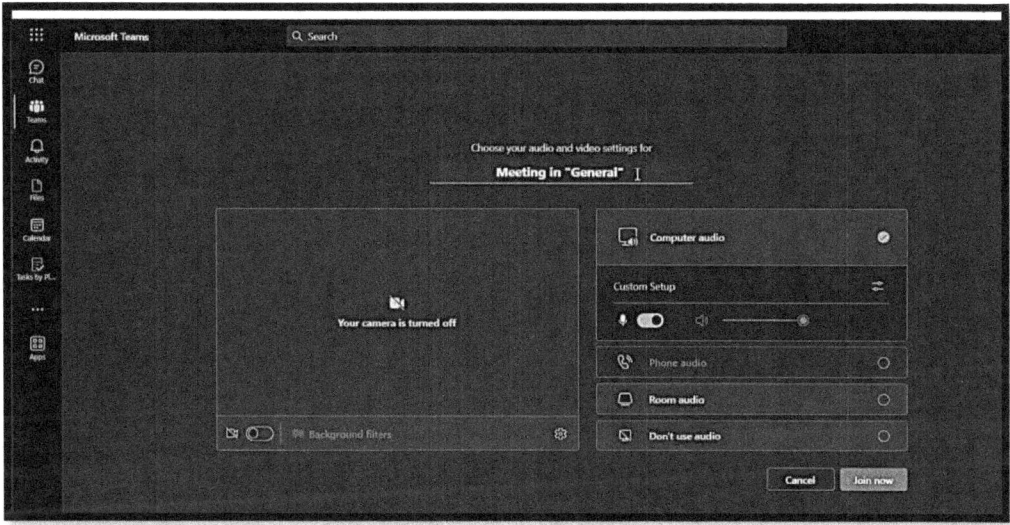

If you're doing some work from home and don't want anyone to see that your desk is a little bit messy, you may use one of these background filters to hide your messy desk or upload your own image. Instead of really adding a photo, you can simply blur the background using the blur option. Disabling your camera is another option you have.

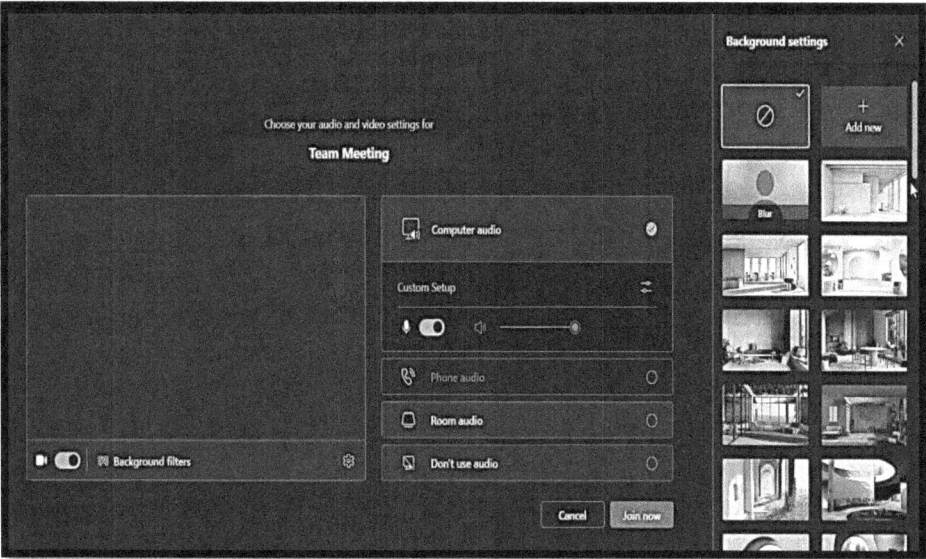

Just make sure that your audio, speakers, and microphone are set to the correct defaults; this will vary depending on your configuration. You can adjust all of these settings by clicking the small Settings icon here. To illustrate, you can utilize a stereo microphone—the default—while simultaneously setting your laptop's speaker. You can use this to connect your headphones to your speakers and microphone simultaneously if you're using a headset; otherwise, you'll need to use a separate microphone. Check that your settings are right by clicking this button.

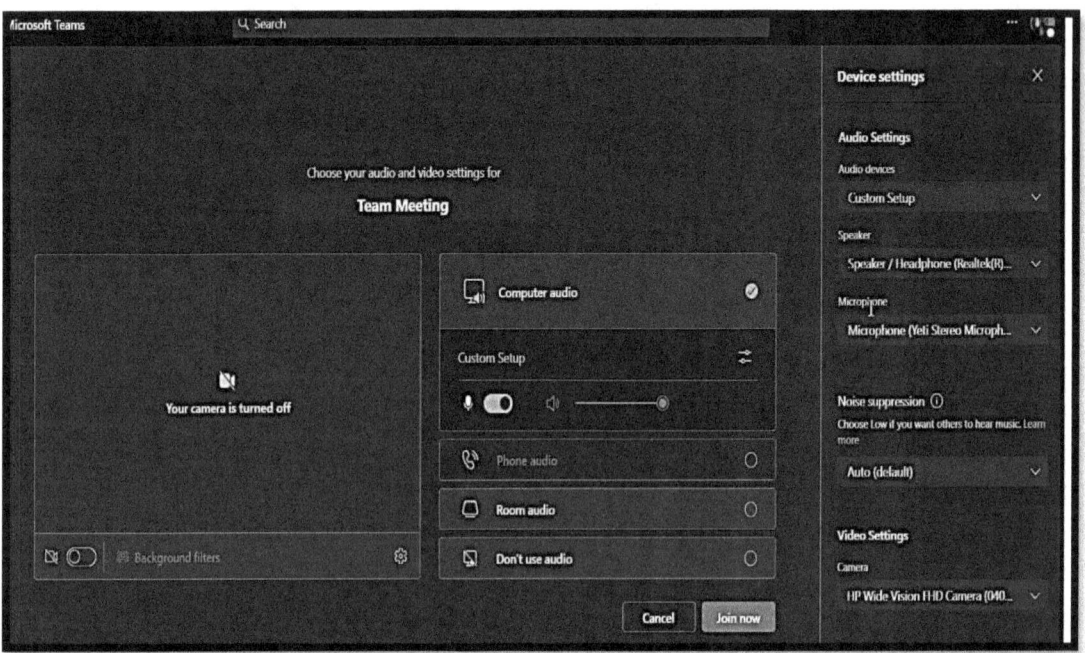

In the Video options, you may choose the camera to use for your video call, whether it's an attached webcam or the one built into your laptop. You can access the meeting by clicking the "Join now" option after you've made these changes. Now you may invite other people to the meeting in a few different ways: by copying the URL and pasting it into a team's Channel, by adding it to an email, or by adding participants directly. So, you've decided to bring someone else into the mix. To make sure everyone is speaking the same language, it will prompt you to confirm.

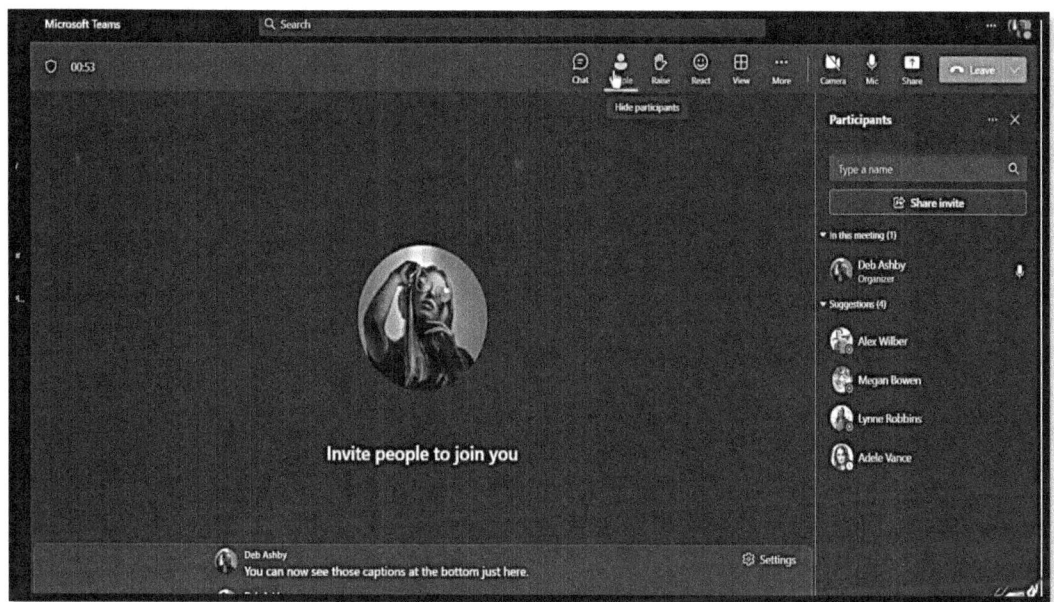

A few things will jump out at you when you're in the meeting. You will notice the captions at the bottom of the page since you enabled them in the previous phase. Plus, you'll see a menu bar across the top with several options pertaining to this team's meeting. When you clicked on "add participants," a window appeared for you to enter the names of those you want to invite to the meeting. Selecting "request to join" will initiate a call to them, and they will be able to join the meeting. Another option is to just type their name at the top and extend an invitation to join.

Another option is a chat panel, which functions similarly to a team channel for chatting. You can use this to have discussions with your team members; it's great for teams since it eliminates the need for audio. What this implies is that while you're talking, others can talk about what they're seeing on the screen without cutting into your presentation. You'll also see other options down below, just like when you're sending a message. Along with files, you can now include images, stickers, emojis, and gifs.

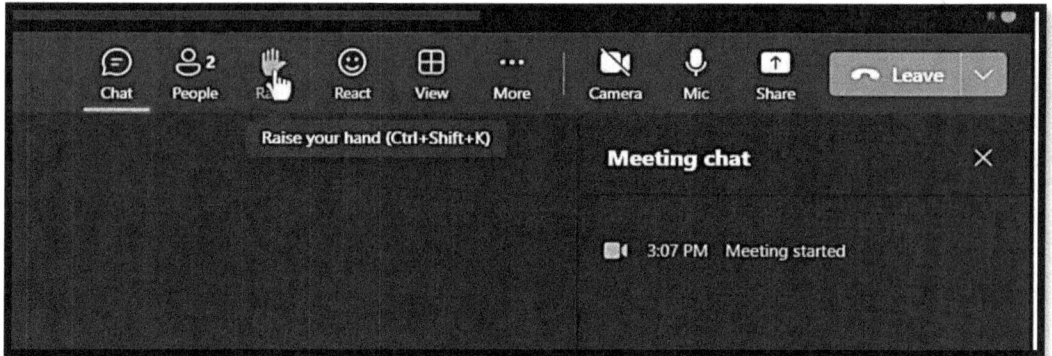

Putting up your hand is the next logical step. This appears frequently in the persons pane, and the keyboard shortcut is CTRL + SHIFT + K. Raise your hand if you wish to pose a question or make a comment during the meeting without disrupting the presenter or organizer's flow of speech; this is a nonverbal cue.

They can lower their hand once it has been dealt with, and if you have them unmuted, you can turn on their microphone if you see their hand raised. A couple of options exist for lowering your hands. To raise or lower your hand, you can either click the Raise button again or use the shortcut CTRL + SHIFT + K. In a meeting, sending a reply is the next possible step. You can let the presenter know how much you admire their work by sending a little heart to the screen, which will display hearts across the screen whenever you find a particularly good area of their presentation. Here we have a delightful example of non-verbal communication. There is an option to adjust your perspective so that this Gallery format is not required. With a little change, you may switch to speaker format, where you can see everyone's faces—even more so when there are more people in the meeting.

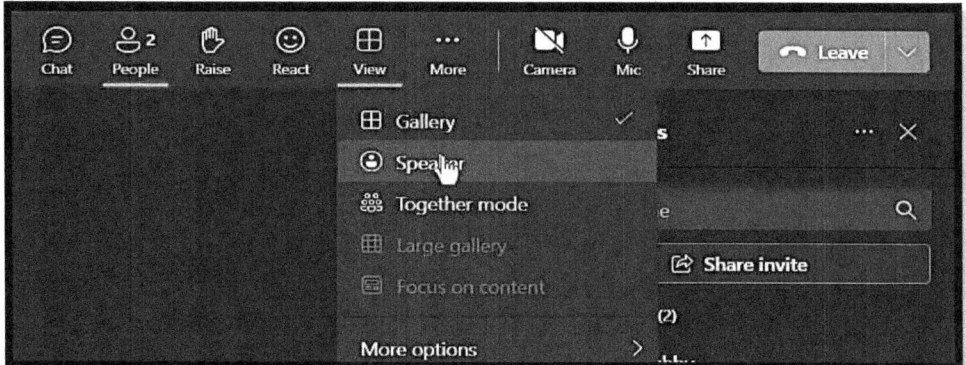

In addition, when you go back and adjust your view, you'll find "together mode." This is a neat little feature that wasn't widely received when it was initially introduced, but was introduced during the epidemic to foster a sense of unity among users. People would be seated in various places if they had their cameras on. While some may adore this setting, others may find it unappealing.

The "More actions" button is where you'll find options to record and transcribe the meeting, among other things. You can find the "Start recording" button here; once you click it, you'll see that in the top right; all you have to do is remember to click the stop button when the meeting is over to record it for later review or to share with others who can't make it.

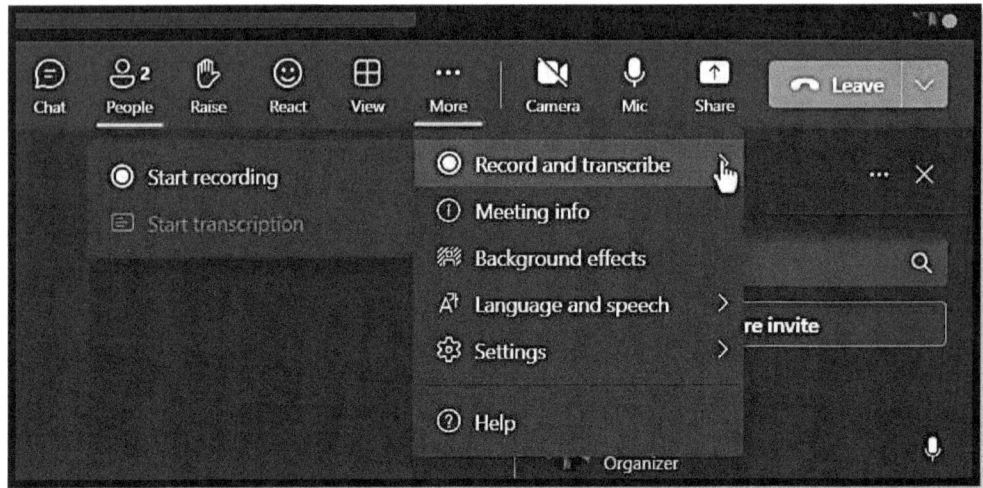

You will find all the links to this meeting under the meeting info area. You can distribute it to other people by copying the "Join info" and pasting it into an email. Background effects can be accessed, once again, from the More Options box. The process is already familiar to you. In addition to the language and speech customization options, there are a number of other settings, including Device settings, Meeting preferences, and Accessibility, that we have previously covered.

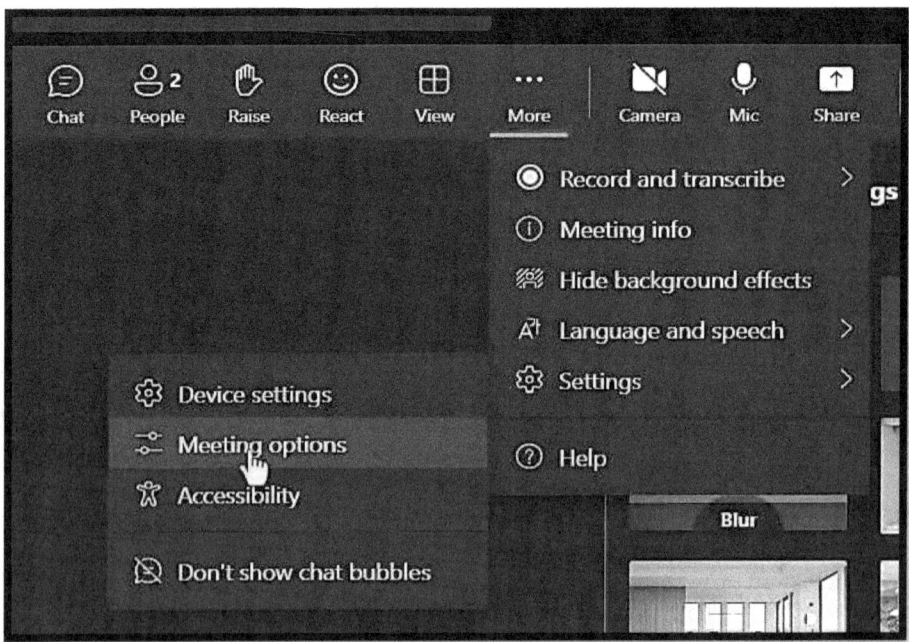

Your small camera toggle is located at the top of this page. The meeting is customizable, so you may turn the camera on and off as needed. In other words, you can't just turn it on once and leave it that way. Simply use this symbol to toggle it.

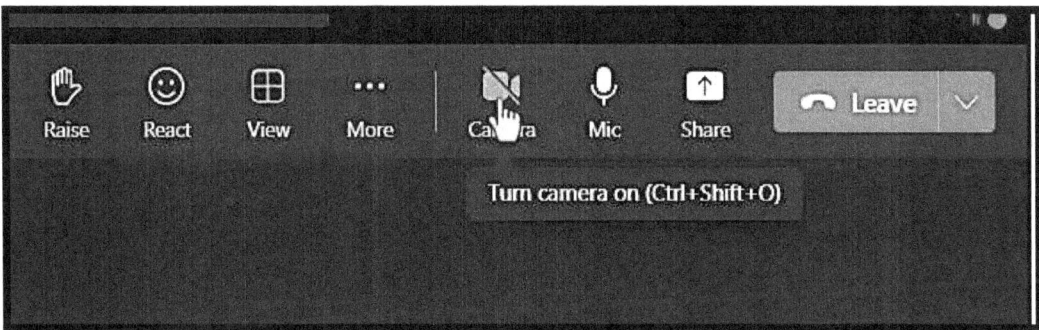

Even your microphone is subject to this rule. From this vantage point, you can manage your own microphone, which is useful if someone is giving a presentation; you can put it on mute while they go over the material, and then turn it off when questions are allowed. Finally, at the very bottom of this meeting, you'll see the "Share" option. Finally, you'll see the "Leave" button. Two choices, "Leave" and "End meeting," appear when you click the drop-down menu.

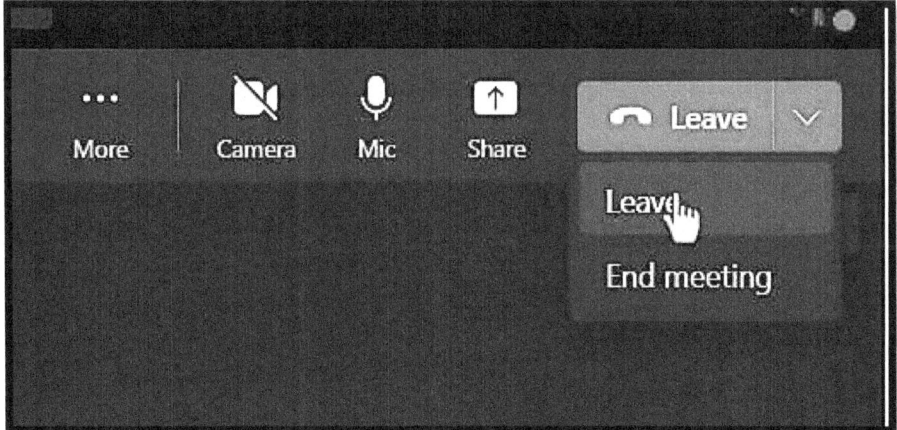

The meeting will continue for everyone on the call after you leave, but it will cease for you and the other participants. The primary difference between the two is this. When you conclude the meeting, the team will close and you will be returned to the channel. You can see that the team meeting has ended and that it took 11 minutes and 53 seconds, depending on the channel you started it in. You may forward it forward and say how good the call quality was. Should you decide to record the meeting, it will also be uploaded to the channel for instant access. If the meeting went longer than expected, kindly be patient; the tape will eventually show up on the channel. It's that easy to start an on-demand meeting using the "Meet now" option.

A meeting schedule

Building on what you learned in the last section about how to start an on-demand meeting with the Meet Now button, we'll look at scheduled meetings in this section and show you how to set one up in Teams and Outlook in Microsoft 365. Moving on to the General Channel. Go back to the corner "Meet" button, but this time, click the drop-down menu and choose "Schedule a meeting." Similar to what happens when you make an appointment or event in Outlook, a calendar invite will appear.

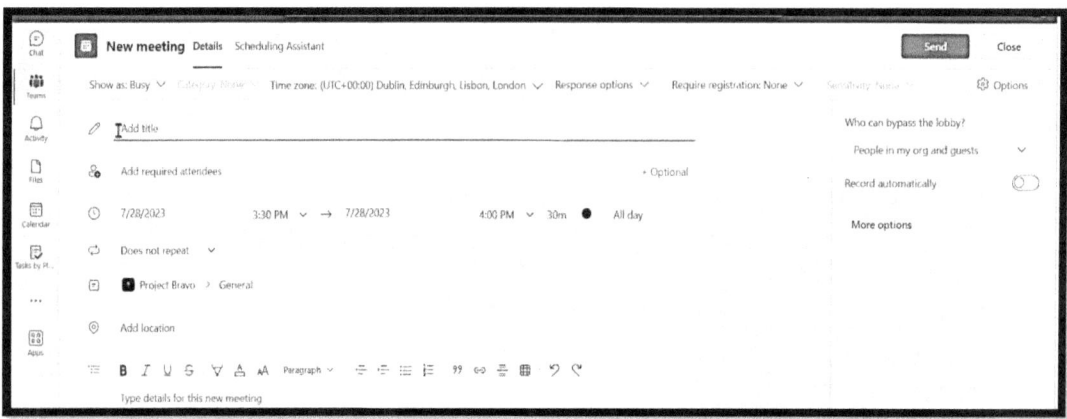

Feel free to include the meeting's title and the necessary attendance. If you're having trouble with scheduling, try using the scheduling helper tab over here. The Scheduling Assistant will display all of the meeting's attendees (you can see their names displayed) and assist you in finding a time that works for everyone. After that, you may choose a start time or date, and if you want to make sure that everyone is free before sending it, you can check their calendars in the Scheduling Assistant. For all your scheduling needs, that is an excellent small tool.

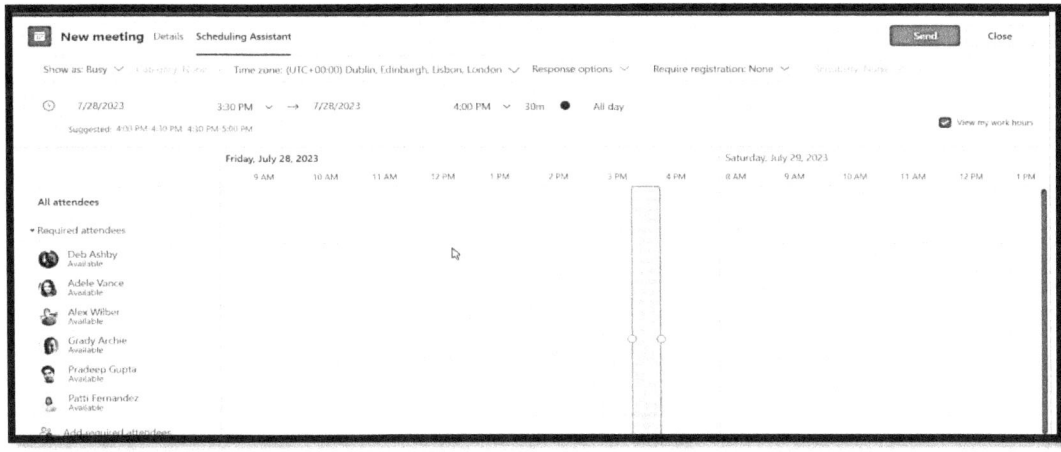

In addition, you can specify which days of the week you would like this to repeat, so you can make it repeat, for example, a weekly team meeting. You can view the channel where this was posted and even add a description and location if you want to. Take note of the small settings button on the right-hand side; this is where you may go to configure who can skip the lobby, as before. You have the option to configure it such that all individuals invited to this meeting can avoid the lobby altogether. Because it's easy to lose track of time when you start a meeting and forget to start the recorder, it's a good idea to set it up ahead so you won't have to worry about it. Another option is to have the meeting recorded automatically.

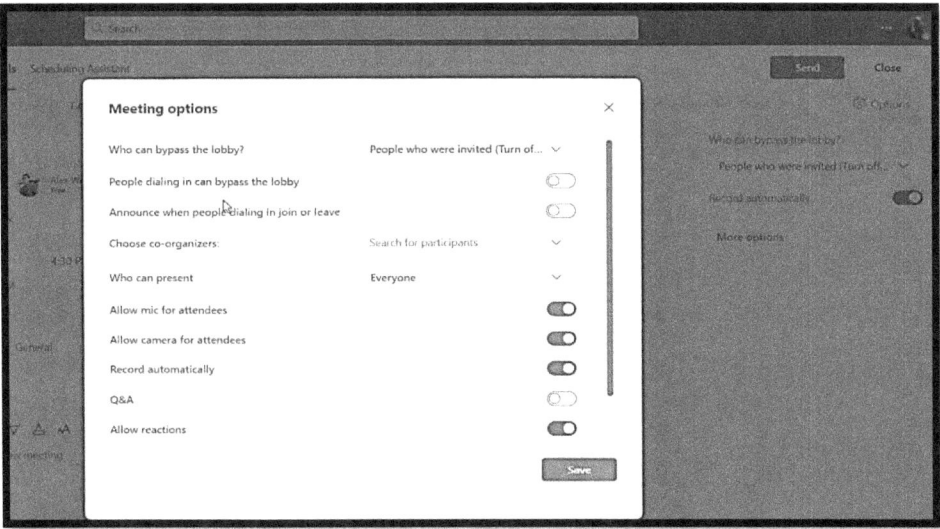

If you want participants to have their microphones on during the meeting, make sure this option is toggled on; if not, click here to view further options and change your settings even further. If you would prefer, turn off the feature that allows everyone to hear the invitation before sending it out. Here, too, you have a few other registration options. You can indicate in the "Require registration" area whether you would like participants to register for this meeting. This will require them to provide their email address upon registration, which is useful for big gatherings when it's critical to estimate the number of attendees. Once you've completed adjusting the parameters and are happy with the outcome, press "Send" to send. You will immediately notice that this meeting has been added to the team channel, making it visible to all channel members. Additionally, it will be put to your team calendar, which you can view by selecting the calendar option from the menu on the left.

Attending a scheduled meeting

Now, there are a few ways for you to take part in this meeting once it begins, as you might anticipate. On the calendar, when you click on the meeting, a join button will show up here. As an alternative, if you're working within the Teams' Channel, click on the meeting here. You'll see a "Join" button in the upper corner. Reopening a mailed meeting will result in some changes to the details. You may now examine tracking information in the details page, which displays the users who have accepted or rejected this meeting invitation, to help you understand the point.

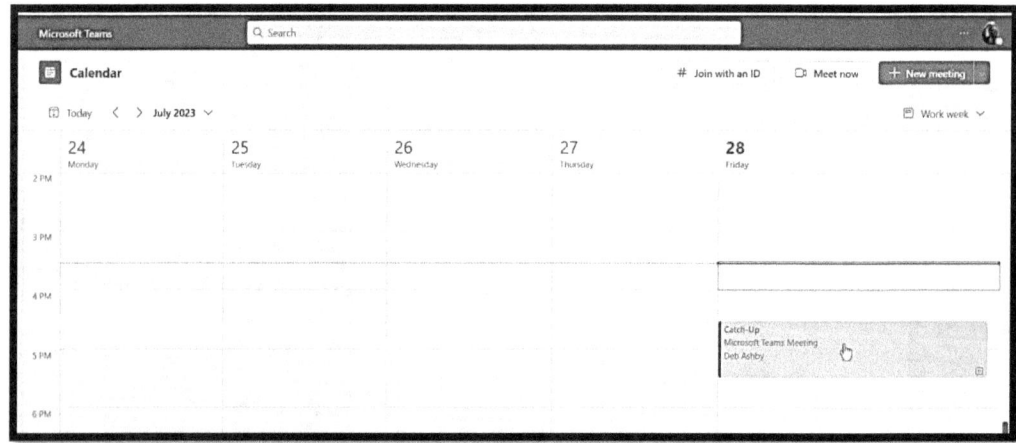

As an additional change, you will now find the meeting details in the email body. These details include URLs that participants can use to attend the meeting. The meeting is still ongoing, so there aren't any entries in the attendance tab just yet. However, when the meeting is concluded, you'll be able to see a complete roster of everyone who showed up. You'll find these extra tabs at the top of the page. Tabs for meeting notes and questions are also at your disposal. You can see that setting up a meeting and then attending it is a breeze.

Keep in mind that Outlook also provides ways to join Teams meetings. By navigating to your Outlook calendar, you will also be able to observe that the newly added team meeting is shown there. To view the details of the meeting, double-click on this. Either use the link within the message itself or go to the top of the page and click "Join Teams Meeting" to join the meeting.

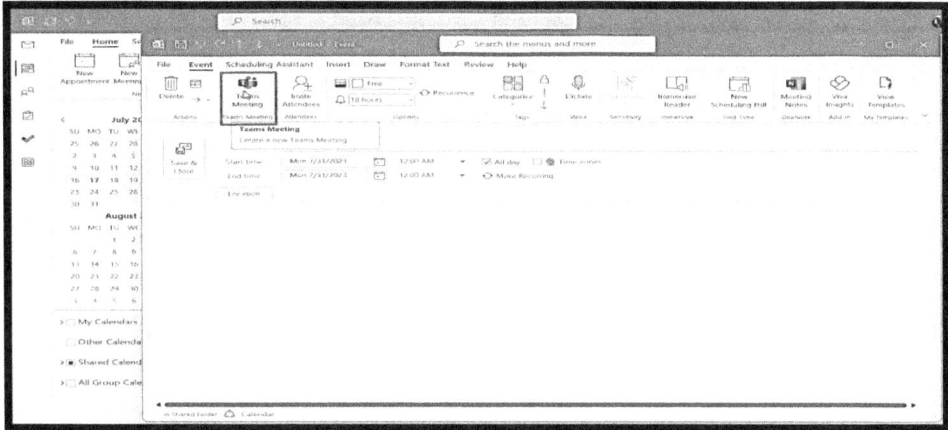

Remember that you can schedule Teams meetings directly from Outlook as well. For instance, if you double-click on Monday of the following week to add an event, you can choose to create a Teams meeting or change this one by selecting the Teams meeting symbol below. With so many possibilities, setting up meetings is simple; take your time and explore them.

Sharing a screen

In this section, we'll go over how to share your screen and files with other team members. Thus, if you would like to share additional content with conference attendees, you will find a "Share" button right here. To open this, use the shortcut CTRL + SHIFT + E. While you can share many other things when you click share, we will focus on sharing a screen, window, or tab.

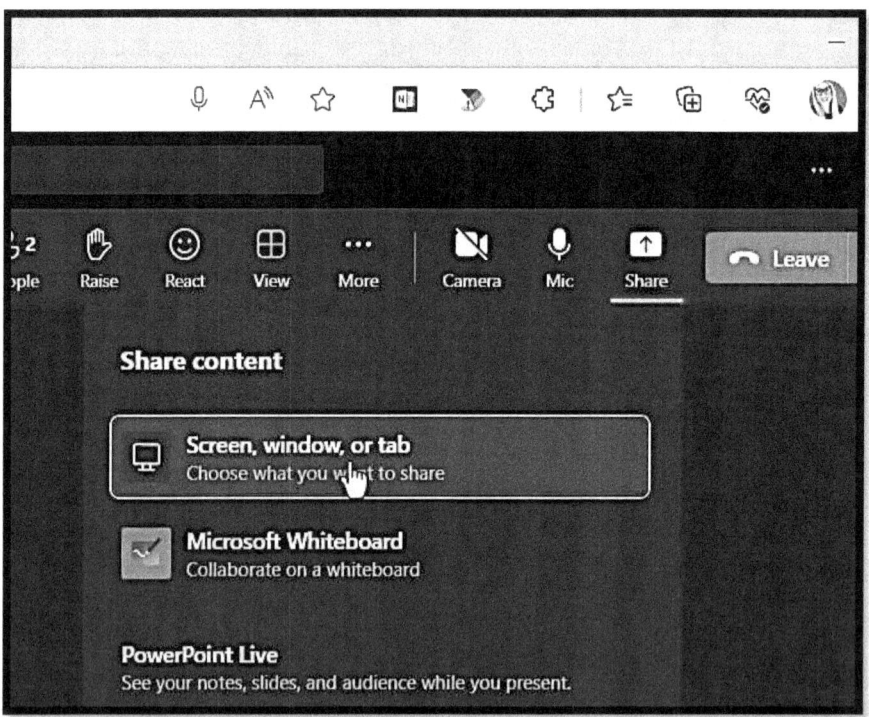

You can choose to share a specific tab in Microsoft Edge, an entire application, or your full screen when you click on this option. A small box will pop up to let you do this. What distinguishes all of them from what the public will observe is this:

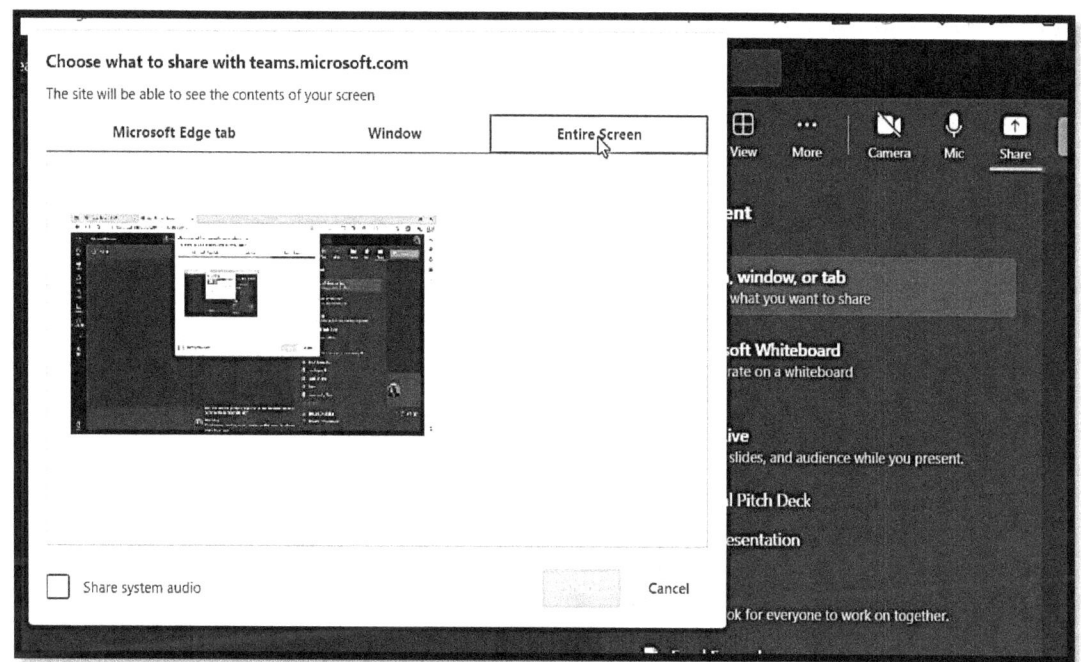

1) Using the Microsoft Edge browser is associated with the Microsoft Edge tab. You have the option to share only the tab that you are currently viewing in Microsoft Edge.
2) By selecting Windows, you will be able to view thumbnails of all the applications currently open on your desktop. For instance, if you wish to demonstrate Outlook while keeping your calendar open, you can share the Outlook window with your colleagues.
3) Finally, you have the option to display the complete screen, which means it will show whatever is currently visible on your desktop.

When you choose to share your entire screen instead of just a window, the meeting attendees will be able to see everything happening on your desktop. For example, if you have Outlook open, they will be able to see all of your emails. Similarly, if you have notifications coming in, everyone will be able to see them. Some people might rather not have others view certain things on their whole screen, so they choose to share just a window instead. By selecting the Outlook window and clicking the "Share" button, you bind it to this window. This means that others will never be able to see any other windows or applications on your screen, including any pop-ups or other windows you may have opened. They won't be able to tell if you're navigating on a variety of other sites. You'll see a hide button at the bottom of the Sharing mode window; clicking it will hide the little panel. When you're ready to end sharing, simply return to this window and click the "Stop sharing" button; doing so will bring you back into the meeting and exit sharing mode.

Take note of what's across the top of the screen while we're here on this screen. Your current status is "Do Not Disturb," it states. It is important to mention that you will only receive notifications for communications that are considered urgent from your priority contacts. Teams has set it to do not disturb, which will limit alerts coming in, because you're in a meeting and presenting. You can see this on your profile image, where the small red icon is over the top.

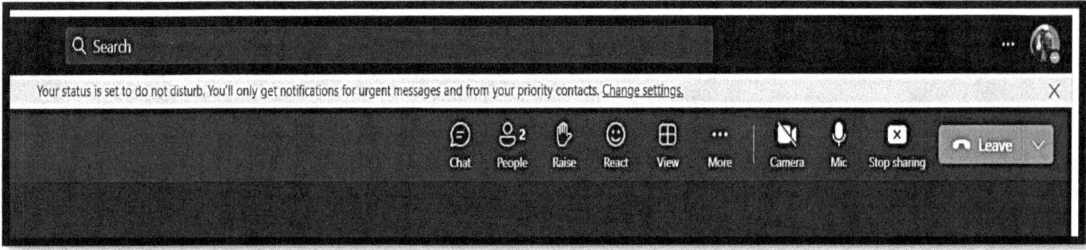

Another choice in this case is file sharing. The parts for Excel Live and PowerPoint Live are located here. At the bottom of this page are the options to explore OneDrive or your computer if you merely want to share a file with everyone. To make a file visible to everyone, simply click Browse My Computer and select the file you want to share. Sharing a window, your whole screen, or any file stored in File Explorer is that simple. You'll also notice that a "Stop sharing" button is located at the top of the window, along with a notice indicating that you are presenting.

Participating in meetings by delivering live presentations

A recent update allows team members to share and modify Excel and PowerPoint files in real time. On top of the Share button, there are two subheadings: "Excel Live" and "Presentation Live."

I'd like to begin by going over PowerPoint. By clicking it, the PowerPoint will disappear, prepare the slides, and then load into the window, so you can easily share it with everyone in the meeting. Now that you're the presenter, you're viewing the presentation in the Presenter View, which also displays all of the PowerPoint slides beneath it, as well as any notes you've contributed. Take note that the other attendees in this meeting do not see this perspective; instead, they perceive the red-highlighted portion.

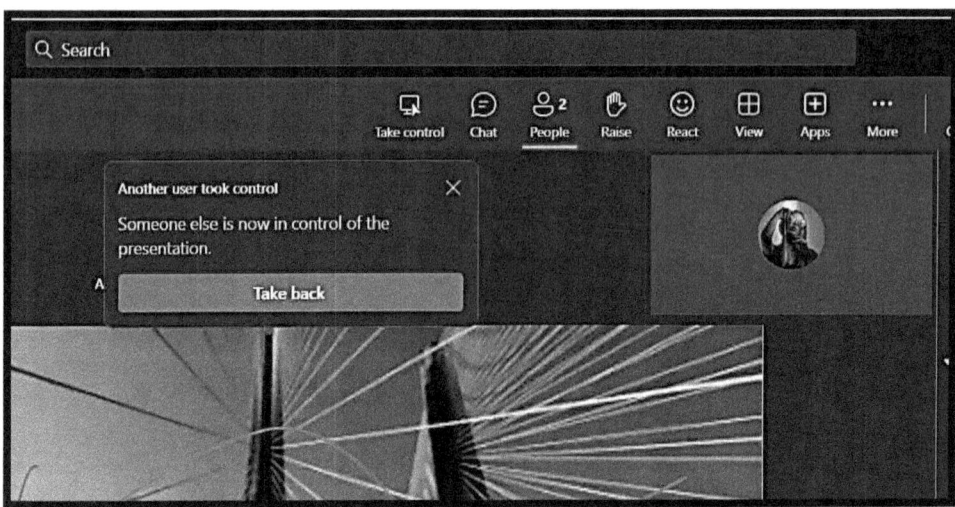

Sharing in this way is essentially co-authoring with other people in this meeting, which is one of the coolest things about working in PowerPoint Live since there are lots of various opportunities to collaborate with other meeting attendees. You'll find annotation tools down below; with a click of the pen, you can begin sketching on this presentation, and everyone watching may see your work in real time. A "Take control" button will appear on the participant's screen; by clicking it, they can essentially seize control of the presentation and go through the slides independently. The presenter has the option to add annotations, end the presentation, or reclaim control by clicking the "Take control" button in the toolbar.

There are a few more options available to you, such as a grid view that provides a somewhat different approach to display these slides. If you want to see what your audience is seeing, you can simply double-click on a slide to return to its original view, and if you click the three dots, you can hide the presenter view. A high-contrast view and translation into multiple languages are also available for the slides. Participants are not obligated to follow your pace through the presentation, which is another great feature. Everyone will see the slide you're currently on while Mary, who wants to read the previous slide, can do so independently of what you're saying on the current slide. This means that she can review the slides at her own pace without interfering with the presentation. We can examine Excel Live. Once again, all meeting attendees will have access to the Excel spreadsheet that you have on hand if you click the Share option.

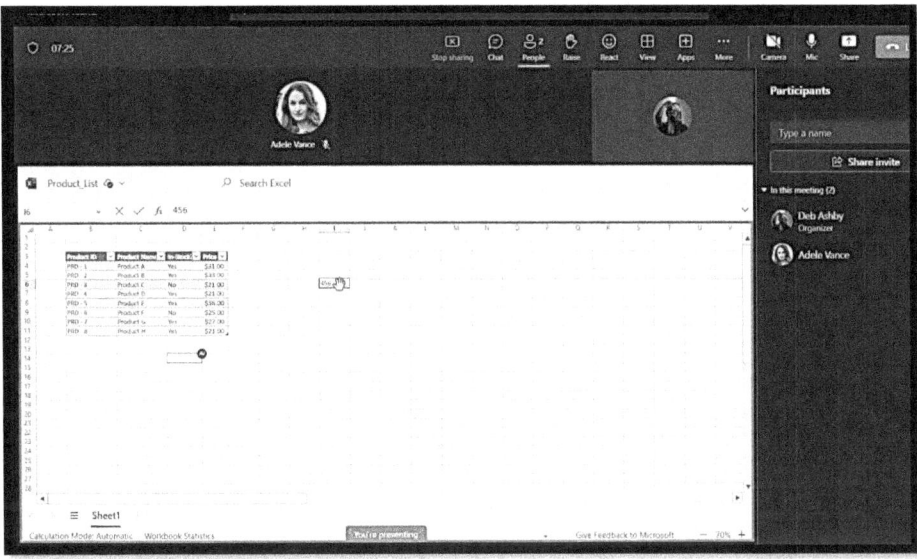

It's fantastic because this is merely a team effort. This spreadsheet allows you to see where other people are clicking while also letting your participants see where you are clicking. While Mary puts other data into the spreadsheet, you can input numbers into one cell; you both get to view the real-time updates. This is comparable to co-authoring a document in Microsoft 365. When you're finished, you can click "Stop sharing" to stop sharing that file. The combination of PowerPoint Live and Excel Live dramatically improves the ability to collaborate with other conference attendees on presentations and spreadsheets.

Generating ideas in a meeting

In addition to files, you also learnt in the previous section how to share a desktop or application during a team meeting. Just in case you remember, there was also the option of having a shared whiteboard for the entire crew. Could you explain what a whiteboard is and how and when you would use it? First of all, you should know that Whiteboard is a stand-alone application in Microsoft 365. To utilize it, navigate to your Microsoft 365 homepage, select the app launcher, and then find Whiteboard in the apps area by scrolling down. A whiteboard, as we can see if we open it and look at it, is just a blank canvas that helps team members and colleagues collaborate on ideas and project planning.

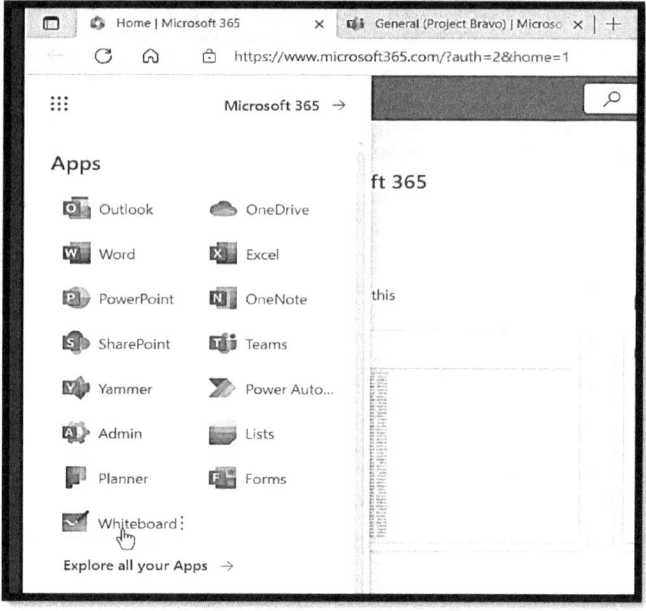

In addition to being able to start from scratch or use pre-made templates to make your whiteboard, there is a small toolbar at the bottom that lets you add annotations and other features. For instance, you have the option to include small sticky notes. By selecting one of them and clicking on the Whiteboard, you will be presented with an image that resembles a sticky note. Stick it anywhere you choose and start jotting down notes.

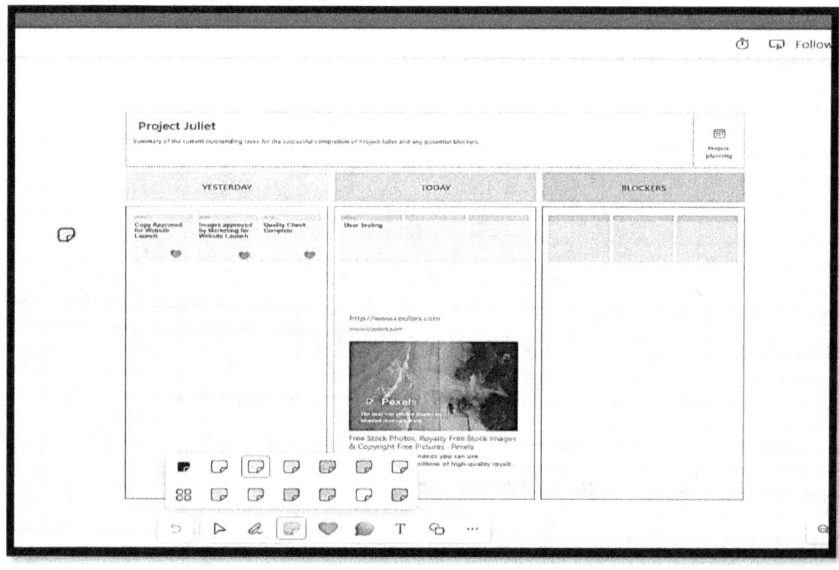

Additionally, keep in mind that you can change the note's color using the little floating formatting bar that appears just above when you enter text here. The note can be deleted, comments can be added, or the text can be better formatted. If you want to add a reaction, you can see what you have by clicking the heart icon right here. For example, if you want to add a checkmark, you can place it wherever on the whiteboard. Like in any Microsoft product, you may add things like comments by clicking and dragging the little comment icon to the desired location; then, you can edit your comment just like any other text in the document. Sure, you can type text wherever on your whiteboard; all you have to do is click and start typing. If the font size is too small, you can easily magnify it using the formatting tools. To facilitate quick and easy text entry, you can also place text boxes on your whiteboard at any desired location. If you'd like to add a triangle, for example, you can do so and then simply drag its corners to make it smaller or larger. Here you may see some examples of the kinds of structures that could be constructed in this area. Having a blank canvas, having individuals scribble comments, and facilitating brainstorming sessions are all viable options for creating diagrams and project plans.

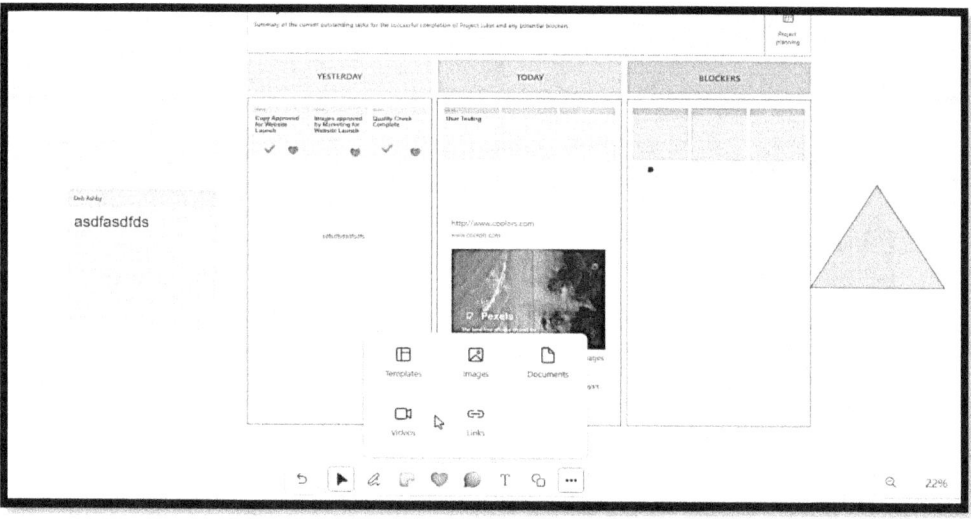

You can access more choices by clicking the three dots. Templates, photos, documents, videos, and links are all at your fingertips. Once you've added all of these elements to your whiteboard, you may customize it whatever you like. When you're satisfied, simply click the name button at the top and enter a new name for your board.

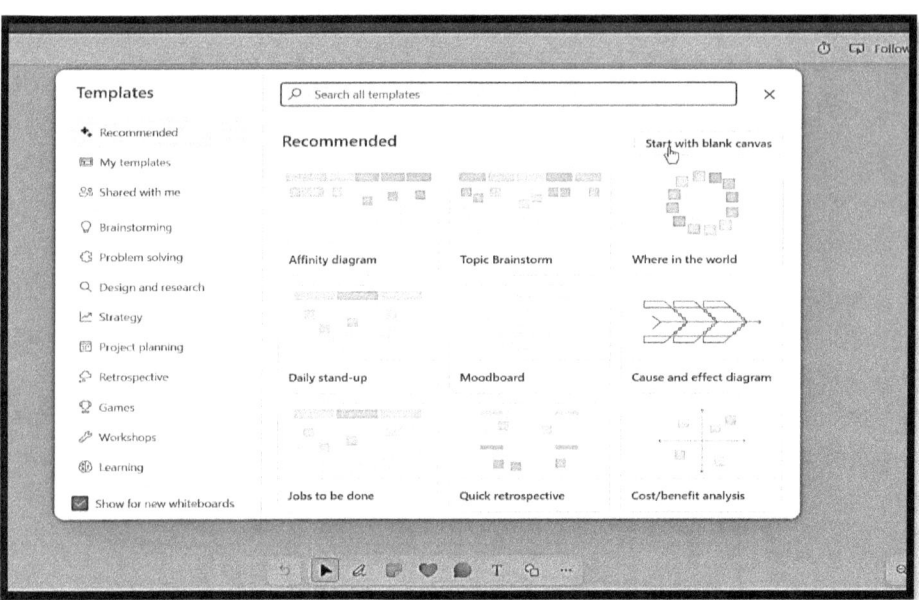

From this page, you may access the "New Whiteboard" button, where you can begin with a blank slate or select from a variety of pre-made templates organized by category. This template is up for grabs if you want to have a look at a preview and decide it suits your needs.

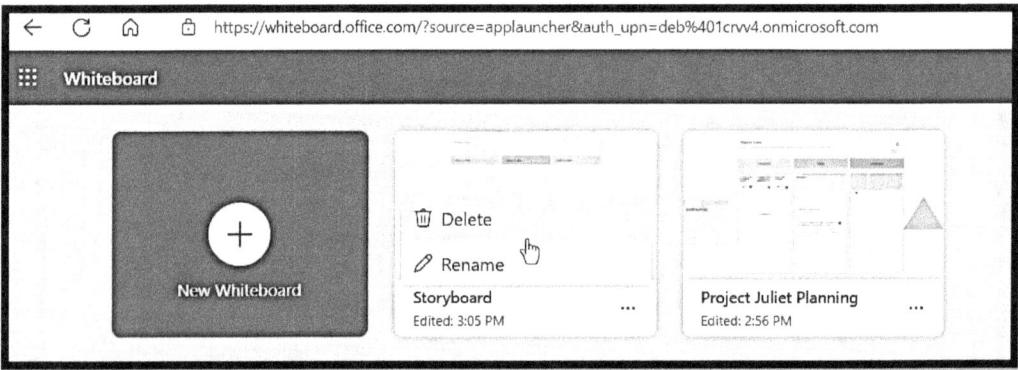

After that, you can decide where to put it, drag and drop it, change its size, and begin personalizing it to fit your team's needs. There are a few things you can do in the Whiteboard app's settings, and one of them is to tap the three dots that appear when you're working inside the program. Remove or rename it as you choose. Keep in mind that while you're using one of these whiteboards, you'll see a Share button in the upper right corner. This allows you to obtain the URL to the whiteboard, so you can invite others to come in and start editing it.

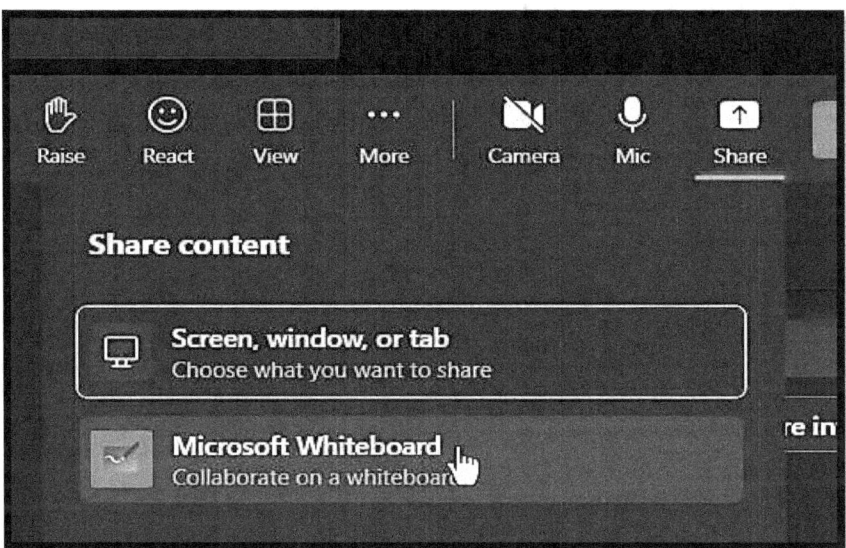

What is the connection to Microsoft Teams here? Imagine a scenario where you're in a Microsoft Teams meeting and you want to start a new whiteboard. Your team members will have a blank slate to brainstorm on, and you can all jump in and co-author the document at the same time. This way, you can make changes, your colleagues can make changes, and you can see those updates on the whiteboard while you work. A second option would be to prepare a whiteboard and make it available to meeting attendees before the event. If you're already in the middle of a meeting, you can still use that whiteboard by sharing it with your colleagues. One can find the Microsoft Whiteboard option by navigating to the Share button located in the upper right corner. To access the app, click on that. Once the app opens, you'll see all of the existing whiteboards. To collaborate on one, simply click the share button. You might not always want other meeting attendees to have editing access to the whiteboard when you share it with them. While you're in the meeting, you can disable that feature for your own whiteboard. If you don't want other people to be able to make changes to the document besides you, you can disable this feature by clicking the gear symbol up top.

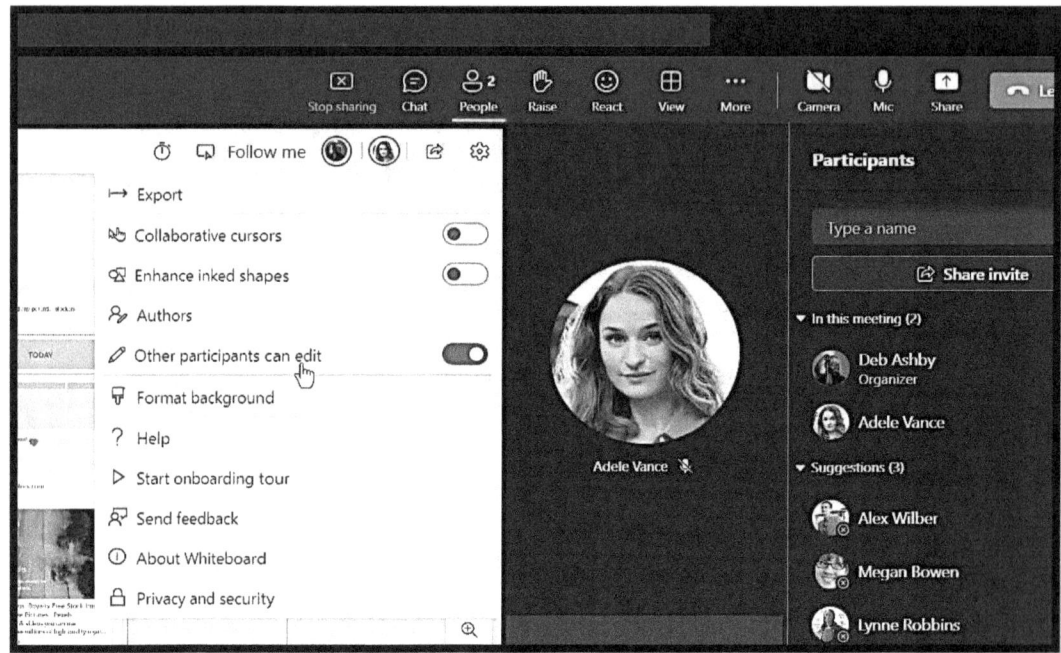

When you're done changing the whiteboard, choose "Stop sharing" to restore all of your changes back into the app. Recall that if you need to rethink your brainstorming session, you may go back to the Share a Microsoft whiteboard screen and begin a new whiteboard from scratch. Click the "New Whiteboard" option without selecting an existing whiteboard.

Complicated meeting circumstances

Conference planners can effortlessly split up large crowds of people into smaller, easier-to-manage groups by utilizing breakout rooms. For example, the facilitator may suggest breaking up the group into smaller groups of four to debate a predetermined topic or work on a group assignment in a meeting with twenty members. It does simulate the actual process of working together, so imagine several seminars happening in different conference rooms. Join me as I walk you through the workings of Breakout Rooms. I should also remark that we have been using the Microsoft Teams online app, which is accessible from the Microsoft 365 website, with success. The desktop version of Teams must be downloaded in order to utilize Breakout Rooms, even though the online software is completely functional. Everything else can be found on the web application. It's vital to note that Microsoft 365 corporate subscriptions are the only way to access Breakout Rooms. The desktop program now has this Room's emblem clearly displayed at the top, as you may have observed. Opening a Breakout Room will let you invite guests because it's usually a terrific spot to host huge gatherings.

Assume for a moment that you are the event planner and would like to set up some Breakout Rooms. A window will appear on the right side of the screen when you click on the Rooms option. From the drop-down menu, you may select up to 50 breakout rooms as your desired number of rooms. We wouldn't recommend it because it will be too much for you to handle as the organizer, but if there are a few members on your team, it would be a good idea to make two or even four rooms.

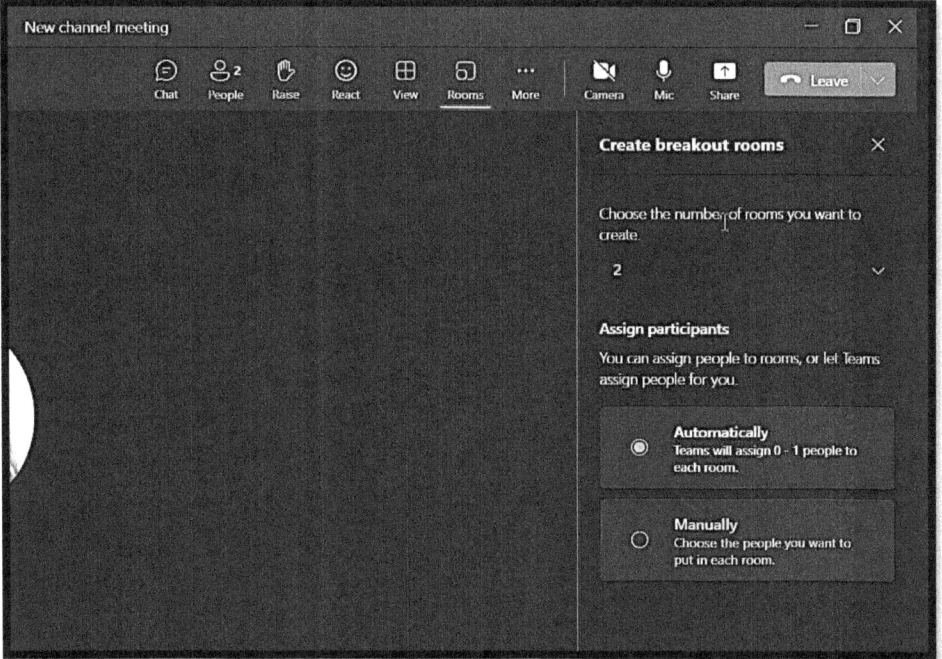

Assigning people to the two breakout rooms you choose is an option that presents you with two possible paths, for example:

a) If you set it to "Automatically," Teams will handle all of the assignment tasks without your intervention. It will randomly divide the attendees evenly between the two rooms.
b) You would select "Manually" if you desire a bit more control and wish to assign individuals to specific teams or have them collaborate with others.

Choosing the second choice will lead you to the "Create rooms" screen. You'll notice that two rooms have been established, but they appear closed with a zero following them. This is because no one has been assigned to these rooms yet. In this case, you can see all of your users' avatars up top, and then you may manually allocate them to rooms.

Keep in mind that there are symbols under "Assign participants" as well:

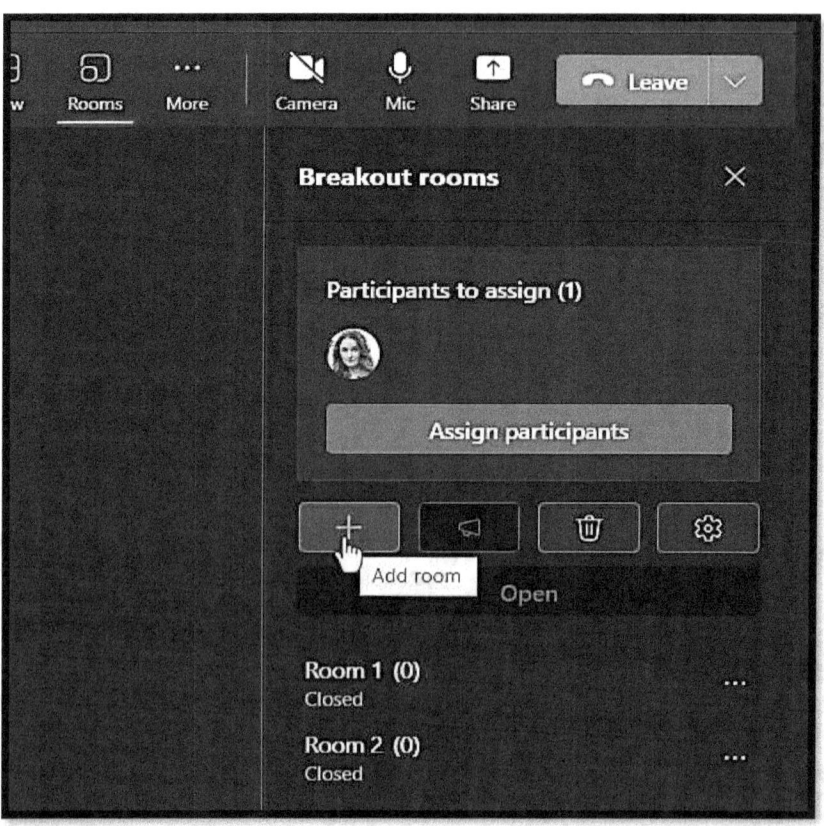

a) Feel free to add one or two rooms if you decide you want three or four rooms because you can make new ones on the fly.
b) An announcement can also be made by you. By selecting this option, the meeting organizer has the ability to effectively communicate with all participants in every room.
c) It is possible to remove rooms.
d) You also have the option to customize our rooms. For instance, you can choose presenters to oversee each room and establish a time restriction for attendees; for instance, after 10 minutes, the system will automatically end the breakout sessions and re-group everyone in the main meeting.

Once you've finished configuring everything, click Save. Now you can see which rooms each person is assigned to. Before the meeting starts, you may configure this such that when it's time to do the exercise or whatever it is, you can open the Breakout Rooms by clicking the open button. This will divide the participants into their respective rooms. After stepping out into their respective rooms, participants vanish from view of the main meeting window; naturally, they will only be able to see the other individuals also assigned to that room.

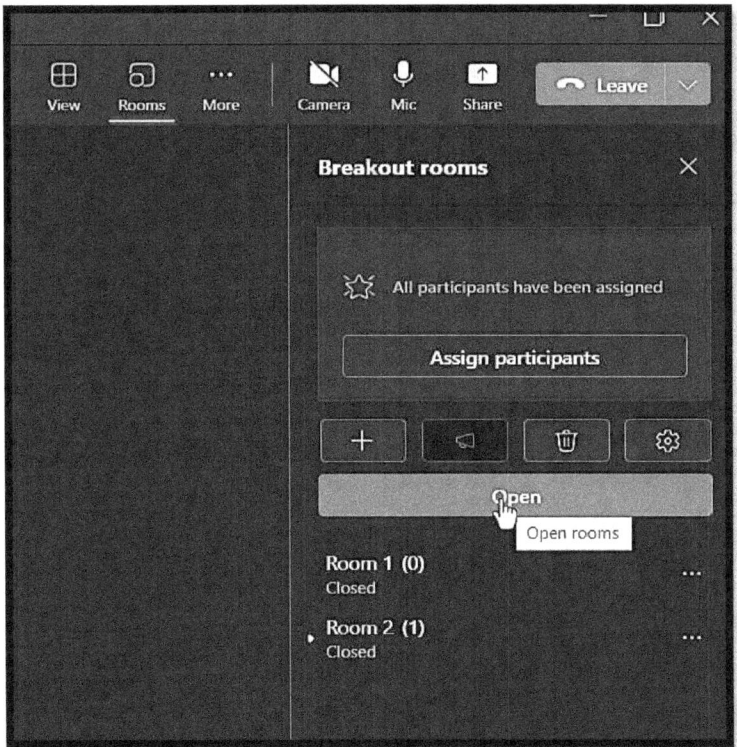

You are free to choose whatever room you wish as the meeting organizer. For example, if you notice that someone is having trouble with an activity in room two, you can join that room by clicking the three dots, which will also bring you into the current room. You can then assist them as needed. Renaming rooms is another option.

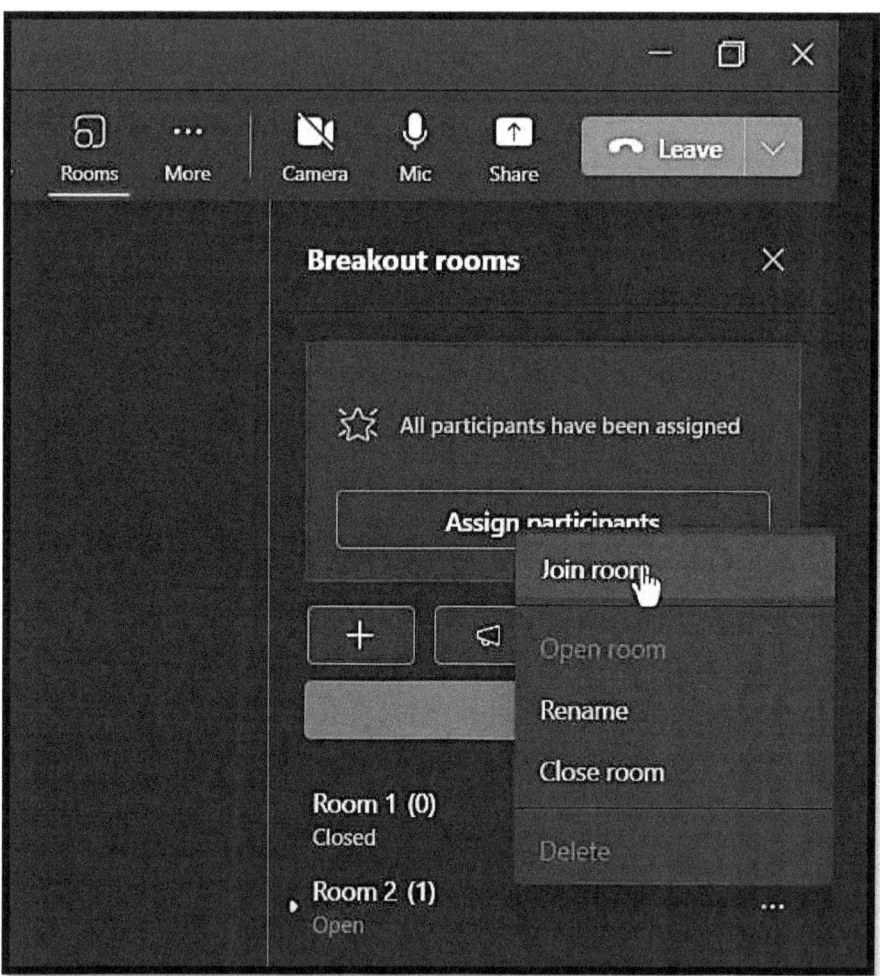

Click the "Make an announcement" option if you'd want to address all teams at once as the meeting organizer. Once you're ready to end the breakout sessions and return everyone to the main meeting, all you have to do is click the close button. All of the participants should be back in the main meeting in no time after you type in your message and send it through.

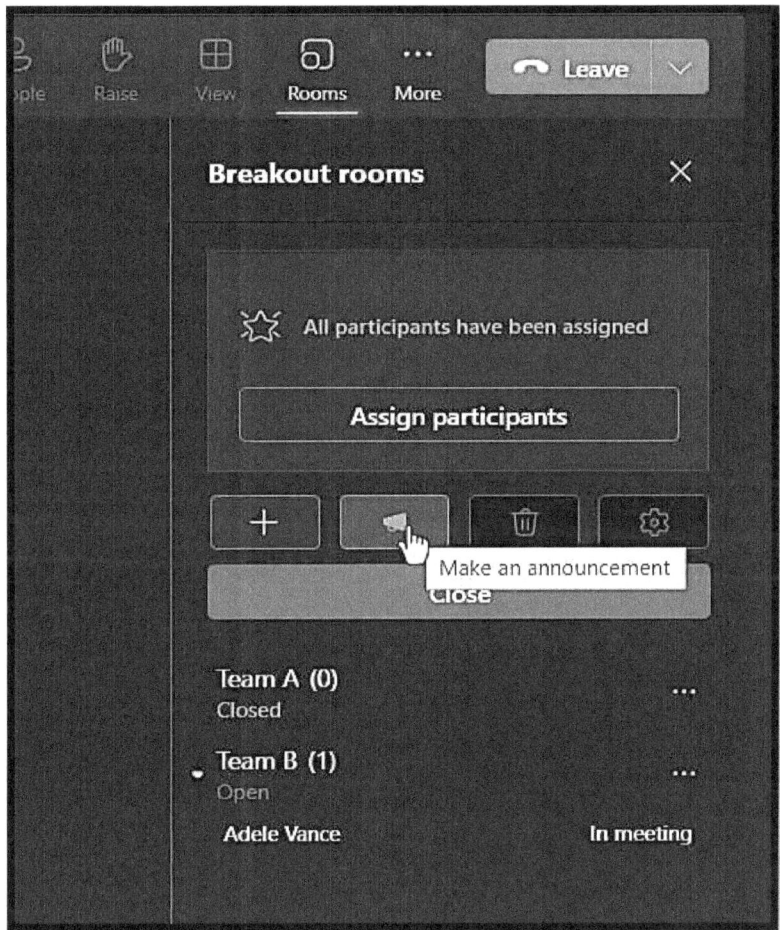

This is the basic premise of Breakout Rooms. The main point to remember is that in order to access the Breakout Rooms feature, you must be using the desktop version of Microsoft Teams. Having more participants makes this feature even better.

Activities

1. Launch the Teams calendar and try setting up a brand-new meeting.
2. Change the meeting's title, date, time, and participants as needed.
3. Keep an eye on the invitees' calendars to see when the meeting is scheduled.

CHAPTER SIX
MICROSOFT TEAMS: MANAGING PROJECTS

Synopsis

Project management using Microsoft Teams can lead to a considerable boost in productivity and collaboration. You will discover how to use external tools within Teams, share files, assign tasks, and promote teamwork in Chapter 6. In this chapter, we'll walk through how to use Microsoft Teams for project management. In case you didn't know, Microsoft Teams has become the go-to tool for managing initiatives, projects, and entire portfolios. It incorporates tasks, meetings, content, communication, and other elements to enhance teamwork, output, and delivery. So, in this chapter, we'll show you how to use Teams to master project management from beginning to end.

The Setting Up

Using teams, channels, and groups to properly build your organizational structure is the cornerstone of Microsoft Teams. The formation of program teams is a part of this. First, let's talk about group, channel, and team structures. The first stage is to form a team at the program level as a whole. If you were running an IT infrastructure program, for example, you would organize a team with the same name. This group would act as the general portfolio container for all of your projects and resources. The second step is to add project channels. Create channels within your program team that are dedicated to each project. You may want to create channels for any project that impacts the entire program team, using our example as a model. Think of channels as differentiable work streams within a bigger team.

The third stage is the creation of project groups. By using groups, you may further organize resources within channels by bringing together the people who are specifically needed for that channel based on department, job, etc. We might create additional groups for the channels we've already built so that the right people have access to the right channels and material. This facilitates team separation. In conclusion, that would be the IT infrastructure example project's software itself. Channels would be used for individual projects, while groups would use resources based on roles. This three-tier hierarchy keeps everything organized and separate even as your portfolio expands.

Regarding the Conversation

The usage of postings for project communication is the next topic. The post tab inside your team channel serves as the main focus for communications for your project. Posts operate in a manner akin to instantaneous chat messages accessible to the entire project team. Unlike emails, posts enable quick conversations, questions, remarks, and status updates. To start creating a post, just click the pencil icon at the bottom of the Post tab. This will open a text field. You can do a lot more things here, like format text, attach other kinds of attachments, @mention colleagues, and incorporate photos using the formatting toolbar. When your message is ready, post it to the channel by clicking the arrow button. To highlight an important notification, click the three dots on your post and select "Mark as important." In order to ensure that readers don't miss it, this will cause the post to be marked with an exclamation point to show how urgent it is.

After that, you can solicit approvals and feedback by including the hashtag #mentioning stakeholders in your post. For prompt attention and input regarding official approvals, click the three dots and select Ask for permission, Assign approvers, and Track status. When your channel fills up quickly, use the search bar to find posts by name or keyword. It is also possible to pin important posts for quick access in the future. In conclusion, posts can be used for debates, announcements, approvals, questions, status updates, and more. It's far faster and more effective than email.

File sharing

Using the Files tab on your channel, you can store and share all of the important project files and supporting documents, including specs, contracts, budgets, presentations, and much more. With Teams' integrated SharePoint connection, you can stop sending files by email and instead make your files available to your team at all times, from anywhere. Create a clear folder structure with subfolders to organize and categorize pertinent project files. We advise using descriptive file names, dates, or version numbers to make it obvious which file is the most recent in order to prevent confusion over the most recent version. With shared files, you may have true real-time co-authoring, enabling several people to work together on the same project at once. By choosing "Share," you can still share files with persons other than your team. This will produce a unique URL that you can share with potential customers. Just remember to set up permissions, expiration dates, and password protection.

Including instruments from external sources

It is possible to incorporate external tools and programs. Teams' extensibility—which allows them to use tabs to directly integrate external technologies into channels—is one of its primary features. Asana and Trello are two popular integrations for project management. You can embed them in addition to using them as web apps, custom apps, SharePoint lists, and much more. Microsoft Teams can now combine work being done on several platforms thanks to this.

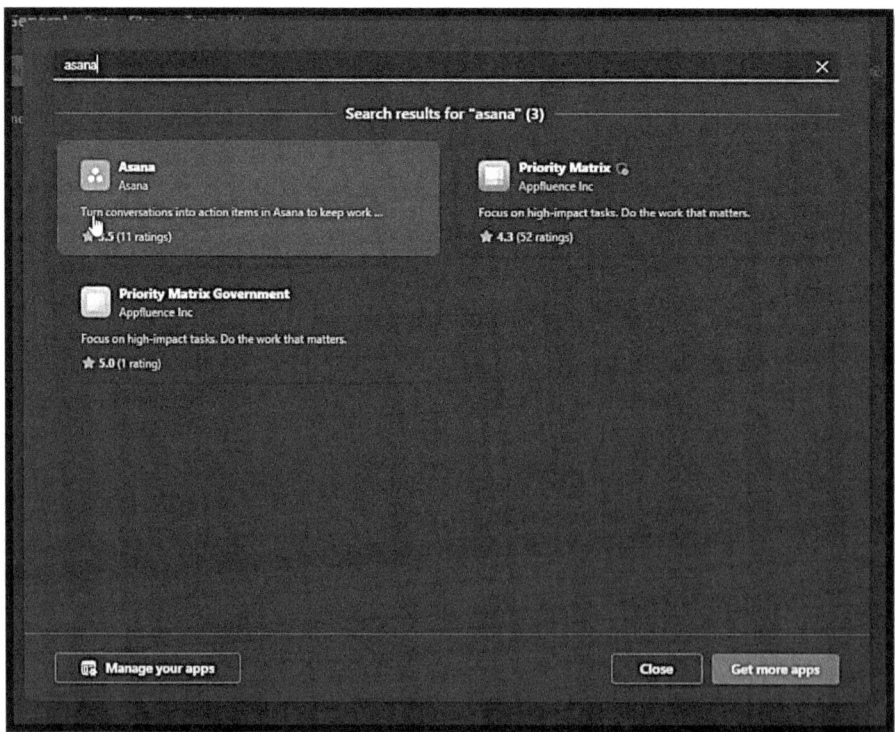

Free software like Microsoft Teams might be a godsend for project managers, as you can see. Initiate the process by forming your team, creating a sample project channel, and documenting your steps.

Activities

1. Establish a Microsoft Teams team dedicated solely to the project management endeavor.
2. Arrange the tabs and channels so they better suit the project's lifecycle and the team's communication requirements.
3. Make sure to invite all the required team members and give them the right responsibilities and access levels.

CHAPTER SEVEN
TEAM MICROSOFT PLANNER USERS

Synopsis

In chapter 7, you will discover the features of Microsoft Planner, a task management application that is a component of Microsoft Teams. This chapter will walk you through the many components of Planner and how they have evolved over time. Task management is consolidated across all apps with the aid of the new Planner on Microsoft Teams, providing you with an easy-to-use job management solution. It has an easy-to-understand navigation menu that combines Planner and To-do into one primary section consisting of three main parts.

Regarding My Day

To begin with, this is just the same as My Day in Microsoft To-do. By default, all of the tasks you were given to perform today will be displayed, together with the source that identifies the origin of each effort. However, if you mouse over a personal plan, nothing displays except the plan name—a new feature we will cover later in this chapter. Next on a Loop page is an icon for a team, and then a task from a task list. If you're interested, we may examine how to manage the tasks that are assigned to you in Loop.

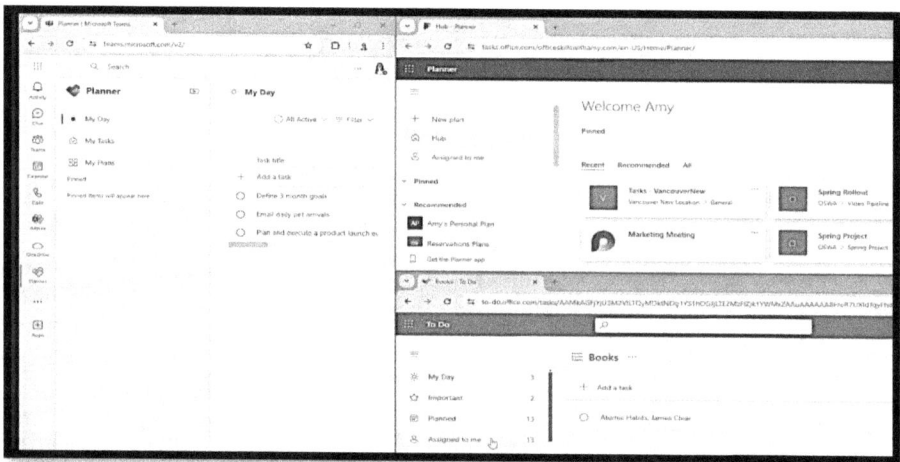

Let's examine the first task there with the help of the above illustration. As you can see, it features a notepad, sunshine, and a small pink icon. The chores that will appear here are all related to the sunshine since they are all part of My Day. However, when we click on one of the jobs, we can see that it has a personalized pink tag attached to it. The note that is attached to the job and any color tags that are defined in any of your plans will also be there. This simply means that when you open the task, notes will be found within it.

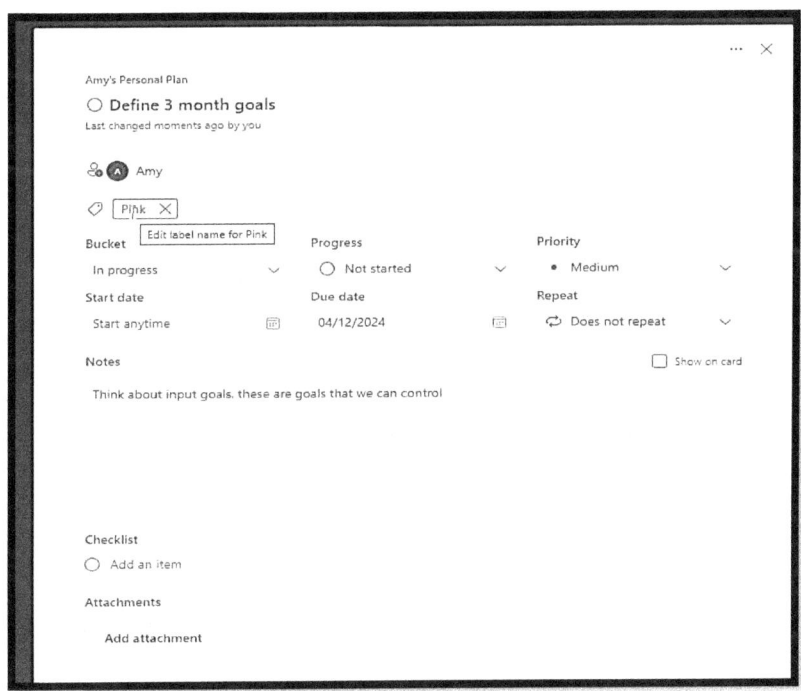

We can simply make a progress bar and indicate, "Hey, this needs to be finished today. It's urgent." When you simply have that day view of all of your tasks, we can see how these produce a great visual impact. If we close this, we can see that the small circle that represents the progress bar and the bell for the priorities has been added. We can update every item listed in the ellipses on the right-hand side as well as from the top menu. They wanted to call your attention to the "Remove from My Day" button because they are the same. This is really useful if you struggle with making decisions. All you have to do is click "Remove from My Day" to get rid of some of the less important things, and then everything will be clear and you can concentrate on the things that really matter.

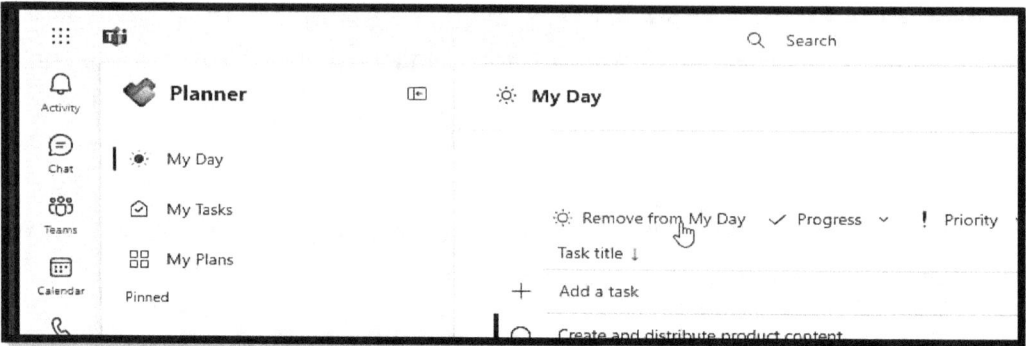

The last feature we want to walk through in this section is the option to add a private task. You'll see that a new private task has been added, and the source is now a private task. These are designed to make it easier for you to quickly jot down to-do lists. To-do has a little completed space below, but we can easily replicate this by filtering for completed items using the top drop-down menu.

Concerning My Tasks

Now let's discuss My Tasks. To-do and Planner users may recognize some of the four predefined filters at the top of this section, which let you review all of the tasks that are relevant to you in one easy-to-reach spot.

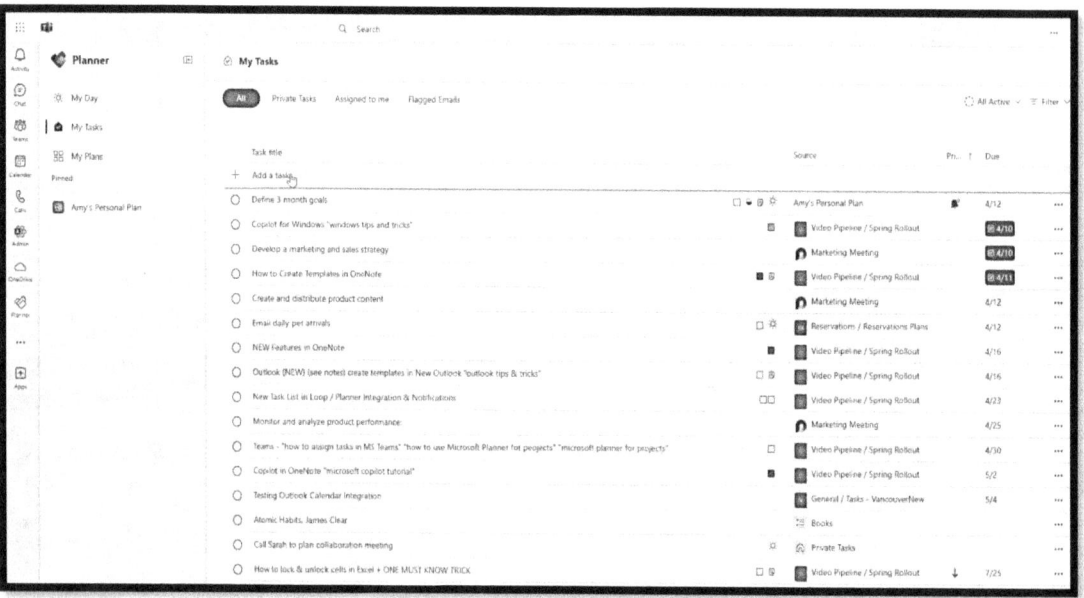

Starting with the Private Job, we can see the small Sun icon next to the newly added private work under My Day. We also have the ability to add new tasks right here. Just pick one, click "Add to My Day," and it will show up under My Day. That's how you assign one to today. By choosing "Assign to me," you may see all of the tasks that have been assigned to you for every date across all of your plans in one easy-to-access spot. Now, depending on how many tasks you have, you may rapidly sort them by title, priority, or due date. Depending on how many tasks you have, you can also choose additional filter options for dates and priorities at the top. Moving on to flagged emails, all we have to do is open the flagged email in Outlook by selecting the "flag this message" option. The source displays Outlook and even has an attachment there. If we click to open this job, we can immediately get back to that email by selecting the attachment here. Under My Tasks, all of the tasks are consolidated. Even the marked email is displayed here, and it will update in the small tag area with an Outlook once we are done.

Concerning My Plans

Now let's go to My Plans, where you can view all of the plans that apply to you in one easy-to-access place. This includes not just the new personal plans feature (which we will talk about shortly) but also lists from to-do plans in Planner. Soon, premium plans will be available; these will need a new membership.

Let's start with shared plans, which are those that are connected to a Microsoft team or other 365 organization and are shared with you. Choose "New plan" and proceed to the left to view all of the templates. Here, we have a variety of templates that provide you a preview of the plan. All of these templates are marked as basic, however some may declare premium in the future and require a different license.

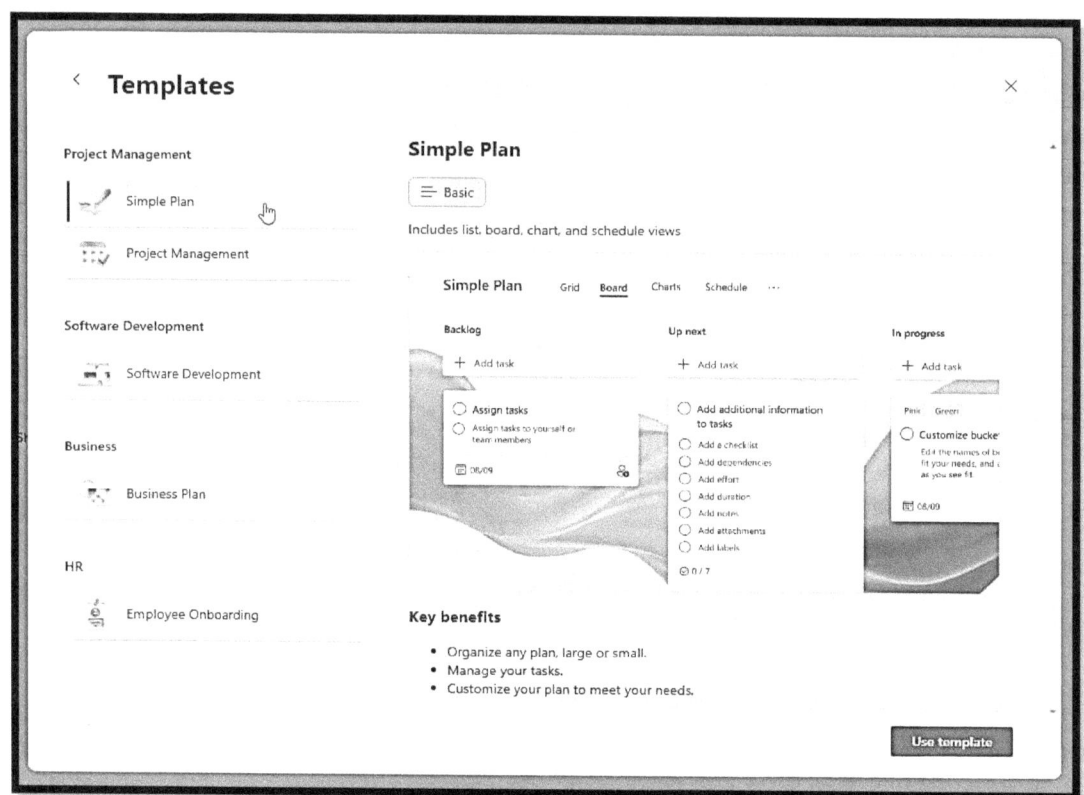

For example, if we are launching a new pet food line, we can choose project management and choose to "Use template at Amy's animal shop." This strategy will be used to oversee the product project. We'll pin this plan to the navigation menu because we'll be using it a lot. Here, we will choose a group from the bottom. As you can see, many of these are your teams in Microsoft Teams, and you can also see if it's public or private. Some of your teams may state private, in which case these are just the group's privacy settings. Now that our plan has been generated, let's move forward and allocate it to the operations.

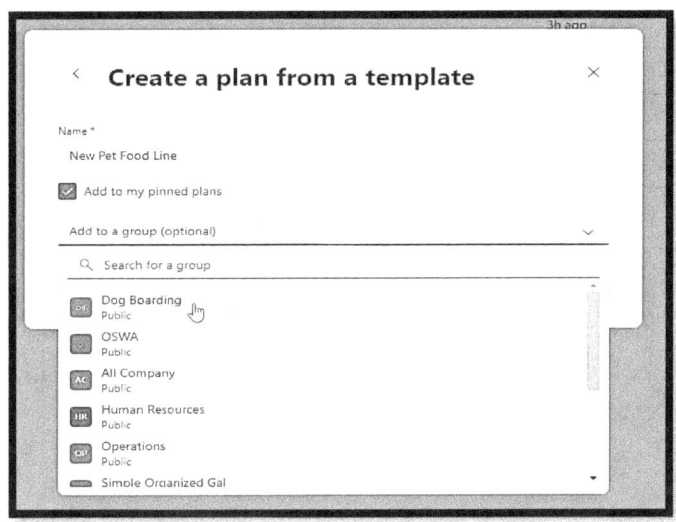

As you can see, this incredible template offers a great beginning point for this project. Additionally, we can see that this plan has been pinned to the left navigation menu and that it appears under the shared section when we navigate to My Plans. This new pet food line plan is available for viewing. Proceeding to the Personal tab, this section comprises your own schedules, the recently launched Planner tool, and Microsoft To-do Lists. We'll also go to the "New Plan" button to make a personal plan. There, we'll find all of those templates, but if we'd rather start from scratch, we may choose "Basic."

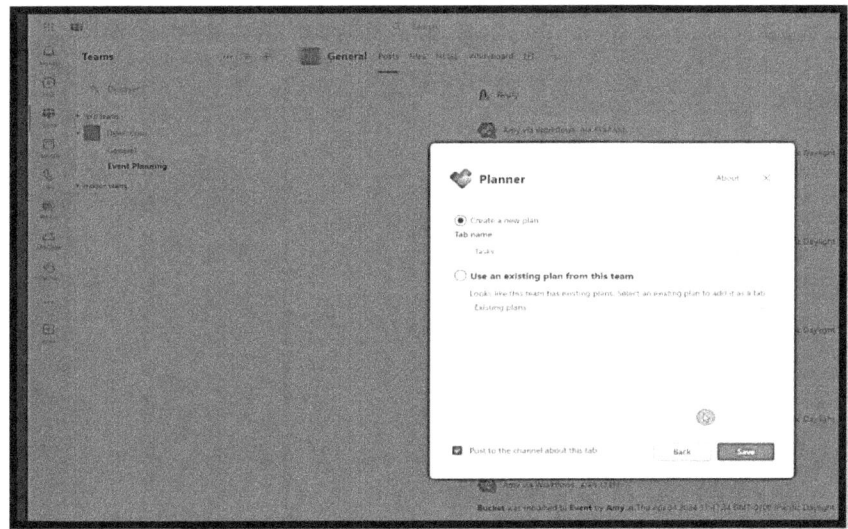

To indicate that this plan will continue to be allocated to a Microsoft group, we're going to leave the spot at the bottom where we assigned it to the group in the previous step blank. We can now proceed with our new plan as we clicked Create. This is amazing because it was previously unfeasible. Before, a private plan could only be allocated to a group. However, with a private plan, you may create your own and enjoy all the benefits of a regular plan, but solely for yourself. You can create a new group or add this plan to an existing one in the future if you decide you would like to add it to one. Next, select a team from the drop-down menu one more time. Our pinned plans match the designs on the menu on the left. It is possible to pin or unpin them.

Accessing My Teams

We then navigate to My Teams, where a list of all our teams that have plans is shown. We can see the plans arranged by team channels if we enlarge any of those teams. We want to overlay the Shared Plans and My Teams here because of how similar they appear. As you can see, though, neither the freshly created plan nor the new line of pet food will be visible under My Teams. Here, under "Shared With," on the right-hand side, you can see whose team they are assigned to. In contrast to My Teams, which provides plans arranged by channel, the channel is not visible.

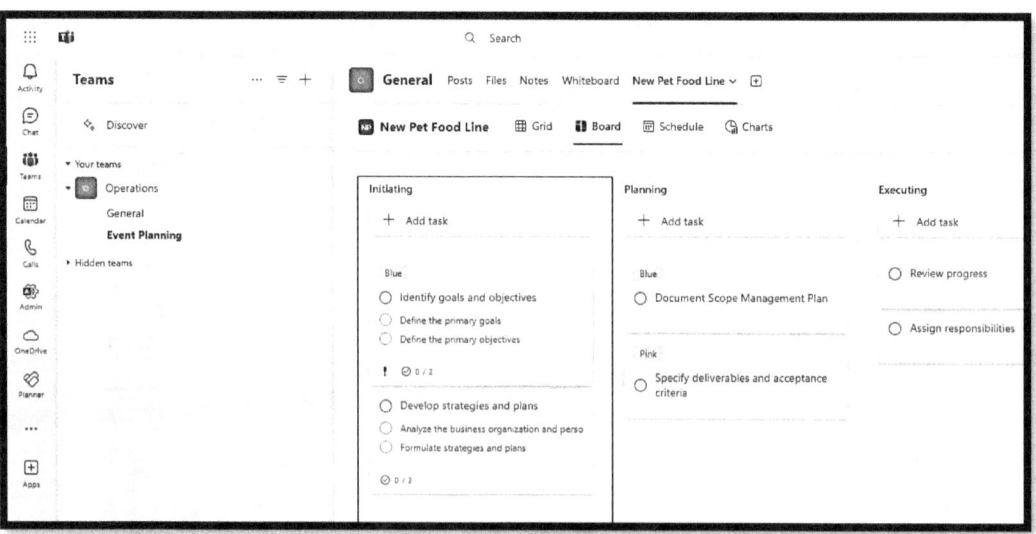

We need to add these plans to a channel in order for them to show up under "My Teams". We can access the Planner here by heading to the "Add a Tab" area now that we are a part of that team (you may look for it here if you don't find it). Now all we need to do is add our strategy. The team has already been assigned to an existing plan, which we could implement, or we could create a brand-new plan from the ground up. In the latter scenario, adding the freshly created plan to a channel would be all that is required. We can see that the amended plan is now in effect after clicking Save. We can see that team and the new pet food line at the bottom by reentering My Plans and My Teams.

Important setups

We would like to highlight a few specific setups. We can modify the plan name from this part on the right if we select the plan name at the top. By choosing it from the bottom, we may also remove a plan from the group area. This is where you may change the parameters for the 365 group. This is also where notifications are provided.

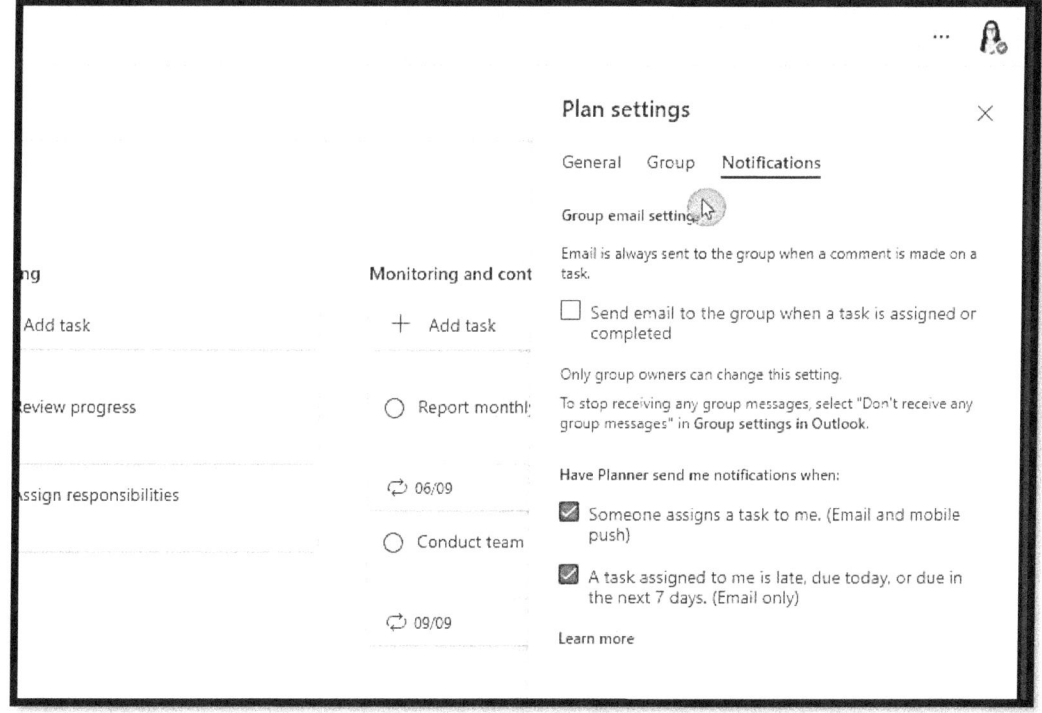

Please be aware that this initial setting can only be changed by owners. Here, you can indicate whether you want to get job assignments by email and mobile post, as well as if the assignment is due today or in seven days.

Comparing new planners to older ones

If we navigate to the old Planner, there are several settings we would rather see in the new one. From the ellipses here at the top, you can see some really remarkable stuff. The plan can first be exported to Excel, which creates a cute little table. After that, we can update someone who isn't directly involved in the details about the plan's development. The last option is to add a plan to an outlet calendar, which incorporates the plan into your calendar and encourages you to check it occasionally.

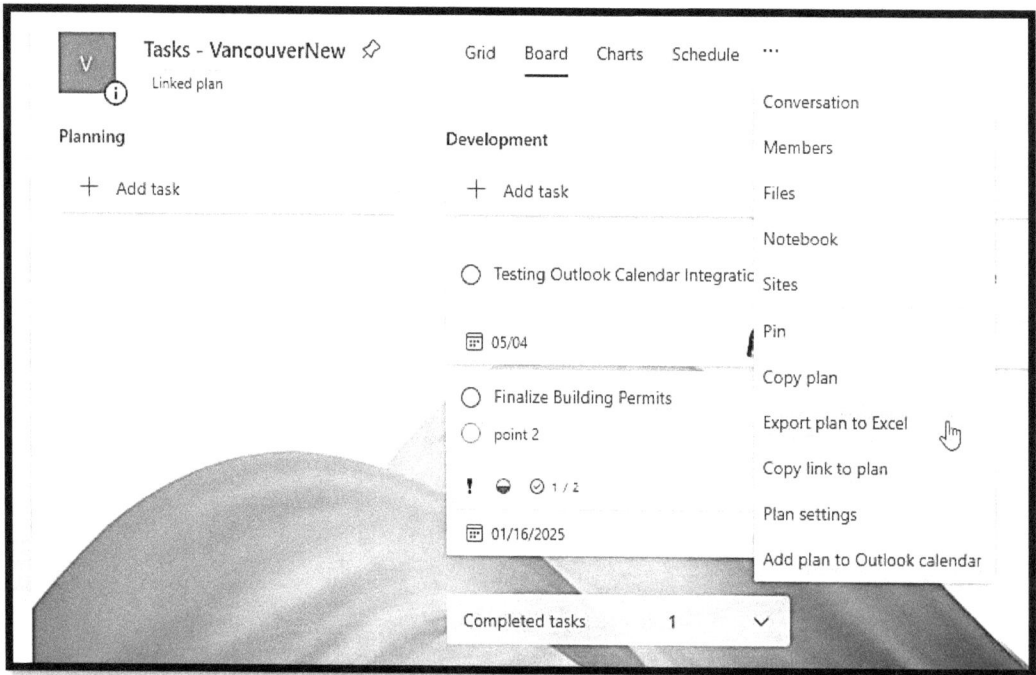

Now, if we navigate to Plan Settings, we see that, like the new version, there are tabs for notifications and the General group at the top. However, beneath the General section, we find these lovely backdrops, which are not currently accessible but should be in the new Planner shortly.

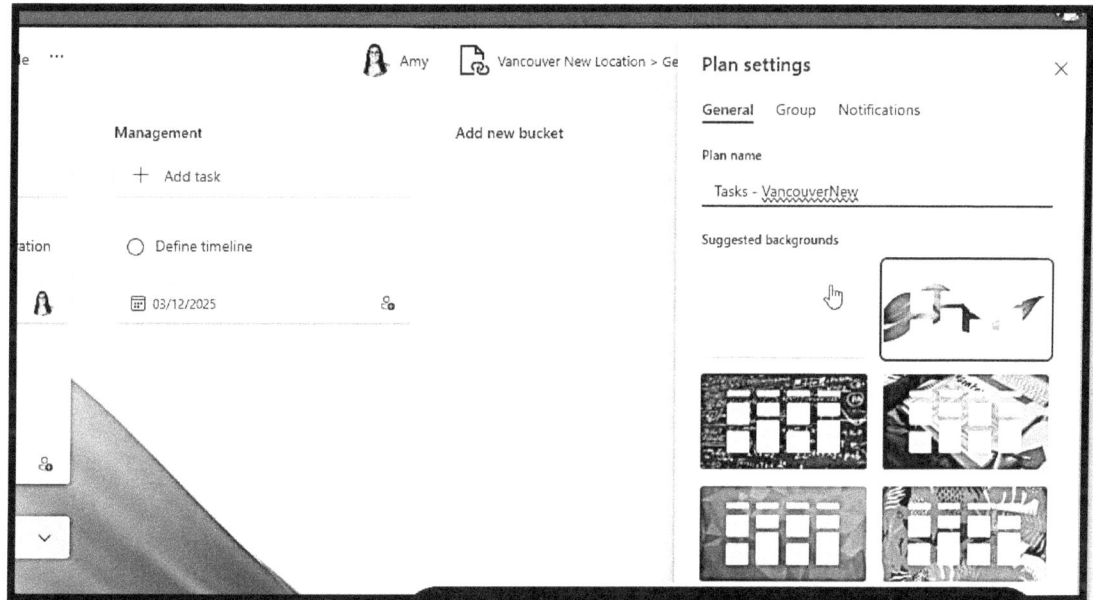

Activities

1. Open Microsoft Planner and navigate to the "My Plans" area.
2. Modify the plan views to your desired design.
3. Take note of how the "My Plans" function offers a summary of your participation in various team- or project-oriented plans.

CHAPTER EIGHT

MICROSOFT EDUCATION: EXPLORATION OF ADVANCED FEATURES

Synopsis

Chapter 8 covers the newest features and tools in Microsoft Teams, designed with educators and students in mind. These tools and features include noise cancellation, annotation, feedback, and reminders. In this chapter, we will walk through the new features in Teams for Education. Along with many other features, this allows you to easily update assignments, annotate PDFs for teachers and students, enhance Reflect, and much more.

Adding notes to a PDF

Teachers have long requested the ability to annotate a PDF in an assignment; therefore this is the first new feature. You will go to the Assignments channel as an educator, choose "Create," and then "New assignment." Give it some instructions and a brief description. Consider the TPS report Explorations as an example. The task should be finished by the students by adding their own TPS report and converting it to a PDF. To proceed, select "Assign."

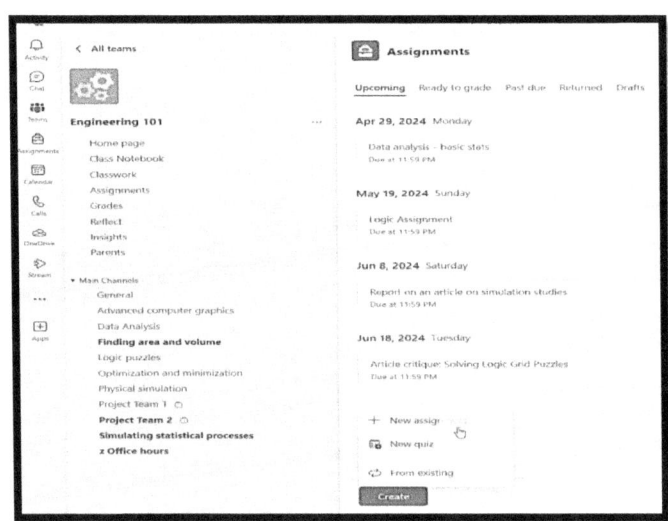

We will now shift our focus to the pupil. Here is where the assignment is located, and we are logged in as students. We will launch this, select "Attach," and include the PDF in this assignment.

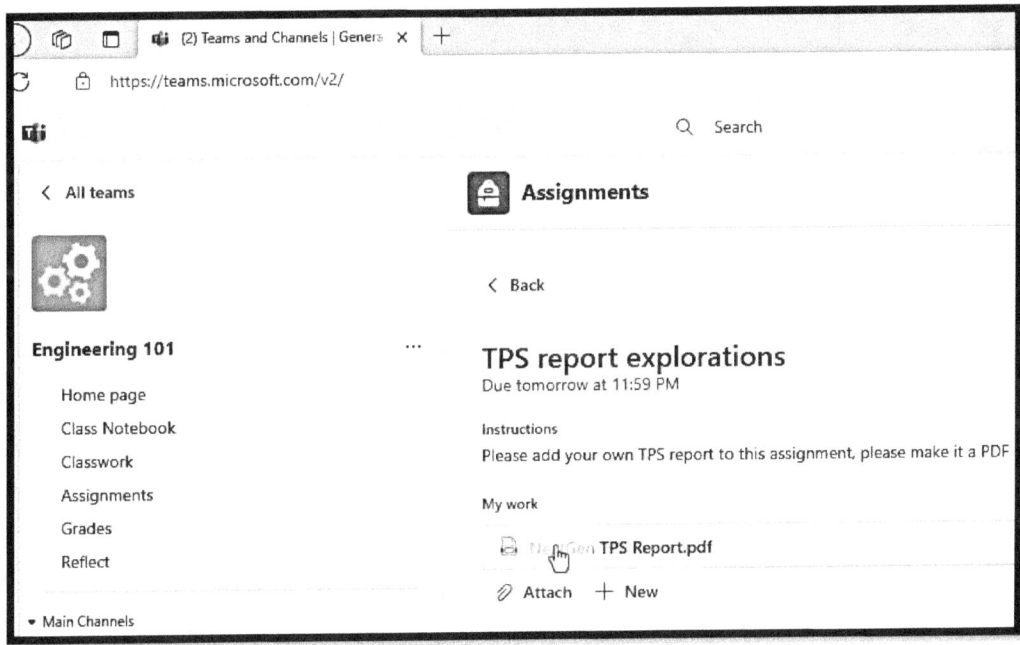

We can click "Edit" after opening this. You can see that you have the ability to modify and annotate your PDF as a student on the right-hand side. Here, we'll click the pen, select a pleasing color, and use the mouse to sign our name. You have a lot of options as a student because you may either highlight or remove certain items.

After that, click "Save changes" to return the modifications to the PDF, and then click "Close" to finish preparing our document to provide to the teacher. We'll navigate to the upper right and select "Turn in" to accomplish that. We'll now return to the educator to demonstrate how it appears in the speed grader. After logging back in as the educator, we will access the report and then scroll down to view the recently submitted assignment. Like we did with the student, we can go back and select "Edit," take out our fancy red pen, and mark up this exact spot on the paper.

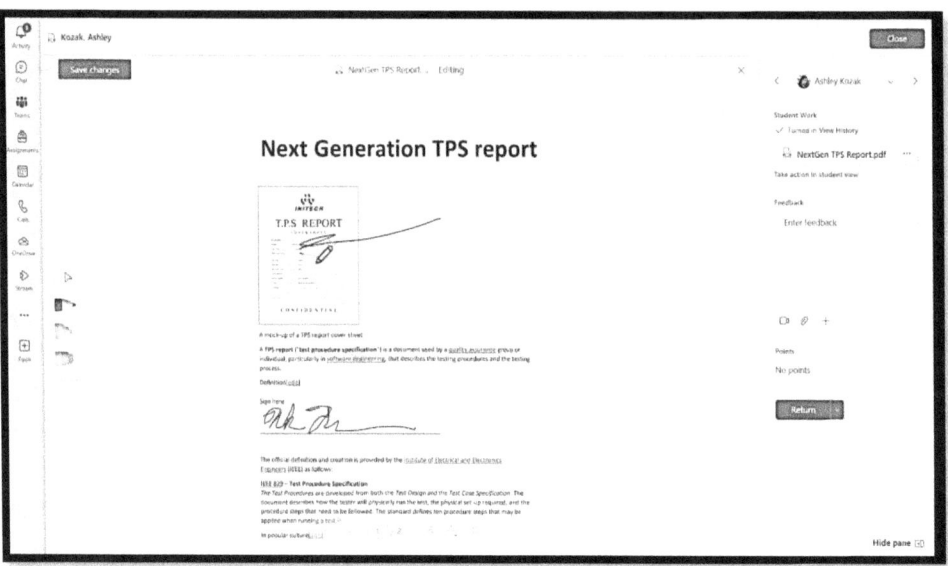

We can use a device to point to the arrow on the report, scroll down, and circle certain areas. Alternatively, you can use a mouse to accomplish all the actions we previously demonstrated. As the teacher, you may now do this in your grade. When you're finished, simply select "Save changes" and go on to the following pupil.

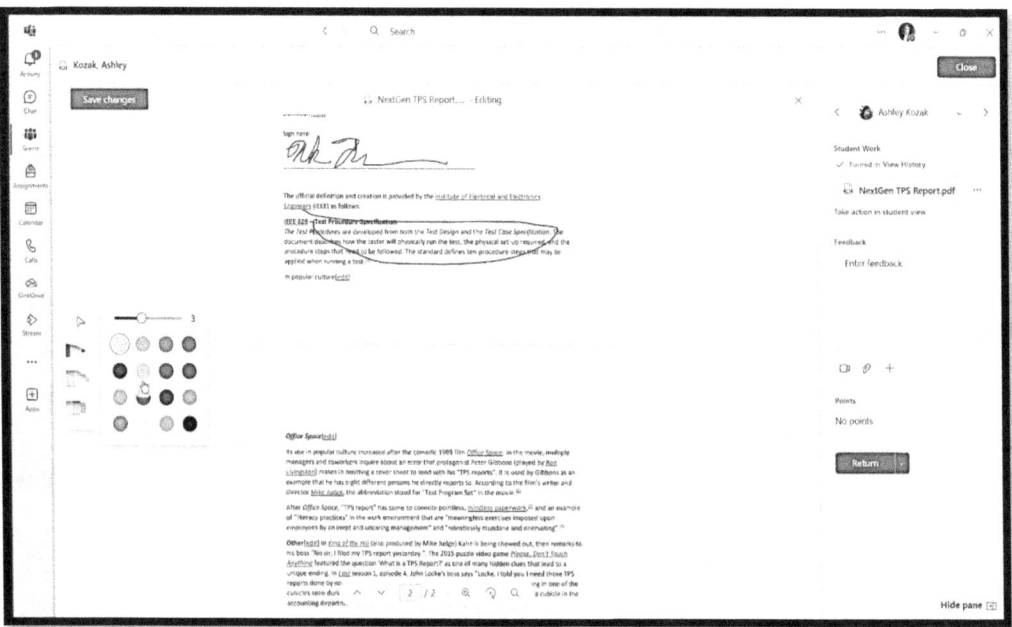

About reminder

Teachers can quickly inform students who potentially have late assignments with the second new function. When you open an assignment that you have already distributed, you will see a list of students to whom you still need to return it in the event that they have not done so. Once you choose these students, you will be presented with a few options. Sending out a reminder is one of the choices.

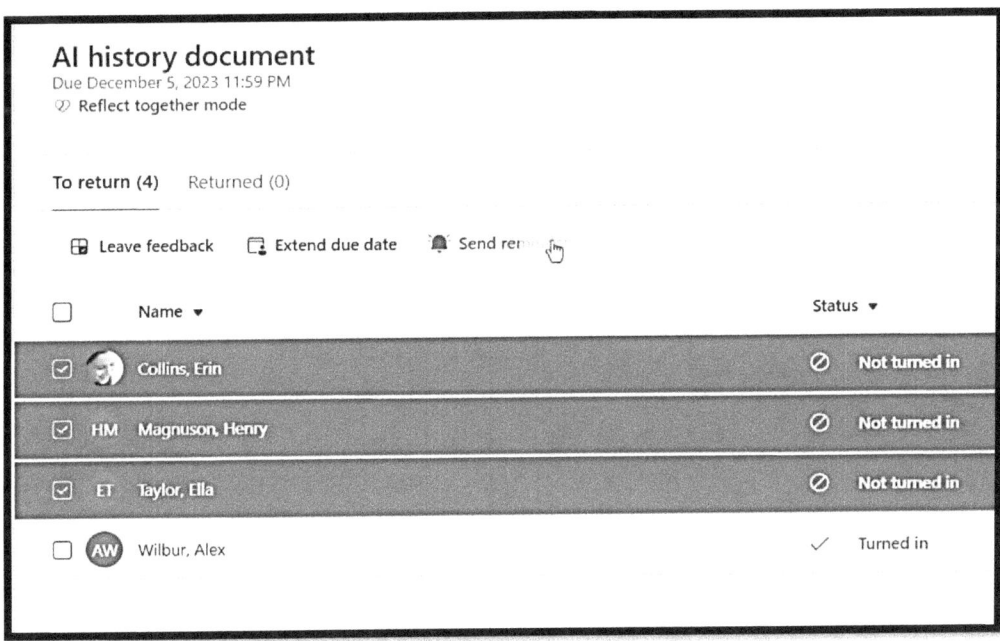

After you click it, a confirmation will appear. A reminder about this will be sent to each of the selected students and will show up in their Activities. When you click Send in Teams, all of those students will now get pings.

Extend the feature until the deadline date

Situated in the same area are the second and third new features. We would like to extend the deadline for the student that we have selected to serve as our example. You'll see "Extend due date" when you select that pupil in this list since we want to offer that child a little more time. We'll select an alternative deadline, enter the day and time, then click "Done."

Now that you know that this kid has an extended due date while the rest of the class has the original due date, it is clear that they have a special due date because it appears right here.

Responses in bulk

The fourth new feature is likewise included in this job list. You can also choose a few students and comment on them all at once. To provide many students with the same type of feedback, simply check this box, type in your comments, and click the Done button.

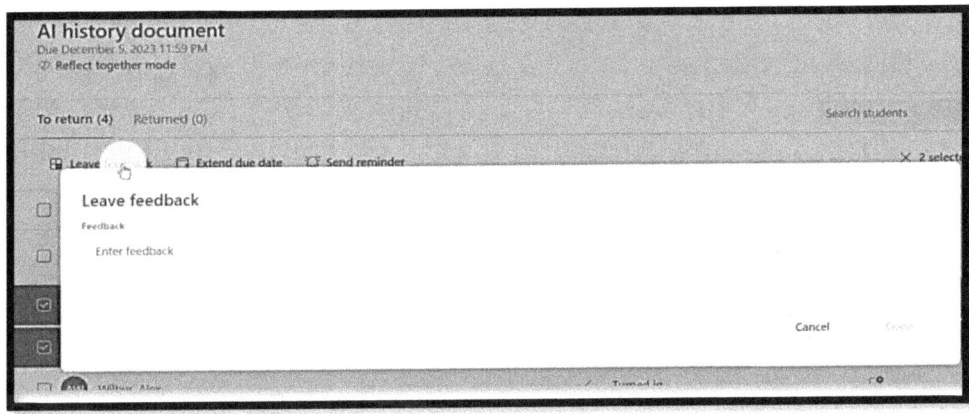

Actually, what happens is that it will apply consistently. You can use this function if a student has turned in their work and you want to leave anything for everyone in bulk. As an alternative, you can utilize it if none of the students submitted their work.

Coloring book that promotes awareness and introspection

Seventh new feature: coloring book Reflect Mindful. In this instance, while still logged in as students, we will navigate over and choose "Reflect". This allows students to use the Reflect feature, where you'll find a new option named "coloring book."

This will direct you to the updated student homepage, which has many entertaining features. The newest one is the coloring book, which we will click to access a variety of emotions, such as focused, frustrated, and joyful, along the bottom. There are several possibilities available to you, so you can select the page of your choice or choose at random.

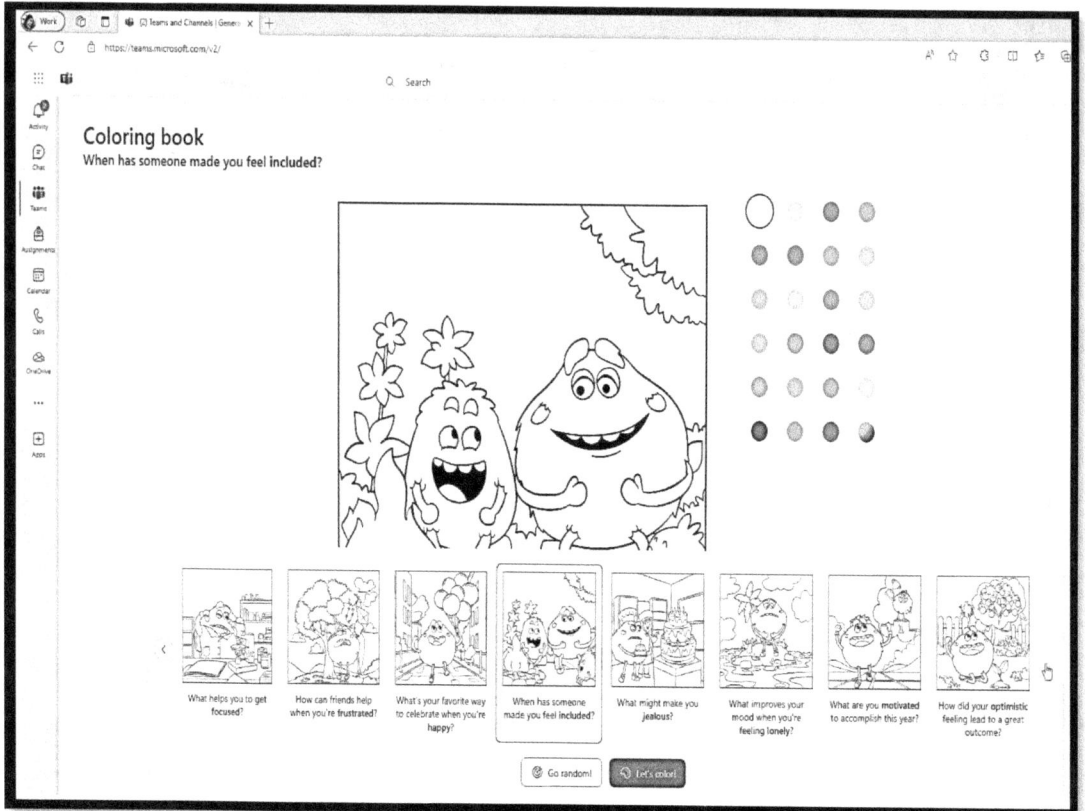

After answering the question, "Why did you feel successful recently?" we'll discuss this feeling and begin selecting the appropriate color. By giving him a red tongue and a lovely sky-blue background with white clouds, we can play about with the colors. It's quite simple to color different sections of it by clicking on them. Making a fun design is really quick and simple. We'll finish this up and add a few more small areas. The wonderful thing is that you can declare "I'm done" after you're all finished. Restart the process or alter the image.

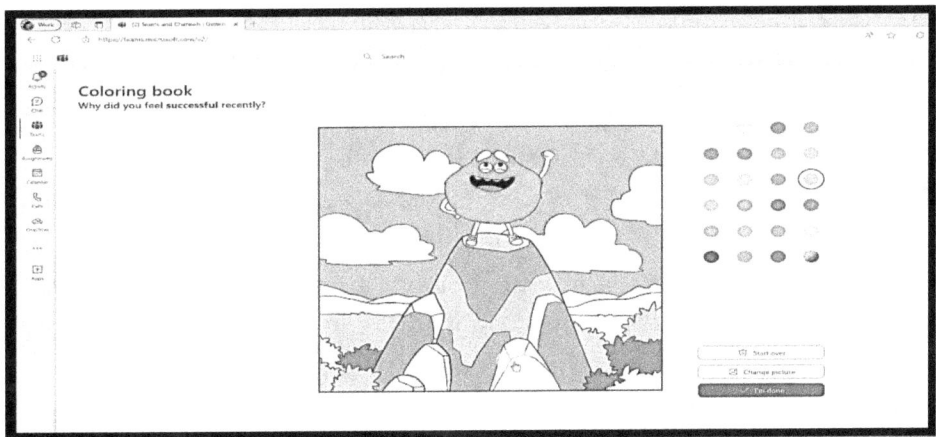

When we choose "I'm done," a little party starts. Saying "Save this" will make a save as an openable JPEG file offer appear. We can choose to share it or try again with another picture. By utilizing the Reflect feature, it becomes clear that this thoughtful coloring book is a fun and relaxing resource for students and adults to enjoy themselves.

About Personnel reflect

Reflect for adults is the sixth feature that Reflect has added. Teams of employees can now use Reflect. Here, we'll use our staff team as an example. When you create a new staff team, you, the owner, will see Reflect at the top.

As the staff account owner, you are able to choose which Reflect check-ins to participate in. To view the Staff Reflect, which is comparable to what you saw in class, click this link. Clicking "New check-in" brings you the alternatives to look into check-in ideas. When you open that, you not only have the well-being of the students but also the well-being of the educators, and these are made with the staff in mind. You may ask about team meetings, the progress your team has made this year, your workload, your ability to handle stress at work, and the situation at your school right now. When you click on it, you can add an option to your check-in and do a preview. Similar to the regular Reflect, which is a similar version of Reflect; staff members can choose these same emotion monsters here and click "Submit." You can set up this check-in and collect all of this information for your staff members using the Reflect feature for staff, just like you would normally do with Reflect in the classroom.

Lowering noise levels to make reading easier

The eighth new feature is noise reduction for improved reading. Reading progress is one of our learning accelerators in Teams that promotes reading fluency. When you go into assignments, open a student's work as the teacher. Let's say your pupil turned in a reading assignment where she recorded herself reading aloud. But the auto-detect AI—which fixes insertions, mispronunciations, and self-corrections—is hampered by the background noise.

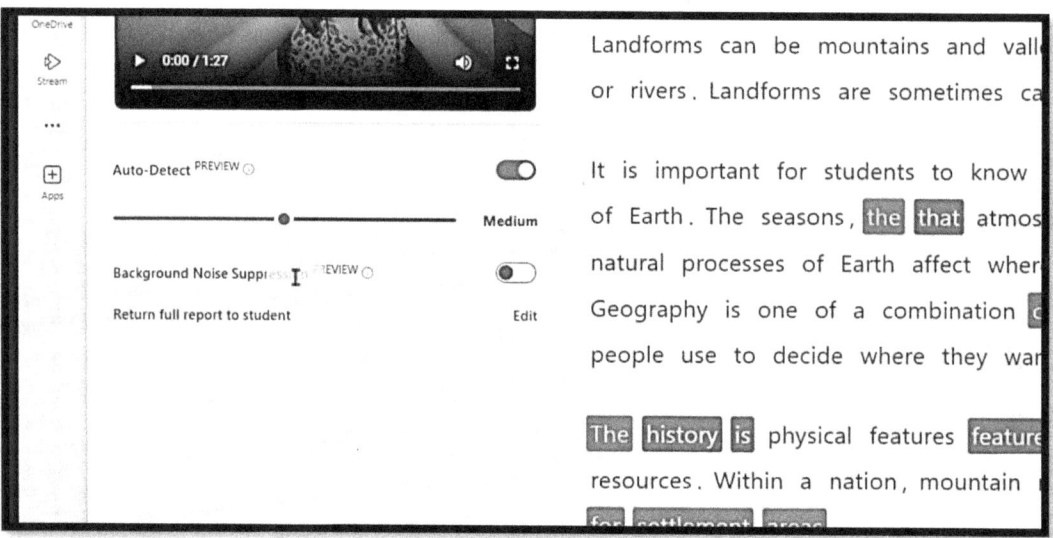

This feature offers background noise suppression, so it can provide a sharper reading of the student if the teacher wishes to build an AI layer on top of it to further minimize background noise. If you are an instructor, just turn the Background Noise Suppression option ON. As a result, the noise suppression layer will be used to recalculate and label the passage.

Notification of missing attachment

The next new feature is a warning for students who have not yet turned in their attached work. By implementing this, teachers will save a ton of time because there will be no need to remind students who forgot. As an educator, click "Create new assignment" and provide a title and instructions. Next, you should include the phrases "attach," "add," and "attachment" to your instructions so that you may ask the student if they attached anything when they turn it in.

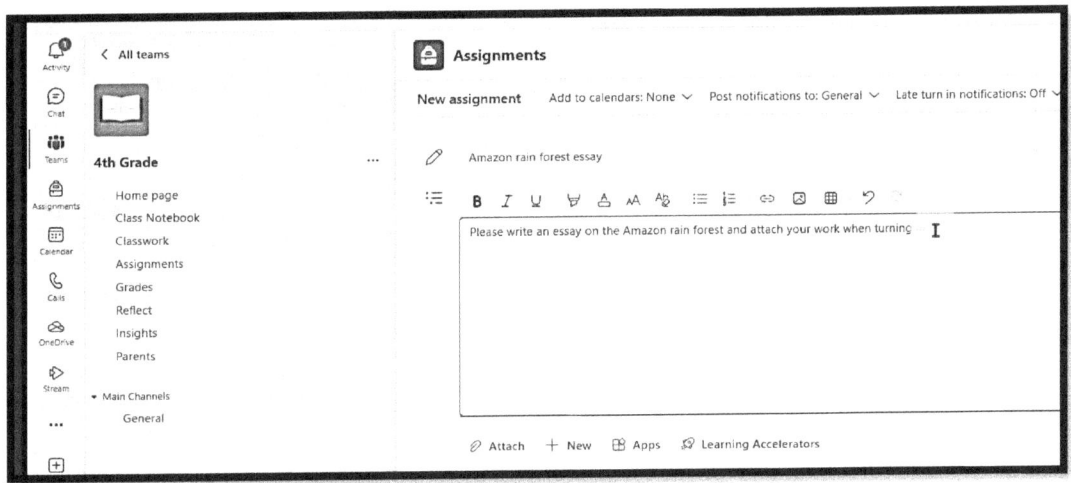

This is how it works: if the student opens the assignment after it has been sent out and realizes they neglected to attach any work, they will receive a small error message informing them that there is no work connected. The student can now select the Cancel button, return, attach it, and click Turn in to complete the process.

A revised feature for student editing

The ninth new feature is a revamped assignment entry point that makes it easy for students to edit their own work. Assume that you have the instructor login. Click "Create," "New assignment," choose Word document, give it a name, and then click "Done." Before, the only way to let students edit their own copies was to choose the three-dot menu and say that it was okay for them to do so. Finding this, though, proved to be challenging for a lot of educators. You can go here and designate that students edit their own copy, and as a result, students will now receive their own copy to edit anytime you send them an assignment. They have now exposed it immediately in front of you on this page.

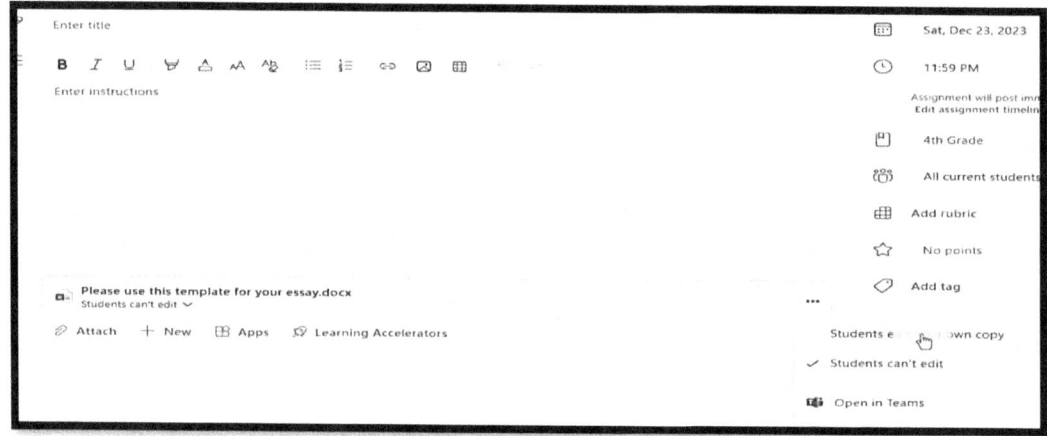

Using tables

This version makes it easier to use tables in assignment instructions. After entering a title, you can select the small table button. This can be clicked to select Insert Table. You can opt to increase the size by adding more columns, adding a row, styling the table, removing all the columns, or removing the columns and rows together.

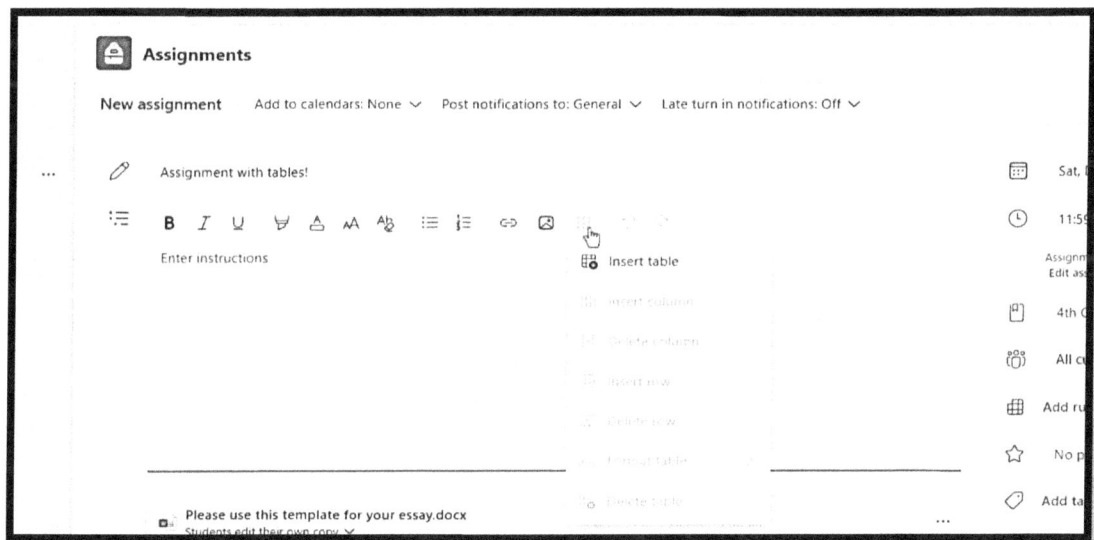

After inserting it, you may now add anything you wish to complete your table. If you'd like, you may also adjust the size to make it larger.

Updated Turn in festivities

The following new functionality is updated. Show off your celebrations. You can see a sample of one of the newest Turn in celebrations, which changes every time a student logs in, when you open an assignment and turn it in. Press the "Turn in" button in the top-right corner to view a fresh little festivity.

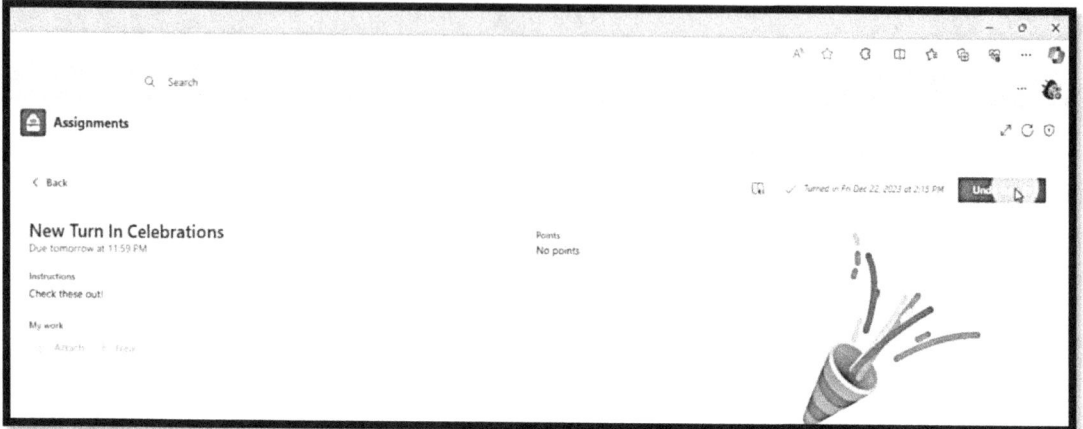

The school connection app

The last new feature is the school connection app, which is incorporated into the Teams mobile consumer app for iPhone or Android. It makes it possible for educators to keep parents updated on their students' development. Remember that this requires authorization from your admin. When enabled, a list of students and a map indicating the parents and guardians to whom they have been assigned will appear. If your school has school data sync, that is the simplest way to do this automatically. Everything pertaining to the pupils and parent emails will be set up after the parent emails are synchronized with the school data.

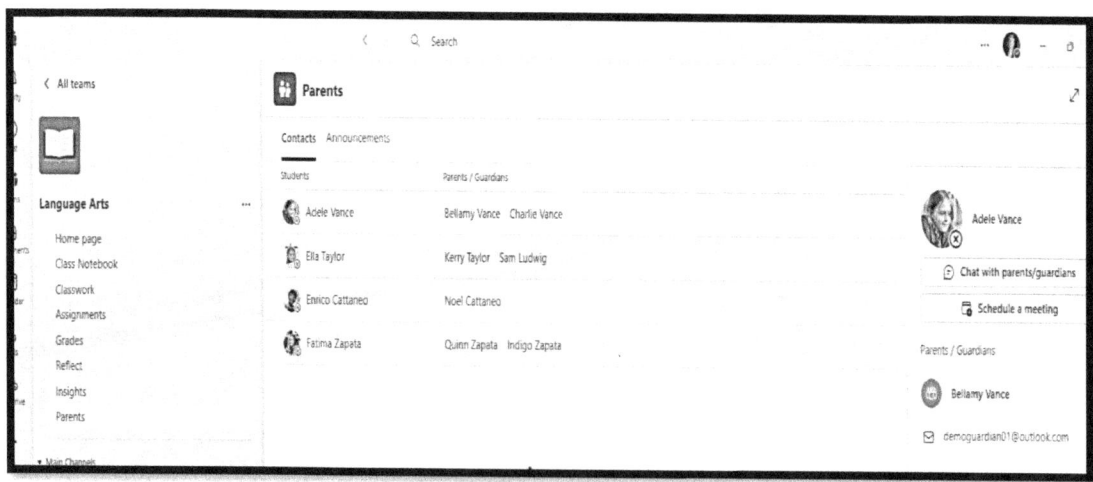

For the purposes of this example, let's assume that a parent and student have previously been mapped. As a parent, you will now utilize a mobile device and open Teams for Education on your iPhone. You will then select your guardian account and be able to log in.

Add the school connection app next. This is the consumer version of Teams; to access the settings, tap the parent's name in the upper left corner of the profile. Now select Settings. The school connection option will appear at the bottom.

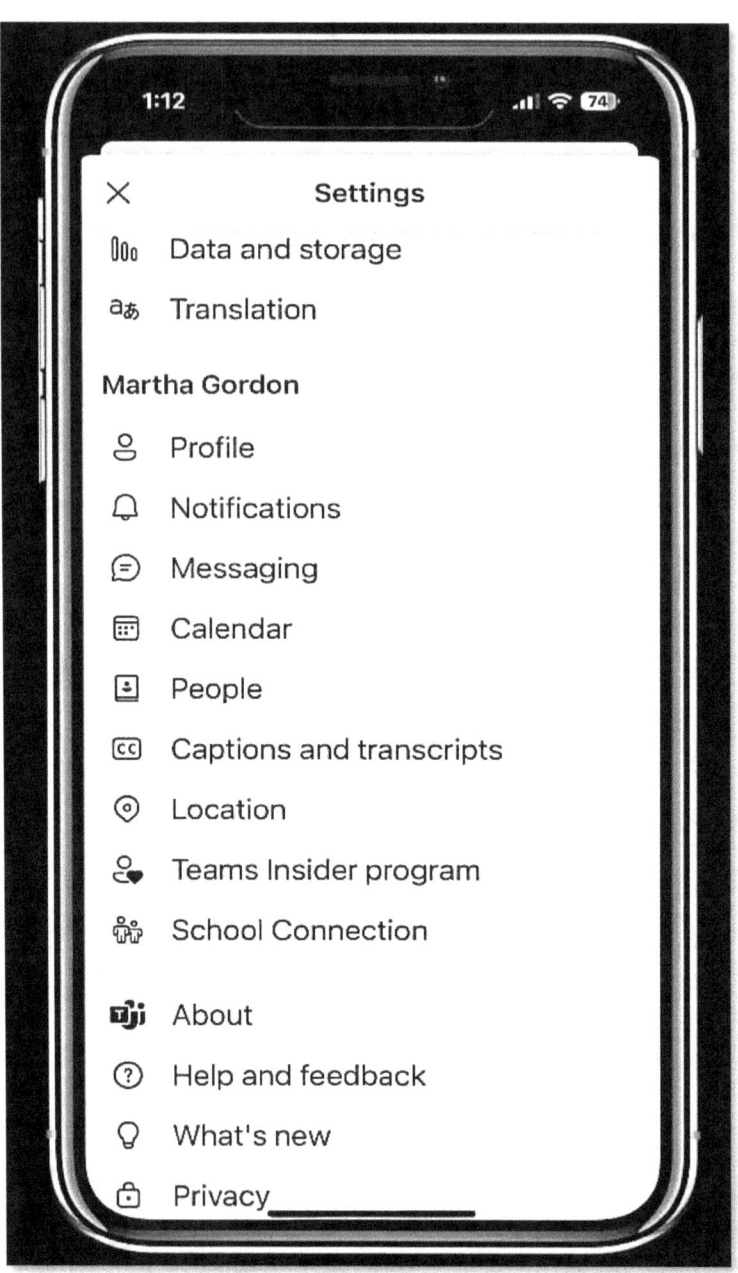

Press that button, select "Enable," activate this, then press return to end the conversation. A small parent and student icon, as well as a small school connection icon, are located in the center of the bottom section. After tapping it, the school connection will load and your child's information will be pulled in.

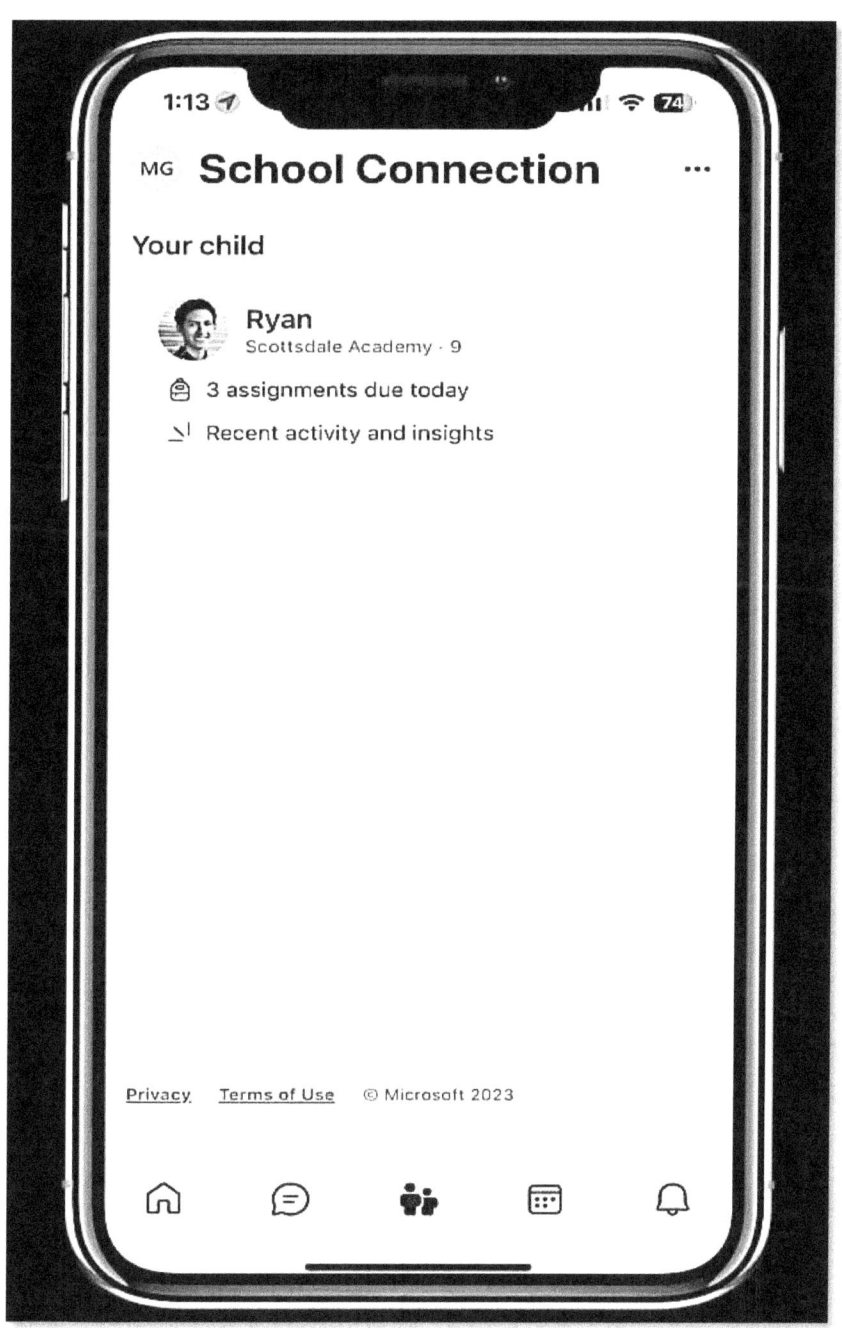

You can see how many assignments your child has to do. If you tap on a child, additional information about what's going on in the class will be displayed. You have access to all of this information as a parent.

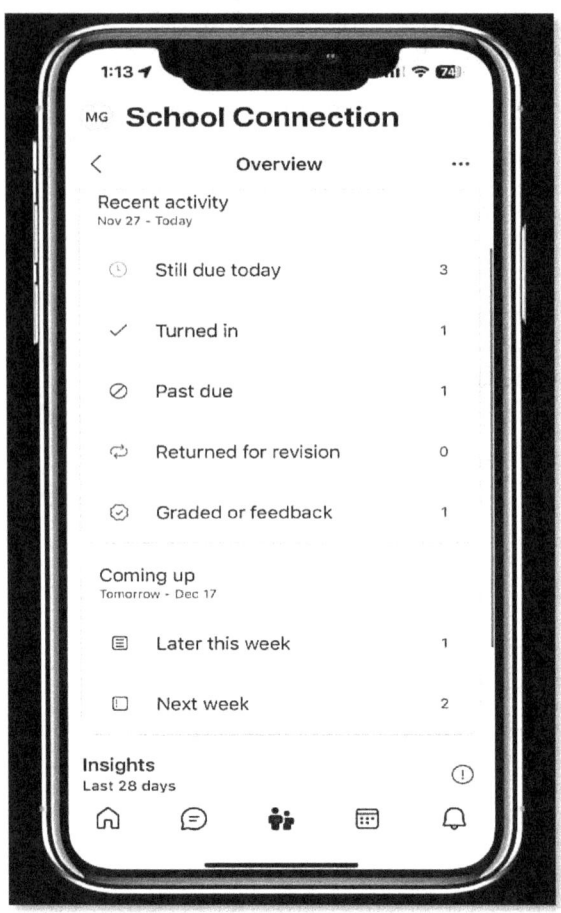

You may also view the assignments that have been handed in by using the Insights bottom. You may check reading accuracy, new practice words, and the kind of digital engagement your student is engaging in if you have learning accelerators like reading progress.

Activities

1. Upload a PDF document to a Teams channel or chat, then practice highlighting, commenting, and drawing on it with the annotation tools.
2. Take note of how the annotations are shared and presented to other members of the team.
3. Talk about how collaborative document evaluation and feedback in an educational setting can be facilitated by the annotation feature.

CHAPTER NINE
UNDERSTANDING HINTS AND TECHNIQUES

Synopsis

Chapter 9 provides several helpful tips and recommendations to help readers get the most out of Microsoft Teams. These cover the creation of tasks from postings, muting of unnecessary discussions, and customizing pop-up windows. This chapter will cover some basics as well as a number of Microsoft Teams hints and suggestions. Additionally, we will discuss some of the new applications that Microsoft intends to offer in 2024.

The essentials

The main goal of teams is to form huge teams—larger than you anticipate being required—and attempt to function with just one team; the others can wait since you'll be operating more in the open and will be simpler or less significant. Making decisions can be done more swiftly and centrally. You have the option to keep your files or complete all tasks in one place. You should begin your file structure in Channels since each channel creates a folder on the SharePoint site that is established at the time the team is formed. After you've done that, the essential Basics in Teams are to use the Teams area only and refrain from utilizing chat. These will simplify everything else in Teams. While chat is acceptable for private or non-work related one-on-one conversation, using Teams' channels will make your life lot easier as many organizations become slowed down by excessive chat usage.

If you are not accustomed to using chat or small-group teams, you may need to modify your behavior in a few ways once you are in a channel in order to get the most of it. It was difficult to tell if you were writing a new post or replying to an existing one in Microsoft Teams in the past because of the small text field at the bottom. That is no longer the case, since a "Start a post" button has taken its place, and clicking it brings up a much larger list of possibilities. They have helped us with that; in the new Teams, we no longer need to click a little button to enlarge this box in order to add a subject and write a message. It's important to remember to include a subject (which, as we previously discussed, can be a little harder to find) every time you start a new post. In this manner, you can quickly ascertain the discussion's subject while participating in it. A new post without a @ mention won't be seen by anyone. If you would like to contribute something to a channel When creating a new post in a standard organization, you should always include a @ mention since if you don't, no one will see it. But, it's acceptable if it's just for informative purposes and you don't give a damn if people see it or not. If you just start typing, it will suggest a few things. When mentioning a channel, you have two options: either type @ and start typing the channel name, or type @ and start typing the channel you are now in. Everyone who hasn't hidden that channel will get a ping in relation to your content.

If your teams and channels are configured properly, people should have hidden channels they don't work in and shown channels they do. As a result, anything hidden in a secret channel is for private information. New threads should always start with a title and a @ mention. Individual @ mentions are also an option. If a thread is open already, click reply. When moving from chat to Teams channels, here are the basics you should know. Most individuals mute a lot of talks while they are pinging everyone in the chat by default, which makes communication challenging. Since some people may have disabled their notifications for that thread, mentioning again in a reply will automatically ping everyone in the information thread above you. If you're applying to a specific person, however, make sure you also include a @ mention in your reply to make sure they receive it.

Mute unrelated conversation threads

If you have a long thread with information in it—for instance, if you added something to someone else's thread and the discussion veered off topic, or if you just wanted to share your thoughts—you can click the three dots, and if there were other users in the thread with you, you'll be able to mute it. It can be used to turn off notifications for that specific topic exclusively.

Turn a post into a task

One can build a task from a message. You can also make a task in the planner, which is right here in the More Options tab, to view the context of what was happening and to construct a task for yourself to finish using that chat thread in

Teams. Alternatively, use "at the time of recording," which is flexible based on changes made to the planner. You can designate that as a personal task so that it shows up in tasks right now. By default, you can see it until you tell us differently. As an alternative, you might add it to a planning board or share it with others. This example is part of a team, so when you add it to your planning board, everyone with permission to see it on the team can see it. You must understand these principles if you want to make the most out of Teams channels.

The hub of activity

The activities that are indicated in the figure below may be seen.

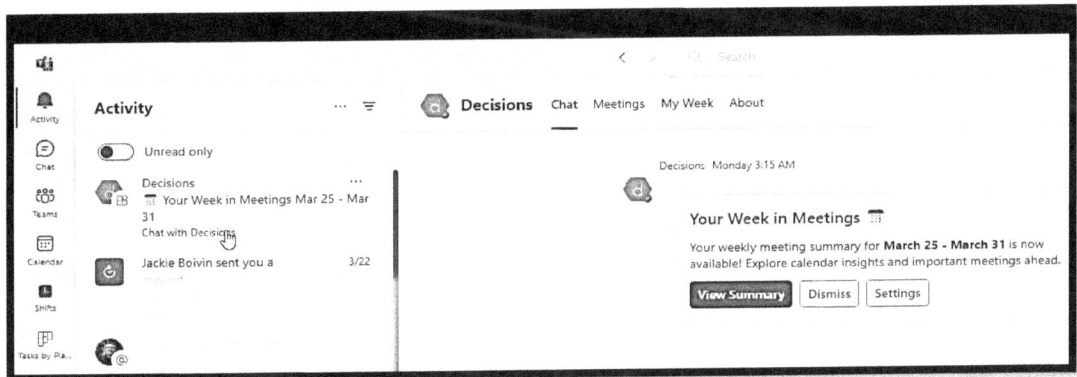

These activities are what have happened recently that maybe you haven't seen. If you click on this little button right here at the top left-hand corner, you can check all the unreads and then if you click it again it'll show everything, even the ones that you have read. Something cool about this is you can filter it so if you click on these three lines on the top right you can choose to type in some sort of filter. Let's say that you only wanted to see things that came from Bobby, you would type Bobby and notice that it would only show the activity for Bobby. This activity center shows the updates for the teams' channels for your chats and anything that goes on inside of any of those.

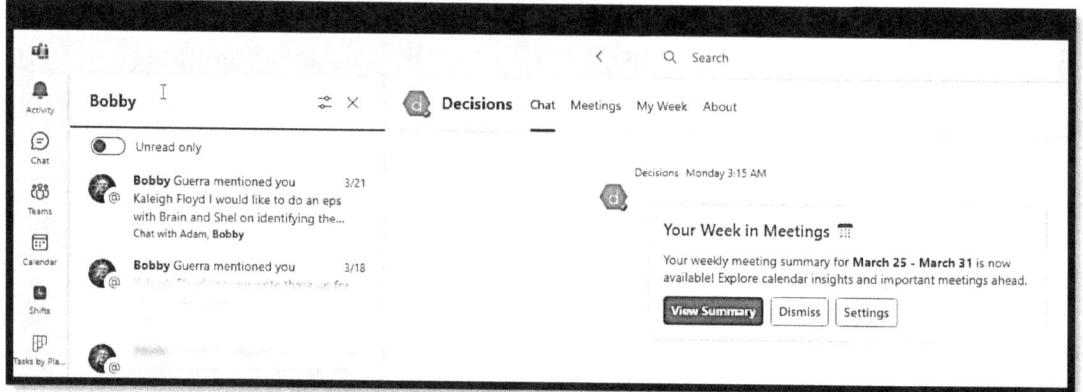

Another neat feature is that you can see samples of different filters by looking at the "more filters" option here. You can even filter it by app. You have further options here if you click the three dots next to activity after leaving that. You have the ability to play sounds with notifications, play noises when incoming calls or meetings, and display messages and content previews on the notification by going to the notification settings.

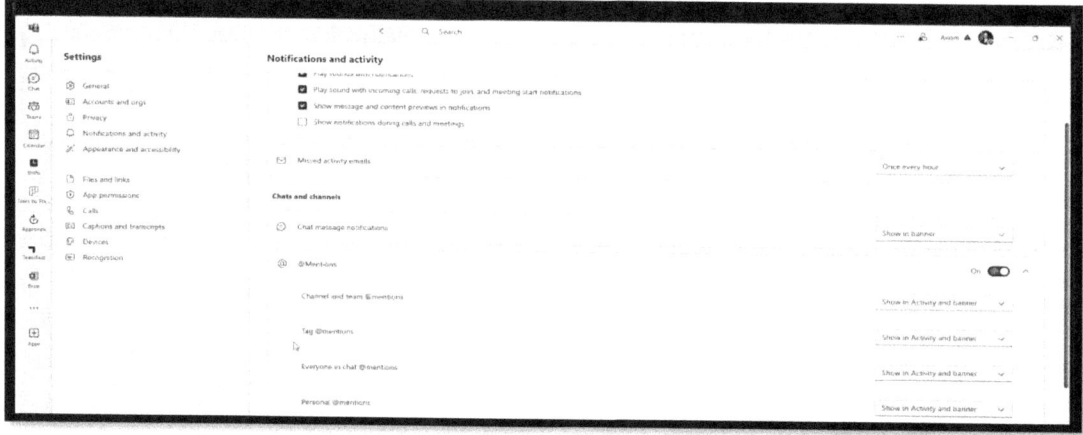

We highly recommend that, if you're new to Microsoft Teams, you review the settings and make sure that all of these alerts and activities are set up to your preference. For example, in this conversations and channels section, you can choose to turn on or off message display as a banner, which will stop chats from showing up on your screen. You can also choose whether you want to be notified when someone tags you in a team chat, mentions you in a channel, or does anything similar. Make sure your notifications are configured the way you want them to be before you start using Teams. By doing this, you'll make sure you get the notifications you need and stay away from the ones you don't want.

How to set up the windows that pop up

When we're in the Settings section, we want to select the General tab. This is important since the Windows creation options are one of the truly great new features of the most recent Microsoft Teams upgrade. One intriguing feature of Microsoft Teams is the ability to "open a new window," which when you start a new chat or open material, creates a separate window especially for that purpose. Let's say someone emails you a link to an Excel file while you are in a chat window with them. It used to bring you into Excel within Teams, giving the impression that you were in Excel yet stayed in Teams, which can irritate certain users. The new feature is that Excel opens in a new window when you click the link. By clicking the "new window icon when opening content inside of Teams" and choosing to launch Excel in a new window, you can configure that. Every time you initiate a new chat, you can click on New window here, and a new window will open just for that chat and the person you are communicating with. Another possibility is a group chat.

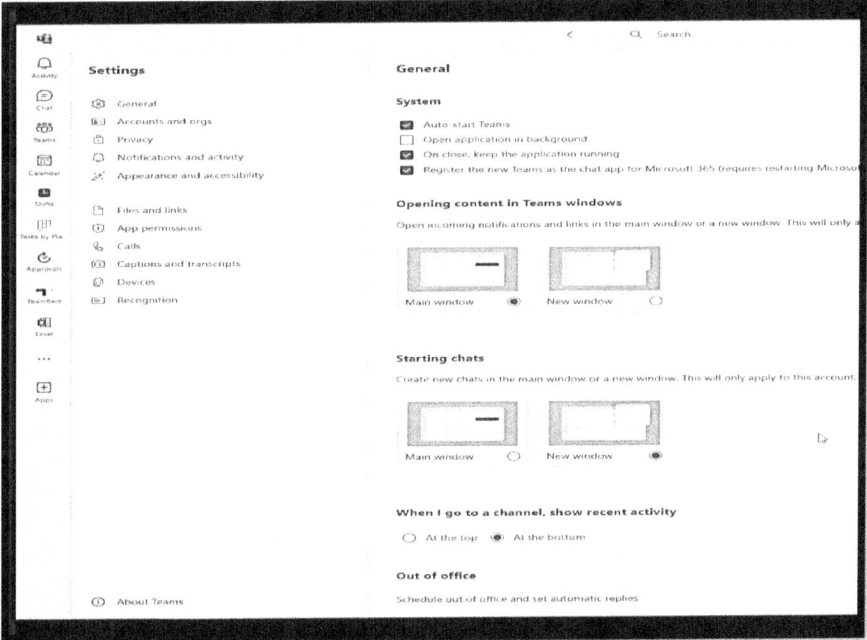

The out-of-office message's scheduling

Lastly, we would like to mention that setting up an out-of-office is one of these general settings' very helpful capabilities. By selecting "Schedule," you can decide to notify your coworkers of your absence and let them know you will be out of town for a week. An automated response for the out-of-office message can also be set up. You can also choose to send responses only to individuals inside the organization or to those outside of it, and to send them only for a certain period of time.

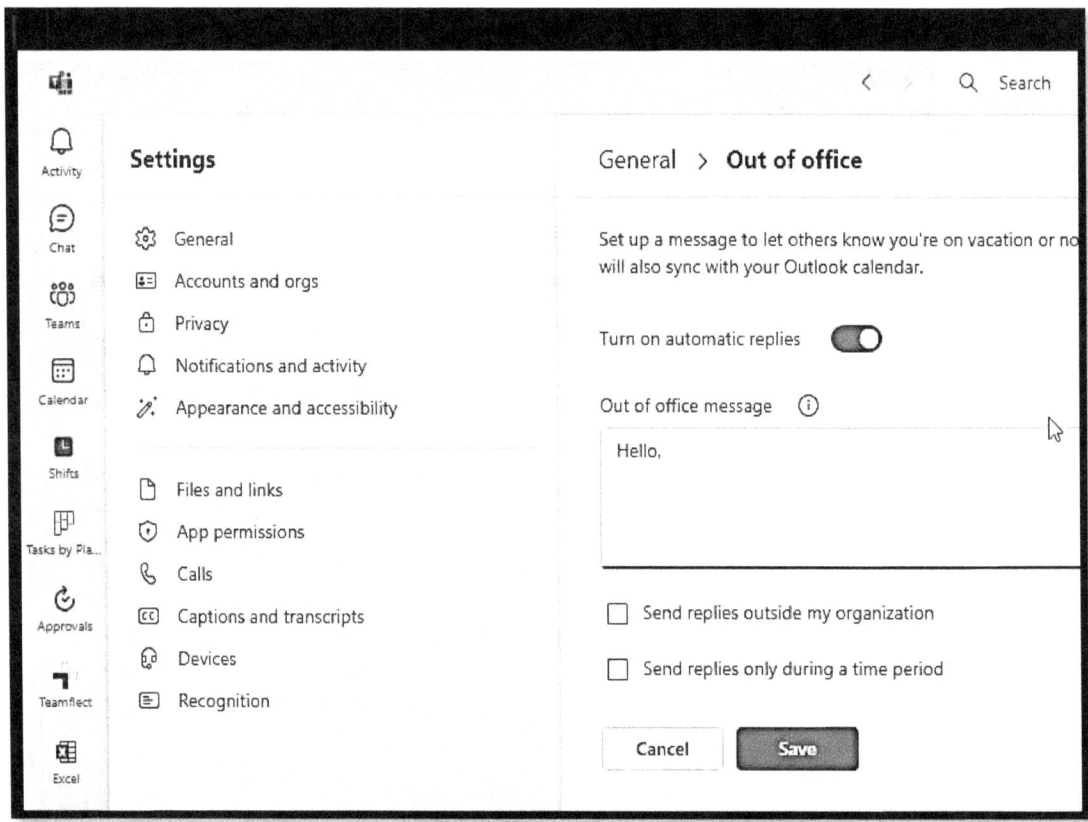

You can specify when you're going to be on vacation and when you'd like this message to be sent to folks when you click on it. These are the fundamental settings that we would advise looking at when you first log into Microsoft Teams. There are other settings that we could discuss.

Adding fresh tabs

Let's talk about including more tabs at the top. In the general channel, the three tabs (Posts, Files, and Notes) each have a little plus symbol (++) next to them. By clicking on the plus sign, you can instantly add a Whiteboard tab to this channel so that users can take notes and brainstorm ideas.

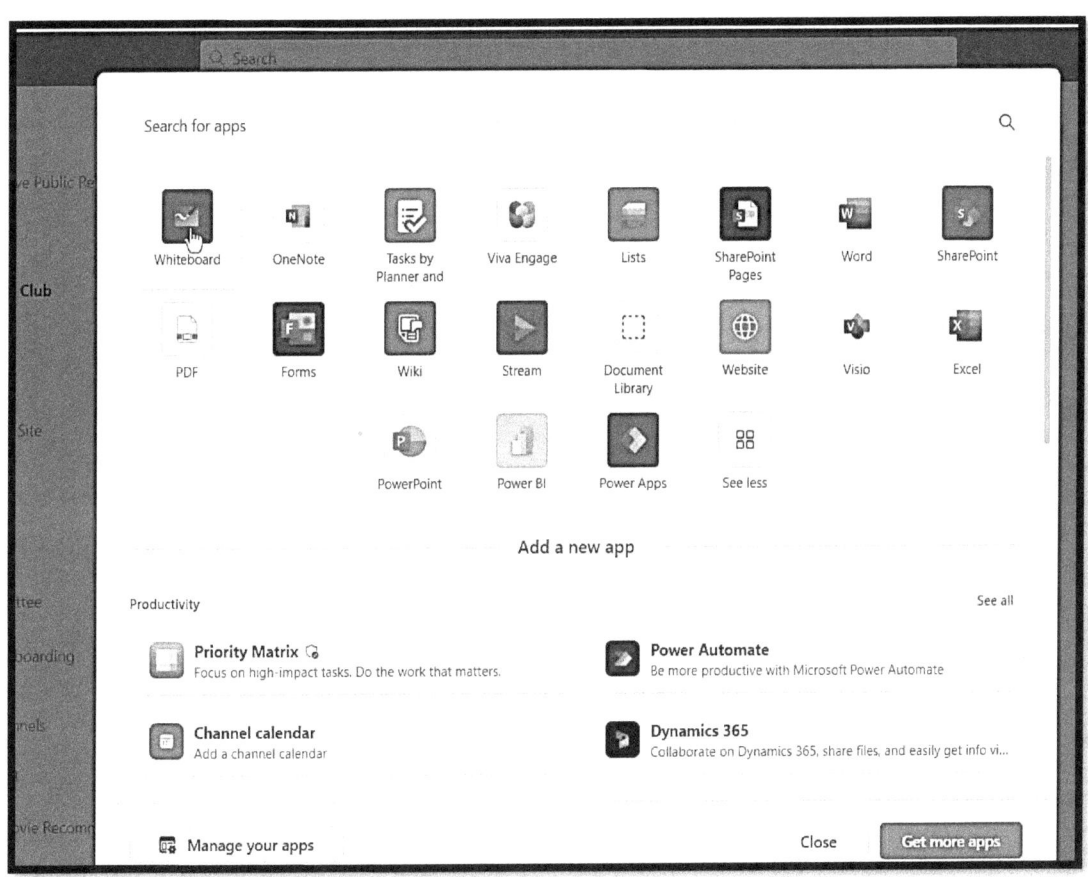

If you select "See All," a lengthy list of all the available apps will appear, and Whiteboard should be included. Let's click on Save after you've added it, given your whiteboard a name, or left it on Whiteboard and posted about it to the channel to let everyone know you've made it. The tab will be created, and a blank whiteboard will load for everyone to utilize just like it would if they were working directly in the Whiteboard app.

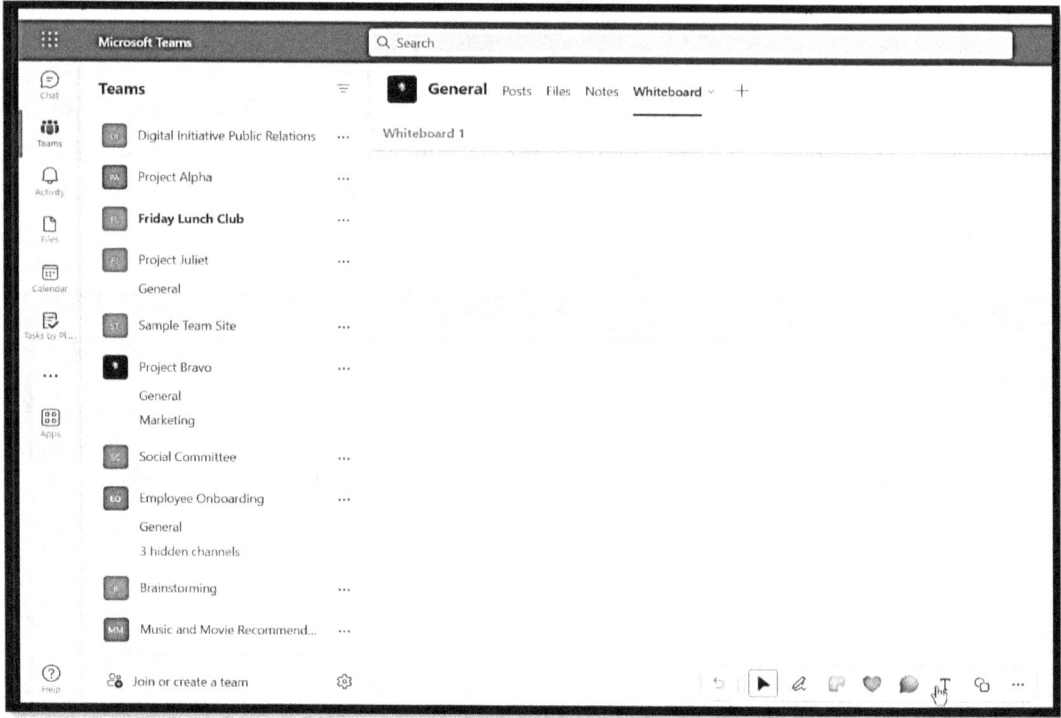

You have a small floating toolbar at the bottom, as you can see. You can add notes, text, photos, and comments using that. How about a real file? Click the addition symbol once again. For example, if you want to share an Excel file as a tab permanently, click the Excel app, search for the Excel file you wish to use in the tab, and then click Save. The Excel spreadsheet will load into that window and a new tab with the file name will be created. Adding applications as tabs is a terrific way to customize your channels and is also a nice method to keep all of your files together within the channel so that everyone can view them and collaborate on them.

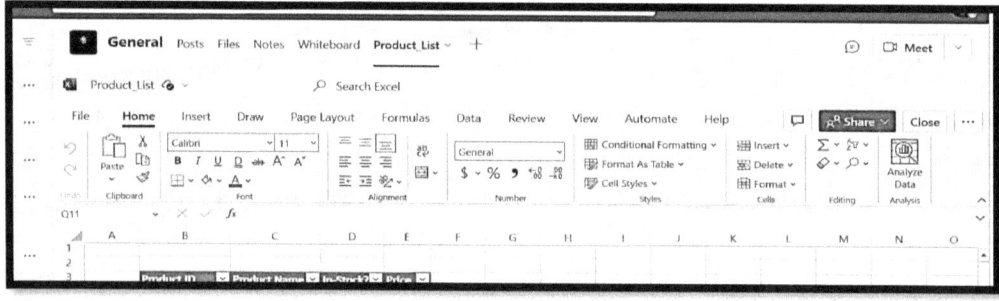

Using the search bar

The second thing we should talk about is the search bar at the top, which contains a few little features that will make your life so much easier. You can search for any kind of material inside teams, including files, individuals, teams, and channels, using this search box.

The text in the search field instructs you to hunt for files, messages, and more, or you can type the forward slash to see a list of commands. Thus, by typing the forward slash (/), you can access a number of shortcut links that let you carry out particular actions. For instance, you can type /away or choose it from this drop-down to rapidly change your status from Available to Away. When you hit Enter, you'll notice that your status has changed to Away. You may immediately set it back to Available if you perform the slash again.

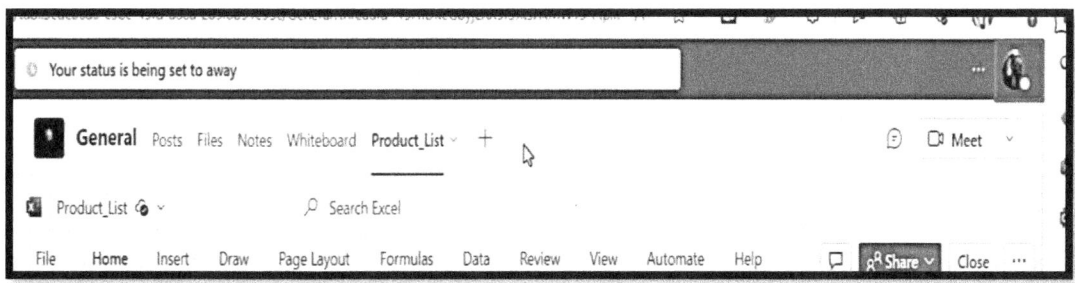

You have a lot of options here, some of which will need your assistance. For instance, you could type /chat to send someone a brief message. After that, it would ask you which person you wanted to message. After deciding on that individual. Since the message is intended only for that individual, you may efficiently type it into the search bar and send it. It will also appear in your private chats.

This forward cut is excellent. You can choose your team or channel by using the /goto option located right here if you want to fast jump to a particular team or channel. We especially like /saved since it provides you with an easy method to go to all of the posts you've bookmarked. In addition to the forward slash, you may now swiftly do other operations by using the @ sign in this place. One simple use of the @ sign is to send someone a message. However, there are other applications for this symbol as well, such as praising someone. Clicking @praise will open the praise application.

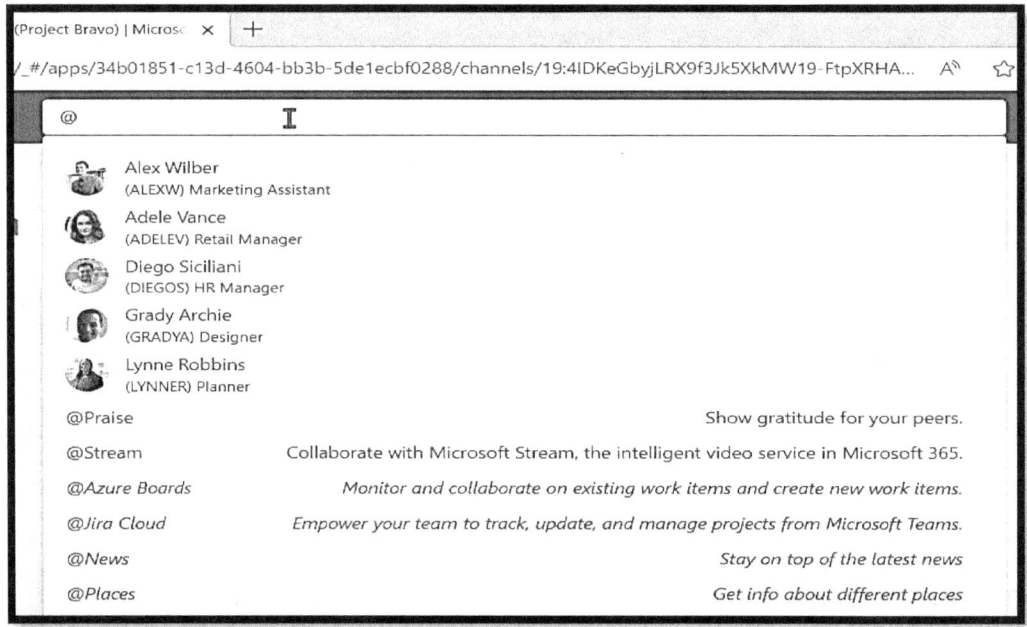

Say you would want to tell Mary how wonderful she is; you may alter the backdrop color, including a personalized message, and send it to her. That's a really kind way to encourage someone and let them know you believe they're doing a fantastic job.

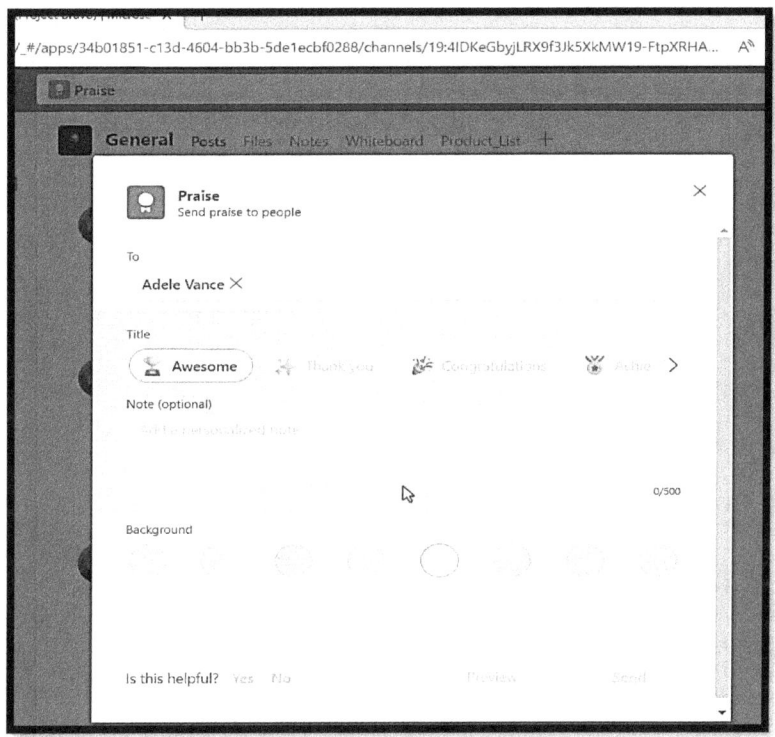

Another really useful feature is that you can search for videos on YouTube and share them by typing the @ sign again. However, keep in mind that Microsoft Teams will prompt you to install the YouTube app if you haven't already. All you have to do is click the "Add" button to begin searching for the video you wish to share. After that, you have the option to share the link in a meeting, copy it, or share it in a chat.

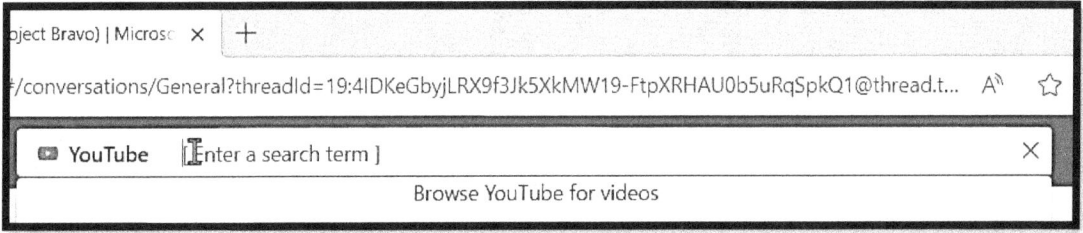

You can share this video and start a team meeting right away by clicking this link. Simply select "Join now" and then "Start sharing," and the video will begin to play in your team meeting.

Activities

1. Become familiar with the Microsoft Teams interface's basic navigation and features, such as the calendar, chat, and sidebar.
2. Get comfortable with utilizing the keyboard shortcuts to swiftly access standard features like launching a new chat window or entering a meeting.
3. Modify the Teams app's settings, including the style, notification options, and default behavior, to your own tastes.

CHAPTER TEN

CONCERNING THE TROUBLESHOOTING OF TEAMS

Synopsis

It's important to troubleshoot common errors, and chapter 10 takes you through the process of fixing problems like spell check and broken Teams. In this chapter, we'll show you how to fix Microsoft Teams not working. In case you encounter any problems with the Microsoft Teams application, we will guide you through the easiest and fastest solutions. In this chapter, we'll show you how to fix it on an iOS smartphone, but the steps are the same for Android devices as well.

Are teams not operating as they should?

When something goes wrong with your iPhone, you should always try restarting it first. If this doesn't work, try reinstalling the Microsoft Teams application: On your home screen, tap and hold Microsoft Teams. Then, choose "Remove app," then "Delete app." Now install it again from the Play Store or App Store.

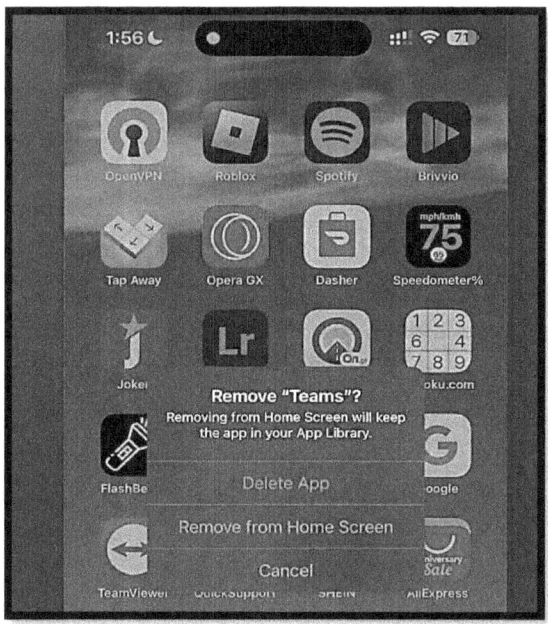

Try changing your network connections if this does not resolve the issue. Try using mobile data if you are on Wi-Fi, and try using Wi-Fi if you are currently using mobile data. Resetting the network settings on your iPhone is the final option. To accomplish this, open your iPhone's Settings, select General, scroll down to "Transfer" or "Reset iPhone," touch Reset, and select "Reset network settings."

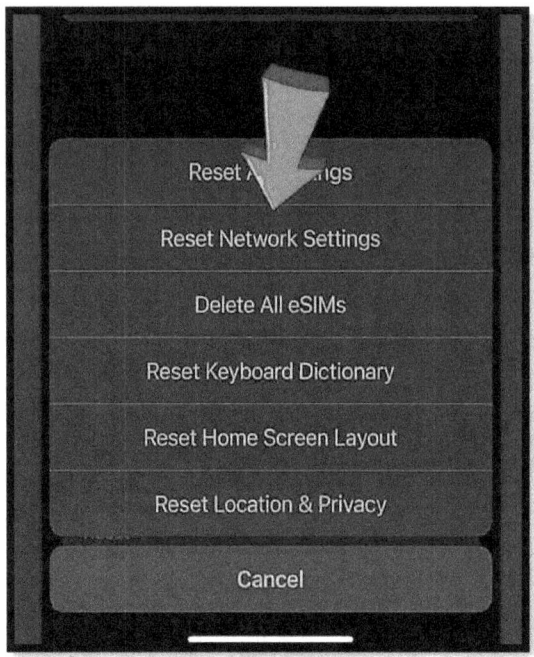

This will reset your network settings after your iPhone restarts, and your Microsoft Teams app should work perfectly after that.

Does spell check not work correctly?

In this part, we'll examine solutions for Microsoft Teams spell check problems. The first solution is to restart spell checking and clear the cache files in Teams. To complete this, simply perform a right-click on the Start icon and select "Run window." You then need to type "%appdata%" and choose "Okay." Simply double-click the Microsoft folder, use the right-click menu to choose the Teams folder, and select the delete option.

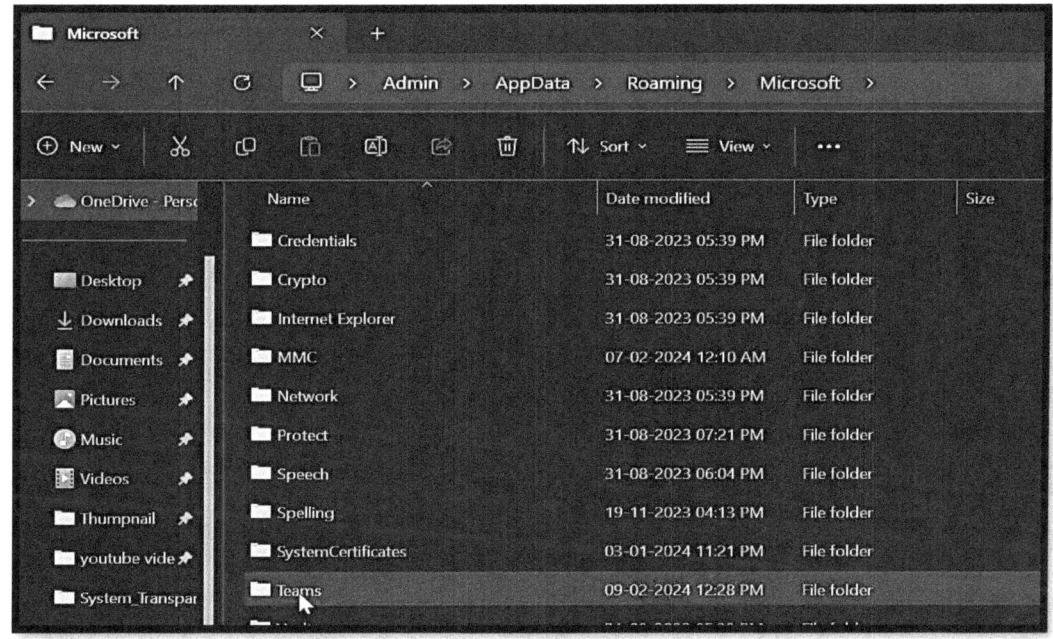

This folder must be removed from the Teams Cache files. Teams will recreate this folder upon reopening. Once the Teams cache file has been deleted, launch Teams, click the three dots at the top, choose Settings, uncheck spell checking, and then shut down.

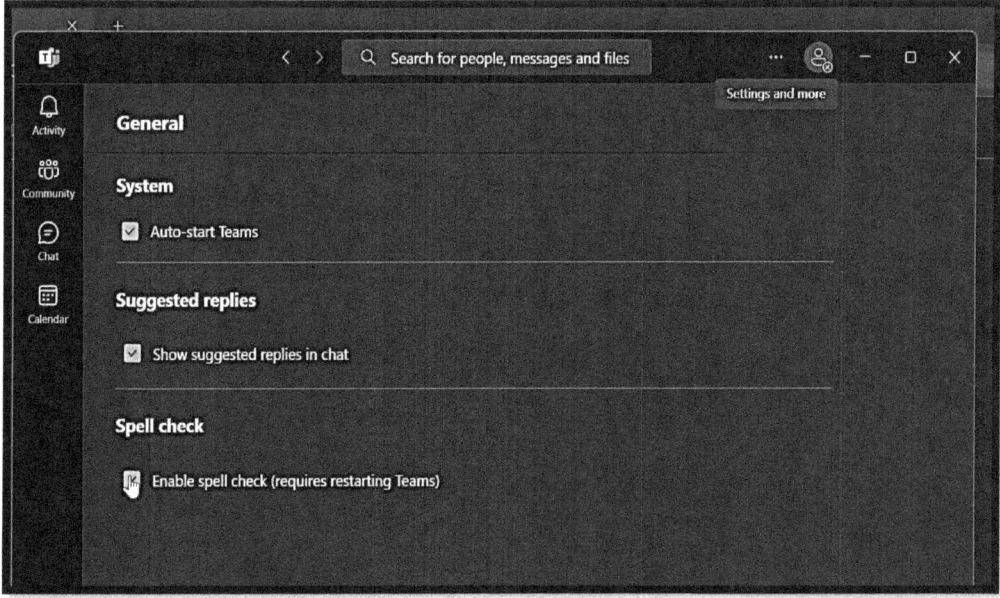

All that's left to do is shut in the background. To quit a team, right-click on it and choose quit. Once you've done that, launch Teams once more. Then, click the three dots at the top, choose Settings, and turn on spell checking. All that's left to do is restart Teams and see if the issue has been resolved. If not, let's proceed to the next fix. Eliminating all non-English languages from your computer is the second option. You will take this action because spell check in Microsoft Teams use the Windows language, and spell check may not function correctly if there are multiple languages selected in the Windows languages area. All you have to do is perform a right-click on the Start button, choose Settings from the menu on the left, and then choose Time and Language.

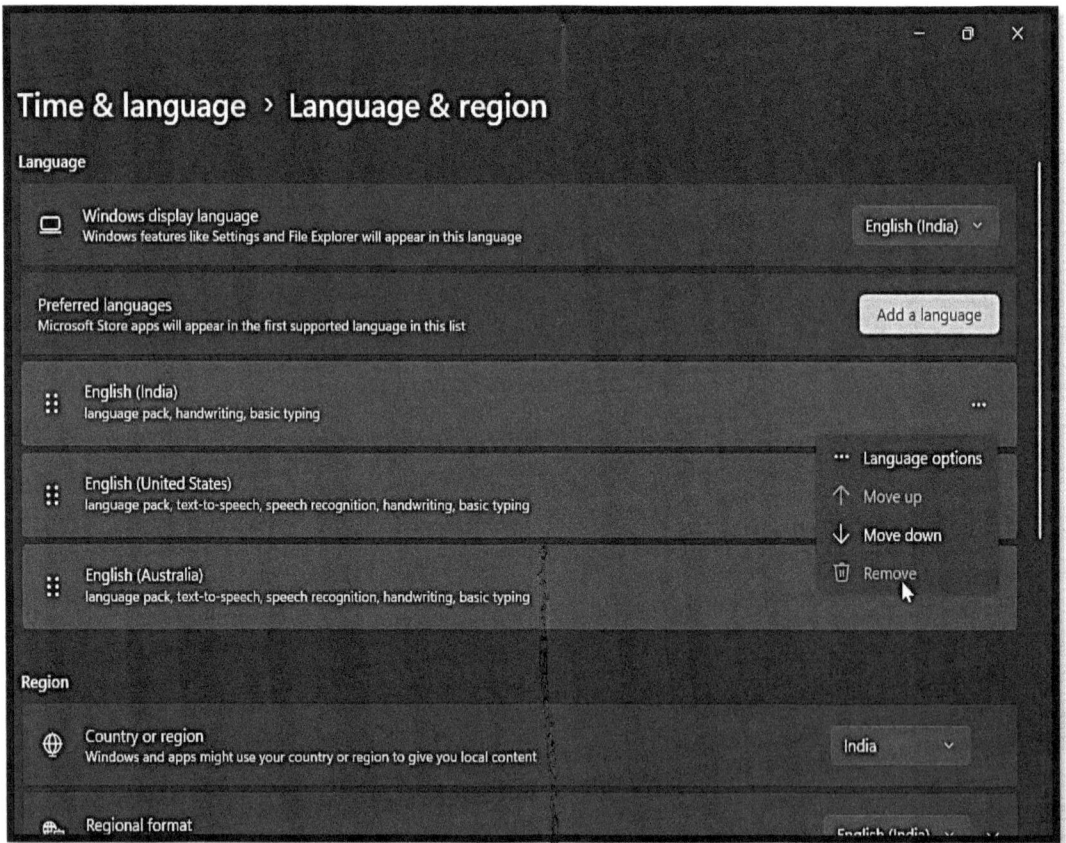

Remove the language other than English from the list of preferred languages by selecting Language and Region on the right. Once you've completed this, close this window and restart your computer to see if the issue has been resolved. Otherwise, let's proceed to the third option. Get the previous iteration of Teams as the third option. If the most recent update is the source of the issue, downloading the previous version will fix it. Prior to downloading, the Teams must be deleted. Simply type Microsoft Teams into the search bar, click Uninstall, and choose Yes.

Once it has been removed, download and install the prior version to see if the issue has been resolved. One of these fixes will take care of your issue.

Activities

1. Determine the typical troubleshooting procedures to follow in the event that the Microsoft Teams app isn't operating as it should.
2. Take some practice troubleshooting a particular issue, like not being able to send a message or join a meeting, and record the actions you take to fix it.
3. Talk about the possible reasons behind problems with Teams.

CHAPTER ELEVEN
ADD-ONS FOR TEAMS APP INTEGRATIONS

Synopsis

You may connect a variety of add-ons and applications with Microsoft Teams, including the Meet app, OneDrive, Planner, Viva Insights, and SharePoint. You may learn more about these integrations and how to take full advantage of them in Chapter 11. You can add a ton of apps and workflows to Microsoft Teams, if you're not familiar with it. If you would like to connect anything like Power BI or Google Analytics, you can choose to link apps inside of this area.

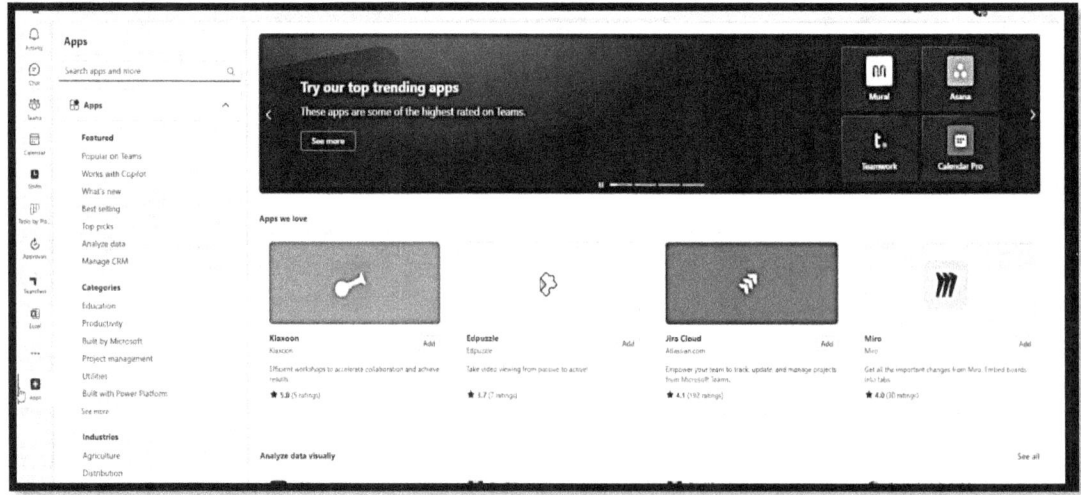

Remember that Teams offers a plethora of apps for you and your team to choose from; ultimately, you and your team will determine which one(s) best suits your needs. You have a plethora of options and connectors at your disposal, but bear in mind that here is the place to look for anything inside of Microsoft Teams if you're new to the program and using it for your team.

App integrations

Now let's take a look at some of the new features from Microsoft 365 that are included in Teams 2024.

Utilizing the Meet application

The first app is called Meet. If you can't find Meet in your three-dot menu, you can search for it. Since this is essentially a new view of your calendar, you might need to click the "Add" option if it isn't already there. You will see your calendar in its standard view by default, which is provided by the Calendar app. In case you missed it, you can switch to an agenda view, which is more akin to your phone app and might be more appealing to you. On the other hand, the Meet app is made to show more specific information regarding your appointments. The Meet app will list all of your Teams meetings, and you can join the meeting right from this screen. If the meeting is almost here, there's a helpful "I'm running late" option that lets you quickly message people to let them know you'll be late. You can also reschedule and message other participants directly from Meet. The meetings you just finished are below that.

Hence, Meet is consolidating all of your meetings, no matter where they are held, rather than requiring you to search through the channel or the chat to find your meetings. If you have Microsoft 365 Co-pilot, you can use the Meet app to access Intelligent Recap. If not, you can purchase Teams Intelligent Recap with Microsoft Teams Premium. This allows you to quickly get to the Intelligent Recap, which shows the meeting notes generated by AI, by clicking on "View Recap". You will also notice any chores that you need to finish. Any files you've shared are then shown on the Meet app's main screen; for instance, if we were using PowerPoint, we could click straight to that slide. If that were the case, the intelligent recap would take over and point out any sites that it thought we ought to check out as well as any instances when other users had brought up our names. Try the Meet app; it's free and rather useful, and you may find that you use it more frequently than a calendar to quickly join meetings and find your summaries rather than scrolling through the chat, which may be engaged with other things.

OneDrive applications

The second new program is OneDrive, which you may have seen has taken the place of Files. Files were the previous name of this program, so even if you've unpinned and hidden it, it can still be visible in your three-dot menu. You may approach OneDrive thinking that these files are private to you and that no one else can access them because they aren't in teams. You'd be right to make this assumption. It is helpful to quickly access files from anywhere in the Microsoft ecosystem if you understand the nuances of where to save them. Not only can you view all of the files at once, but you can also quickly access the most recent ones on Teams, OneDrive, SharePoint, or any other place within the Microsoft ecosystem. If you set your default to open in the app, you can get it to ping out into Word, PowerPoint, or Excel. If you haven't already, you can change the default by clicking the three dots and opening it in Teams, an app, or a browser, depending on your preferences.

Two very useful new capabilities that OneDrive has added are now simpler to reach in Teams: Users browsing files: You can easily respond to people with whom you've shared files once you see who they are. Through gatherings: It functions similarly to the Meet app in that it shows the meeting-related files. By selecting the files that you exchanged and going to the recording or replay, you may watch every prior session that has taken place.

Examining the organizer Planner is a worthwhile endeavor. Microsoft Planner is a great tool to help your business get things done. You may pin it to a team tab, which will cause the sidebar app to show you everything that is assigned to you as well as all of the plans for any team you are a part of. As you can soon see, access to practically every app in the Microsoft 365 ecosystem is provided by using Teams. Teams make the other apps easier to use, so that's why we usually start there. When you give someone a job with a deadline, the planner will follow up with them multiple times before the deadline is met. This is how it follows up with individuals on your behalf. It will follow them until they finish the assignment or meet the deadline if they don't. You never miss an assignment in this manner. Use Tasks by Planner (shortly to be Microsoft Planner) as much as possible.

The Viva's insights

Again, since it's not default, this one may show up on your three-dot menu. You can now access many materials for free thanks to this.

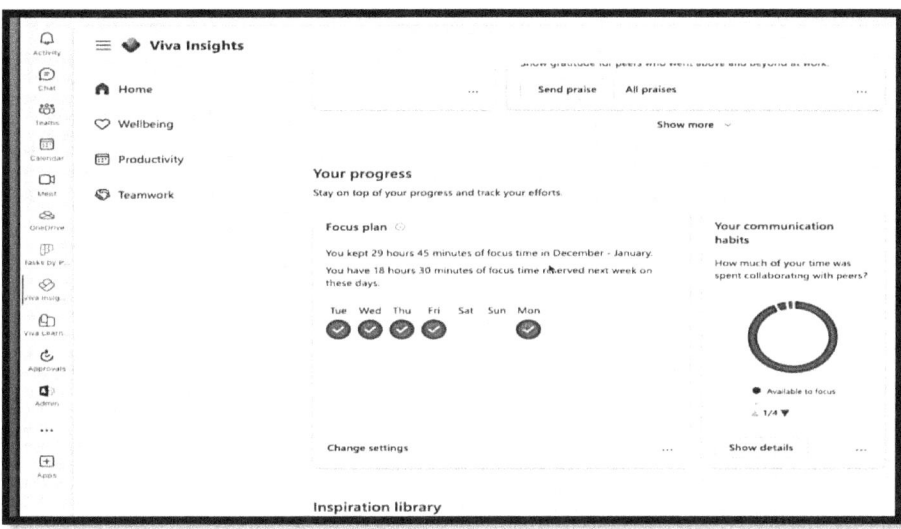

It features Zoom out, Lo-Fi times, and Focus that is currently suggested for us. Though most people don't use Focus Plan, it's the most beneficial feature of Microsoft Teams that can provide you with some insights about your meetings. You don't need to have it turned on if you prefer to work straight through and don't typically eat lunch. However, if you have a concentration plan already set up, you can set some lunch hours for you to block out time for lunch.

If you would like to turn off meetings on certain days, you will need to purchase an additional license. Nonetheless, you can control your own attention time to have large blocks of time to concentrate and complete tasks for free. If you do all of that and specify the days you want Focus time on, it will attempt to block that time out on your calendar. You can also set it to silence notifications from Teams while you're in that Focus period.

The Microsoft SharePoint

The last item is nothing new, but many people overlook it: when you create a team, a lot of things are automatically set up for you, including a fully functional SharePoint site where it manages all of your documents and many of your pages, giving you access to a complete internet.

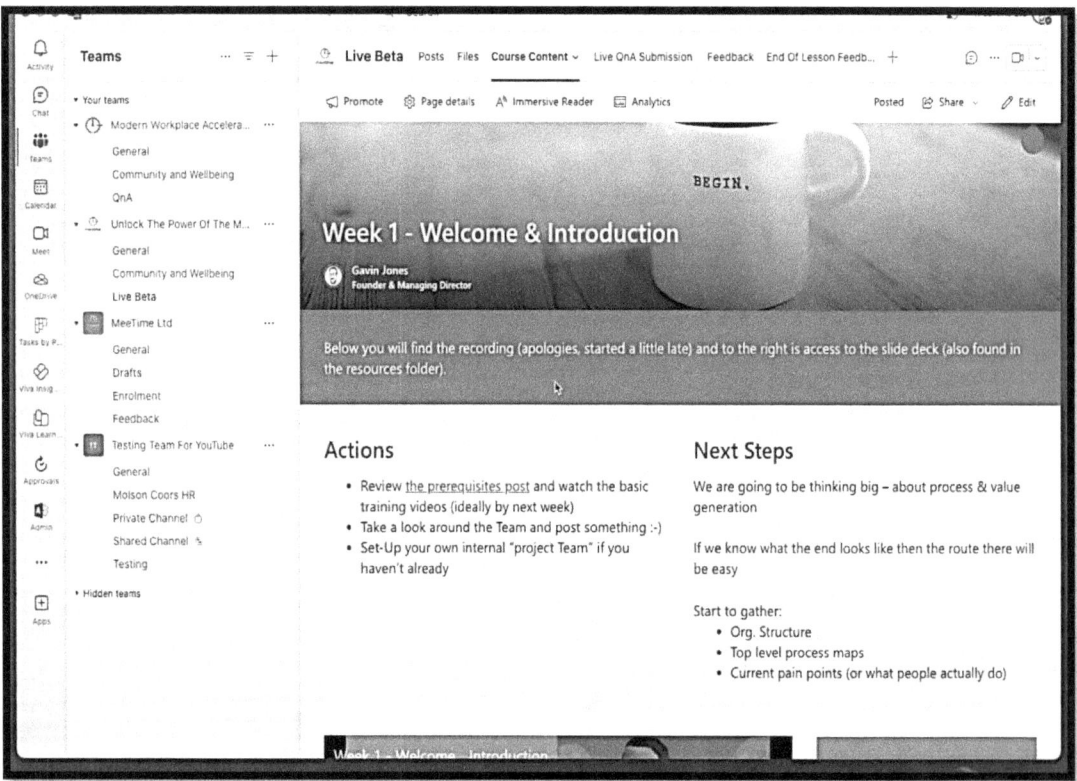

Each team may use it to bring material to life because it has the same power as the entire company's internet, and anyone can create whatever kind of page they desire. To make your content more engaging, you may create a brief course overview and content that includes several web pages, actions and steps, links to videos, and links back to papers. In order to create meeting minutes, outputs for meetings, prepare for meetings, or work on anything else together; you can also use external links and embedded forms.

Think about different ways that you would like to consume content, and people that you are collaborating with might want to consume content as well. Then, bring it to life with a little more content, just like you would in your personal life. Instead of attaching a PowerPoint slide to an email, you can now bring and start to put out an internet linked web page with pictures, videos, or rich content. One can be pinned to your channel so that others can view it and contribute. In this manner, you begin to develop a really strong knowledge foundation inside your team. There are many things that SharePoint pages can accomplish for you. Even though it has been since Team's founding, many individuals still fail to notice this.

Activities

1. Locate three third-party apps in the Microsoft Teams app store that can be incorporated into the Teams ecosystem.
2. Install and configure the chosen add-ons as you go, paying attention to how they work with the Teams interface.
3. Talk about the advantages of using Microsoft Teams to integrate apps.

General summary

You now have all the resources and knowledge needed to make the most of Microsoft Teams thanks to this book. So whatever the reason for your need for this book, there's something here to help you become a better team user. You can work with teams more productively and achieve more if you know how to use this guide. This book provided you with eleven chapters Take your time and read through each chapter and do the tasks that follow, and apply the lessons to your daily job if you want to get the most Microsoft Teams. You'll become an expert at leveraging Microsoft Teams to boost team output and effectiveness in no time. **Congratulations!!!**

INDEX

"

"Create a team" button, 24

A

A Brief Overview and Exploration of Teams, 5
A component of my collaborative Loop system, 13
A meeting schedule, 68
a notification or alert in the activity area, 31
A QUICK LOOK, 1
A reminder, 105
ABOUT CHATS AND CONVERSATIONS WITHIN THE TEAMS, 41
About Mark Team Notifications, 16
About Personnel reflect, 109
access Breakout Rooms, 83
access levels., 91
access many materials, 138
access method, 5
access the Analytics section, 37
accessed via browsers and mobile apps on iOS, 4
Accessibility, 4, 58, 66
Accessing My Teams, 98
achieve more, 1, 141
activate the Microsoft Teams app, 4
Activities, 12, 22, 40, 55, 87, 91, 101, 105, 118, 130, 135
add a new tag, 36
add an emoji, 46
Add Channel, 38
add members, 33
adding a photo, 61
adding a title, 10
Adding fresh tabs, 125
Adding notes to a PDF, 102
adding participants, 62
additional change, 71
additional information, 117

ADD-ONS, 136
ADD-ONS FOR TEAMS APP, 136
ADD-ONS FOR TEAMS APP INTEGRATIONS, 136
Addressing a specific person, 49
adjust your perspective, 64
adorable little window, 42
advise verifying a few settings, 56
alternative option available, 26
Android devices, 4
annotate PDFs, 102
annotate PDFs for teachers and students, 102
annotations, 76, 78, 118
announcement, 85, 86
Announcements, 29
Another neat feature, 122
Another option is to have the meeting recorded automatically., 69
App integrations, 136
app store, 141
application, 9, 12, 72, 128
applications on your screen, 73
Are teams not operating as they should?, 131
Are you feeling ready to use Microsoft Teams?, 1
arrange content, 23
arranging a Teams meeting, 58
Asana and Trello, 90
assign individuals to specific teams, 84
Assigning people to the two breakout rooms, 84
assignments, 105, 117, 118
Attending a scheduled meeting, 70
audio and video calls later., 53
audio and video chats, 2
availability status, 54

B

backdrop color, 128

Background effects, 66
background filter, 61
background filters, 61
background using the blur option, 61
become an expert, 141
become an expert at leveraging Microsoft Teams, 141
begin adding tasks, 14
beneficial feature, 139
blank canvas, 77, 79
blank slate, 80, 81
bookmark, 49
boost team output and effectiveness in no time, 141
Both Windows and Mac users, 4
brand-new channel, 38
Breaking up with a team, 39
Breakout Rooms, 82, 83, 85, 87
broken Teams, 131
budgets, 89
bullet points, 47
bypass the lobby, 11

C

Calendar app, 137
calendar of a team, 9
calendar of a team is also available to us, 9
carrying out actions, 7
Change picture, 34
change the font's color, 47
Change the meeting's title, 87
change the parameters, 99
changing your network connections, 132
channel configurations, 23
channel management options, 32
channel metrics, 38
Channels, 4, 37
Channels and chat both now support components, 13
Channels offer a disciplined method, 4
CHATS AND CONVERSATIONS, 41

chatting with your coworkers and attaching files, 44
child's information, 116
Choose "New chat" from the menu, 41
choose Settings, 133, 134
choose to share a specific tab in Microsoft Edge, 72
Choosing the second choice, 84
click "Create" after adding a description, 28
click Settings, 21
click the emoji button, 46
click the format option, 47
Click the Open button to begin installing Microsoft Teams, 3
click Uninstall, 135
Clicking "New chat" opens a new window, 53
Clicking @praise, 128
Clicking Apps, 9
clicking on the Whiteboard, 78
clicking the "Join now" option, 62
Clicking the "New" drop-down, 8
clicking the gear symbol, 81
clicking the small Settings icon, 62
clicking the three dots, 23, 31, 38, 39, 79, 86, 138
co-authoring a document, 77
collaborate on ideas and project planning, 77
collaborative loop component, 14
collaborative workgroup techniques, 1
colleagues can make changes, 81
colleagues collaborate, 77
coloring book, 108
Coloring book, 107
coloring book Reflect Mindful, 107
Coloring book that promotes awareness and introspection, 107
comment icon, 79
commenting, 22, 118
commenting and work assignment., 22
communicate with coworkers, 4
communicate with coworkers one-on-one or in groups, 4

communication, 1, 2, 23, 29, 41, 64, 88, 89, 91, 120
company's internet, 140
Comparing new planners to older ones, 100
complete roster, 71
Complicated meeting circumstances, 82
component from a task list, 14
components of Planner, 92
COMPREHENDING MEETING AND CALL CONFIGURATION, 56
concentration plan, 139
Concerning Channels, 36
Concerning My Plans, 95
Concerning My Tasks, 94
CONCERNING THE TROUBLESHOOTING OF TEAMS, 131
Conference planners, 82
configuring everything, 85
Congratulations, 141
connect a variety of add-ons and applications, 136
consumer version of Teams, 115
content, 36, 72, 88, 120, 122, 123, 140, 141
contextual menu, 6
contracts, 89
Conversation, 4
Conversations that take place within Teams, 41
co-organizers, 11
copy components, 14
copying the URL, 62
create a group, 27
Create channels, 88
create new meetings, 10
Create rooms, 84
create tags, 23
Create team, 32
created the team, 28
creates a new window, 42
creating a sample project channel,, 91
Creating and managing Teams and Channels, 23
creating diagrams, 79
creating diagrams and project plans, 79
CREATION OF TEAMS AND CHANNELS, 23

currently using mobile data, 132
Customize a pre-established list of responses, 17
customized invitation, 11
cutting into your presentation, 63

D

decipher a variety of accents and voices, 58
declare premium, 96
default behavior, 130
delete a team, 39, 40
Delete team, 40
deleting entries, 49
deliver a message, 57
Delve into the many calendar views and options available in the Microsoft Teams app, 12
depending on your preferences, 138
description, 38, 69, 102
desired location, 79
desired number of rooms, 83
desktop program, 83
Determine the typical troubleshooting procedures, 135
different conference rooms, 82
different filters, 122
different license., 96
different sections, 108
direct connection, 15
Disabling your camera is another option you have., 61
display hearts, 64
documenting your steps., 91
documents, 4, 8, 48, 79, 140
Does spell check not work correctly?, 132
download and install the Microsoft Teams desktop application., 12
Download app for desktop, 2
Download Microsoft Teams Desktop, 2
download the desktop application, 5
download the desktop version of Microsoft Teams, 4
downloading the previous version, 135

drawing on it with the annotation tools., 118
drop-down menu, 38, 67, 83

E

easier-to-manage groups, 82
easily integrated with Teams, 4
easily update assignments, 102
easy-to-use calendar, 10
Ecosystem for apps, 4
Edge Browser, 20
Edit button, 57
edit your comment, 79
editing, 49, 51, 81, 112
Editing, removing, and bookmarking posts, 49
educational institution, 2
educational setting can be facilitated by the annotation feature, 118
elements of your task list, 15
email or channel., 32
emoji categories, 35
emojis, 4, 44, 63
Employee Chat, 29
English languages, 134
enhance our functionality, 9
enhance Reflect, 102
enhance teamwork, 88
entertaining features, 108
Establish a new channel for an already-existing team., 40
Establishing a group, 24
everyday work, 1
examine bookmarking, 49
Examine the possibilities in a chat for sharing files and other items., 55
Examine the ways in which Collaborative Loop, 22
EXAMINING INNOVATIVE FEATURES IN GROUPS, 13
Examining the organizer Planner, 138
Excel Live, 74, 75, 76, 77
Excel, and PowerPoint., 4
expand our experience., 9
expiration dates,, 90

EXPLORATION OF ADVANCED FEATURES, 102
EXPLORING MICROSOFT TEAMS, 2
extend customized channels, 30
Extend the feature until the deadline date, 105

F

facilitating brainstorming sessions, 79
feedback, 118
Feel free, 68, 85
Feel free to add one or two rooms, 85
Feel free to include the meeting's title, 68
few alternatives, 24, 45, 54
few more options available, 76
few options, 38, 105
file sharing, 47, 56, 74
File sharing, 89
Filter Profane words, 58
filter the files, 8
final strategy for team formation, 29
floating formatting bar, 79
formatting styles, 55
formatting tools, 79
forming your team, 91
forward slash, 127, 128
fourth new feature, 16, 106
framework, 25
fresh little festivity, 113
fun and relaxing resource, 109
Fun Stuff, 35
functionalities, 2
functionality of the newly launched OneDrive, 17

G

Gallery format, 64
General, 26, 29, 44, 60, 68, 100, 123, 132, 141
General summary, 141
Generating ideas in a meeting, 77
Get comfortable with utilizing the keyboard shortcuts, 130
get the most Microsoft Teams, 141

Getting files and sharing them via chat, 47
gifs, 35, 44, 63
giving a presentation, 67
Google Analytics, 136
greater detail in a moment, 8
grid view, 76
group's privacy settings, 96

H

handy method, 20
Hide a team from view, 39
Hold off while Microsoft Teams downloads, 3
home screen, 131
homepage in the main web area, 19
how to create Teams, 23
How to set up the windows that pop up, 123
how to use Teams, 88
huge corporation, 2
hunt for files, 127

I

important project files, 89
Important setups, 99
improve the productivity and effectiveness of your team, 1
improvements and changes to Microsoft Teams, 1
Improvements to the live captioning, 21
including a personalized message, 128
including Device settings, 66
Including instruments from external sources, 90
including more tabs, 125
including specs, 89
including the style, 130
including Word, 4, 14
incorporate external tools and programs, 90
incorporates tasks,, 88
increase productivity, 1
Increasing the enjoyment of your conversations, 45
Individuals must be granted permission to join a private group., 27

input your message, 53
inside of Microsoft Teams, 136
Install and configure, 141
installation process, 3
Installing and downloading Microsoft Teams, 2
integrate apps, 141
integrating with other Microsoft Office programs, 4
Integration with Microsoft 365 Teams, 4
integrations, 4
interface's basic navigation and features, 130
iOS smartphone, 131
iPhone's Settings, 132
It is possible to remove rooms., 85

J

join a public group, 27
join a public team, 27
join button, 27
Join or create a team, 24, 31
Join Teams Meeting, 71
join the meeting, 63, 71
joining and forming teams in the public and private domains., 32

K

Keep an eye on the additions, deletions, and role changes that occur within the team., 40
Keep an eye on the invitees' calendars to see when the meeting is scheduled., 87
Key characteristics of Microsoft Teams, 4
keyboard's Enter key., 44

L

Launch a fresh chat session in the Teams app with a coworker., 55
launch Teams, 133, 134
Launch the Teams calendar and try setting up a brand-new meeting., 87

launching a new chat window or entering a meeting, 130
launching a new pet food line, 96
learning accelerators, 118
left-hand side, 5
lengthy list of all the messages, 51
Let's start with shared plans, 96
links back to papers, 141
list checklist, 14
little extra assistance, 1
little more content, 141
live captioning, 22
Locate three third-party apps, 141
Locating chat rooms or channels is made easy, 16
Lo-Fi times, 139
look at our app launcher, 5
Look for a Microsoft Teams, 2
loop component, 14
lovely sky-blue background, 108
Lowering noise levels, 110
Lowering noise levels to make reading easier, 110

M

main channel, 14, 37
main goal of teams, 119
main meeting, 85, 86
make our team public., 30
make your content more engaging, 140
make your whiteboard, 78
making collaborative loop component creation simple., 14
Making use of the template, 29
Manage team, 34, 38
manage your own microphone, 67
manage your teams, 23
Management of Teams and Channel, 32
managing initiatives, 88
managing projects, 1
MANAGING PROJECTS, 88
managing your teams and channels, 7
many channels, 5

many third-party integrations and apps, 4
marketing channel, 38
marketing collaborate, 5
Meet app, 18, 19, 136, 137, 138
Meet now, 10, 60, 68
MEETING AND CALL, 56
meeting and exit sharing mode, 74
meeting attendees, 73, 76, 81
meeting details in the email body, 71
meeting invitation, 11
meeting organizer, 57, 85, 86
meetings, 4, 57, 60, 71, 122, 139, 140, 141
Meetings, 4, 57
meeting's attendees, 68
meeting's organizers, 11
meeting's specifics, 11
member of your organization, 27, 28
members of an organization, 2
merging your conversations, 20
message or join a meeting, 135
Message sending and receiving, 43
messaging everyone in the channel., 7
method of forming a team, 26
microphones, 57, 70
Microsoft 365, 4, 16, 20, 22, 26, 68, 77, 82, 137, 138
Microsoft 365 group, 26
Microsoft 365 group set up, 26
Microsoft 365 homepage, 77
MICROSOFT EDUCATION, 102
Microsoft Planner, 92, 138
Microsoft Stream, 19
Microsoft team or other 365 organization, 96
MICROSOFT TEAMS, 88
Microsoft Teams 2024 can assist you, 1
Microsoft To-do Lists, 97
mobile apps, 4
moderators, 36
modify the apps within the chat, 42
Modify the plan views to your desired design., 101

Modify the Teams application's design to your taste., 12
Modify the Teams app's settings, 130
more information, 49
more loop components, 14
More Options box, 66
multiple languages, 76, 134
multiple private chats, 53
Music and Movie Recommendations, 31
Mute unrelated conversation threads, 120

N

navigate to Plan Settings, 100
navigate to the old Planner, 100
navigating to your Outlook calendar, 71
navigation menu, 96, 97
necessary attendance, 68
new assignment, 14
new channels, 38
new feature, 92, 102, 110, 111, 112, 114, 123
new features in Teams for Education, 102
new functionality, 20, 113
New Meeting Schedule, 10
new Planner on Microsoft Teams, 92
New Whiteboard, 80, 82
new window, 42, 123
newly added team meeting, 71
newly created teams, 6
nine applications, 29
Notification of missing attachment, 111
notification options, 130
notification settings, 122
notifications, 42, 57, 73, 74, 100, 122, 140
notifications are provided, 99
notify your coworkers, 124
numerous new caption settings, 21

O

obtain the URL to the whiteboard, 81
Onboard Employees, 29

OneDrive, 4, 13, 17, 18, 47, 48, 74, 136, 137, 138
OneDrive applications, 137
online software, 82
Open Microsoft Planner and navigate to the "My Plans" area., 101
open Microsoft Teams, 5
open Teams for Education on your iPhone, 115
openable JPEG file, 109
Opening of the meeting, 59
opening the "Calendar" section of the app., 12
operations, 96, 128
opportunity to speak with attendees, 11
option to create private channels, 37
option to customize our rooms, 85
organizers and co-organizers, 11
Organizing the conversations, 46
other amusing items, 44
other applications, 128
other Microsoft 365 services, 4
Out of a collection, 26
Outlook, 4, 14, 26, 68, 71, 72, 73, 95
out-of-office message, 124
outside parties, 4

P

participants, 63, 71, 84, 85, 86, 87
Participants, 76
participants vanish, 85
Participating in meetings by delivering live presentations, 75
particular actions, 127
particular tasks, 4
Partnerships, 4
password protection, 90
paying attention, 141
pending invites, 23
perceive the red-highlighted portion, 75
permissions, 37, 38, 90
Permissions for members, 34
personalized pink tag attached, 93
personalizing, 80

Planner, 97, 100, 101
Planner and To-do, 92
planner or to-do list, 15
Play around with the various Collaborative Loop features, 22
Play Store or App Store, 131
plus symbol, 125
popular platform for teamwork, 1
possible paths, 84
Posting and receiving messages in groups, 43
Posts, 6, 44, 89, 125
Power BI, 136
PowerPoint, 4, 17, 74, 75, 76, 77, 137, 138, 141
PowerPoint Live, 74, 76, 77
PowerPoint slides, 75
Practice Exercises, 91, 101, 118, 130, 135, 141
practice highlighting, 118
Practice utilizing various emoticons and formatting styles in your chat messages., 55
preferred languages, 134
presentation, 64, 76
presentations, 8, 56, 77, 89
Pressing CTRL+F, 16
previous step blank, 98
primary features., 90
Prior to downloading, 135
private conversation, 53, 54
private discussion, 54
private messages, 52, 53
Private messages exchanged, 52
private team requires an invitation, 24
private teams are concealed from view, 24
process of fixing problems, 131
produce a great visual impact, 93
product of Loop, 15
project management, 91, 96
Project management, 88
project managers, 91
project-oriented plans., 101
project's lifecycle, 91
provide you a preview of the plan, 96

providing audio and video conferencing features, 4
Public and private teams, 24
Public and private teams are the two types of teams, 24
public team, 28, 30, 31, 39
publish a message or chat, 52
purple-highlighted, 5
Putting up your hand is the next logical step, 64

Q

quotes, 47

R

reading progress, 118
real challenge, 58
receive a pop-up notification, 46
recent update, 135
recently launched Planner tool, 97
record and transcribe the meeting, 65
record the actions you take to fix it., 135
recording features, 4
recording features are supported, 4
Reflect for adults is the sixth feature, 109
Regarding My Day, 92
Regarding Teams Calendar, 10
Regarding the Conversation, 89
reinstalling the Microsoft Teams application, 131
reminders, 57
remote work and virtual cooperation, 4
Remove from My Day, 93
Remove the language, 134
Renaming rooms, 86
Reopening a mailed meeting, 70
request to join, 63
Require registration, 70
Reset iPhone, 132
Reset network settings, 132
Resetting the network settings, 132
resources and knowledge needed, 141

respective rooms, 85
Responses in bulk, 106
Restart the process, 108
revised feature, 112
Right from the start, 27
right responsibilities, 91
right-click on the Start button, 134

S

Save changes, 103, 104
Schedule a meeting, 60, 68
Schedule a meeting and Meet now, 60
Scheduling Assistant, 68
school connection, 114, 115, 116
school connection app, 115
school data., 114
scratch necessitates, 25
Screen sharing, 4
Screen sharing,, 4
scribble comments, 79
search bar, 128, 135
search box, 33, 127
search for the Excel file, 126
second new program is OneDrive, 137
see other options, 63
select "Download Teams for home", 3
select a team from the drop-down menu, 98
select Teams, 3
select Teams for work or school, 3
select the app launcher, 77
select the delete option, 132
select the next option, 30
select the page of your choice, 108
select your preferred language., 21
selecting "Copy Component", 14
selecting Manage Team, 31
selecting Windows, 73
separate microphone, 62
Setting up Tags, 36
Settings tab, 31
Seventh new feature, 107

several employees, 36
several platforms, 90
several possibilities available to you, 108
several seminars, 82
several team members, 4
share a specific tab, 72
share an Excel file, 126
Share button, 75, 81
share files,, 4
shared access, 14
shared files, 8
shared locations, 14
SharePoint, 4, 37, 89, 90, 119, 136, 138, 140, 141
Sharing, 74, 76
Sharing a screen, 72
sidebar app, 138
sign in using your Microsoft account, 4
sign up with your ID, 10
simultaneously setting your laptop's speaker, 62
small conversation box, 44
small floating toolbar, 126
small parent and student icon, 116
small pink icon, 93
small Saved button, 51
small school connection icon, 116
small settings button, 69
software, 91
speakers and microphone, 62
specific ID, 10
specific information, 137
specific team member, 52
spontaneous meeting, 10
Start a fresh Collaborative Loop and extend an invitation to your group to participate., 22
start a new chat, 44, 47, 123
start a new whiteboard, 81
Start an on-demand call, 60
Starting a new conversation, 44
starting from scratch necessitates adding each member of the team by hand, 25
stickers, 4, 35, 37, 44, 63

stickers and memes, 37
Stop sharing, 74
students and adults, 109
subchannels beneath the main channel, 23
subsequent addition, 15
summary of your participation, 101
supporting documents, 89
swiftly access other files, 17
swiftly access standard features, 130
switch to speaker format, 64
symbols, 84
Synopsis, 2, 13, 23, 41, 56, 88, 92, 102, 119, 131, 136

T

tables, 14, 47, 113
Tabs for meeting notes and questions, 71
take a look at some of the new features from Microsoft 365, 136
Take control, 76
Take note of how the "My Plans" function, 101
Take note of how the annotations are shared and presented to other members of the team, 118
Take some practice troubleshooting a particular issue, 135
Take your time and read through each chapter, 141
Taking a group out, 39
Taking part in a group, 31
Talk about how collaborative document evaluation, 118
Talk about the possible reasons behind problems with Teams., 135
tap and hold Microsoft Teams, 131
tap the parent's name, 115
tasks and projects, 2
Tasks app, 16
Teachers can quickly inform students, 105
Teachers have long requested the ability to annotate a PDF in an assignment, 102
team channel, 5, 43, 52, 53, 63, 70, 89
team meeting, 60, 69, 129

team member, 39, 52
team members, 5, 23, 26, 38, 63, 72, 75, 77, 81, 91
TEAM MICROSOFT PLANNER USERS, 92
team or channel, 128
team output and effectiveness, 141
team owner, 24, 31, 39
team with a code, 24
Teams are quite intriguing, 23
Teams Cache files, 133
Teams can improve their experience and connect with other tools, 4
team's Channel, 62
Teams channels, 14
Teams' Chat section, 52
Teams discussion, 20
Teams enable users to arrange and participate in meetings with coworkers, 4
team's file library, 8
Teams folder, 132
Teams group discussions, 4
Teams group discussions and documents, 4
Teams interface, 4, 141
Teams meeting, 81
Teams' meetings, 58
Teams of employees, 109
Teams offers a plethora of apps, 136
Teams recognize your identity in meeting transcripts and captions automatically, 58
Teams screen, 24
ten chapters, 141
terrific way, 126
text in the search field instructs, 127
The "More actions" button, 65
The Browser integration, 20
The calendar for your Team is another place you can initiate a meeting, 60
the calendar, chat, and sidebar, 130
The essentials, 119
The hub of activity, 121
The installation process should take one minute, 3
The latest version, 17

The management of the teams, 33
The Mobile App Stream, 19
The out-of-office message's scheduling, 124
the platform offers, 4
The school connection app, 114
The school connection option, 115
The Setting Up, 88
The Viva's insights, 138
the Whiteboard app, 80, 125
There are numerous new caption settings on the right, 21
third-party app, 9
thoughtful coloring book, 109
three dots appear on the side of the screen, 6
three dots will take you to additional options, 54
three-dot menu, 16, 21, 112, 137, 138
thumbs up button, 46
titled Tasks by Planner, 9
To-do list links that are easy to recognize, 15
tools and information, 1
touch Reset, 132
TPS report, 102
transcript and onscreen captions, 58
Transcripts, 58
Transcripts and closed captions are also available, 58
transmit date and time of the message, 43
true real-time co-authoring, 90
Turn a post into a task, 121
two popular integrations for project management, 90
type in your message, 86
typing in the list of previous conversations, 52
typing the @ sign, 129

U

uncheck spell checking, 133
understand navigation menu, 92
UNDERSTANDING HINTS AND TECHNIQUES, 119
Updated Turn in festivities, 113

Upload a PDF document to a Teams channel or chat, 118
Upload button, 17
URLs, 71
use a template, 29, 31
use Teams to master project management, 88
Use template at Amy's animal shop, 96
use the Reflect feature, 107
user interface of the new Teams was harmonized, 13
Users of Microsoft Teams, 4
using a headset, 62
Using a pre-made template, form a new team., 40
using gifs, 4
using Microsoft Teams, 1, 37, 88
using mobile data, 132
using Teams, 119, 123, 138
using the /goto option, 128
Using the Files tab on your channel, 89
Using the Microsoft Edge browser, 73
Using the search bar, 127
using Wi-Fi, 132
using your browser, 2
utilize a mobile device, 115
utilize Breakout Rooms, 82
utilizing breakout rooms, 82
utilizing Microsoft Teams in 2024,, 1
Utilizing the Meet application, 137
utilizing various emoticons, 55

V

variety of pre-made templates, 80
variety of small GIFs, 46
various categories, 46
various file kinds, 8
various methods for joining and forming teams, 32
various team, 101
Video options, 62
video solution, 19
view the details of the meeting, 71

view the range of tools, 32
view your teams' stats, 23
viewing the presentation, 75
viewing the presentation in the Presenter View, 75
virtual backdrops, 4
Viva Insights, 136

W

We can see the team for music and movie recommendations, 31
We can start from zero and build a simple team, 25
web application, 82
website, 20, 82
what are some of the key benefits of Microsoft Teams?, 4
whatever the reason for your need for this book, 141
whiteboard, 77, 79, 81, 82, 125
whiteboard a name, 125
wide range of formatting options, 43

Wi-Fi,, 132
Windows language, 134
working together and maintaining the order of conversations., 4

Y

You can access the meeting, 62
you can adjust the font size, 21
You can browse by meetings, 17
You can now join meetings and start conversations, 4
You can work with teams more productively, 141
You have additional options, 42
you may share a link or upload a copy, 48
You may view all of the channels, 37
You will get knowledge on how to create Teams from various sources, 23
your full screen, 72
your own tastes, 130
Your small camera toggle, 67
your team meetings, 56

www.ingramcontent.com/pod-product-compliance
Lightning Source LLC
Chambersburg PA
CBHW062313220526
45479CB00004B/1153